DATE DUE

Disputing the Subject of Sex

Curriculum, Cultures, and (Homo)Sexualities
Edited by James T. Sears

Editorial Advisory Board:
Dennis Altman, Warren Blumenfeld, Deborah Britzman, Diane DuBose Brunner, Debbie Epstein, Pat Griffin, Glorianne Leck, Peter McLaren, William Pinar, Eric Rofes, and Mariamne Whatley

Getting Ready for Benjamin: Preparing Teachers for Sexual Diversity in the Classroom
Edited by Rita M. Kissen

Troubling Intersections of Race and Sexuality: Queer Students of Color and Anti-Oppressive Education
Edited by Kevin K. Kumashiro

Queering Elementary Education
Edited by William J. Letts IV and James T. Sears

Beyond Diversity Day: A Q&A on Gay and Lesbian Issues in Schools
By Arthur Lipkin

Sexual Orientation and School Policy: A Practical Guide for Teachers, Administrators, and Community Activists
By Ian K. Macgillivray

Disputing the Subject of Sex

Sexuality and Public School Controversies

CRIS MAYO

ROWMAN & LITTLEFIELD PUBLISHERS, INC.
Lanham • Boulder • New York • Toronto • Oxford

ROWMAN & LITTLEFIELD PUBLISHERS, INC.

Published in the United States of America
by Rowman & Littlefield Publishers, Inc.
A wholly owned subsidiary of The Rowman & Littlefield Publishing Group, Inc.
4501 Forbes Boulevard, Suite 200, Lanham, MD 20706
www.rowmanlittlefield.com

P.O. Box 317, Oxford OX2 9RU, UK

British Library Cataloguing in Publication Information Available

Library of Congress Cataloging-in-Publication Data Available

ISBN 0-7425-2658-5 (cloth : alk. paper)

Printed in the United States of America

♾™ The paper used in this publication meets the minimum requirements of American
National Standard for Information Sciences—Permanence of Paper for Printed Library
Materials, ANSI/NISO Z39.48-1992.

Contents

Acknowledgments

Thanks to my many helpful readers, especially Kal Alston, Walter Feinberg, Paula Treichler, and C.L. Cole, whose comments on earlier drafts greatly helped improve this text. I would also like to thank colleagues for their assistance and commentary: Natasha Levinson, Megan Boler, Audrey Thompson, Lisa King, and Alicia Rodriguez. Gloria Filax, Maureen Ford, and Arthur Lipkin all provided helpful responses and suggestions to previously published versions of chapters. Suzanne de Castell, Jenn Jenson, Carolyn Riehl, David Blacker, Eugene Matusov, and Maria Alburquerque Candela provided important guidance through long conversations and collaboration on related projects. I am also grateful to my mother, Jane Franck, an outstanding art teacher, whose participation her district's HIV/AIDS review board provided practical insights. Jim Sears continues to be a great help to all of us involved in the study of education and sexuality and I greatly appreciate his work and his help improving mine. Thanks also to the Foote family, Peter, Deb, Zak, and Krystina, for all their warmth and generosity. My greatest thanks go to Stephanie Foote for providing intellectual energy, incisive criticism, and pleasant distraction.

Introduction

Disputing the Subject of Sex: Sexuality and Public School Controversies

Early predictions that the AIDS crisis would dramatically alter discourse about sexuality have proven to be simultaneously true and false. Since the passage of the Welfare Reform Act, abstinence-based education has had money heaped upon it, despite the fact that abstinence until marriage curricula fully exclude the needs of sexually active heterosexual students and utterly ignore gay, lesbian, bisexual, and transgender students. On the other hand, schools have found themselves increasingly held liable for their inaction against homophobic harassment and thus have increasingly begun to implement policies protecting students. While most of this book will focus on conflicted discourses about sexuality and schools during the early years of AIDS, the conflicts are no less heated today. Sexuality is increasingly addressed by public schools, but it is often addressed in a way that marks sexual minorities as only quasi-legitimate members of the school community.

The National Education Association (NEA), the largest teachers' union in the United States, has recently passed a resolution calling for public schools to include lesbian, gay, bisexual, and transgender students and school employees in their nondiscrimination policies. The NEA also firmly supports efforts by schools to provide factual, up-to-date, age appropriate information on sexual minorities. The NEA's resolution constitutes a strong statement of support for the educational rights of sexual minorities. However, in at least two states, Massachusetts and Maryland, laws attempting to protect gay and lesbian students from harassment have been crafted specifically to prohibit their use as a mandate to bring curricular materials positively representing gays and lesbians into public schools. In other words, both states attempt to prevent harassment through a tolerance that dare not speak its name. In Maryland, school board members and legislators have raised concerns that school antidiscrimination policies may bring too much information on homosexuality into public schools. Apparently a "technical glitch" in the policy means that the state school board may have unintentionally opened the door to curriculum addressing gay and lesbian students.[1] School board members are caught between trying to protect gay and lesbian students from harassment, as they must do in order to follow the state antidiscrimination policy, and also trying to avoid opening a loop hole allowing the introduction of gay and lesbian issues into the curricula. As of the summer of 2002, they are working together with lawyers to eliminate this "glitch" that might bring gay and lesbian issues into the classroom.

This same attempt to prevent discrimination and prevent curricular representation was settled by the Massachusetts legislature. It passed an antidiscrimination policy including protection for sexual orientation to its equal educational opportunity law that included clauses minimizing the degree to which curricula could represent gay and lesbian issues. The state now calls for schools to start "active efforts" to address and prevent discrimination on the basis of sexual orientation.[2] While original drafts of the law called for schools to "counteract" bias found in curricular materials, the state board revised the law to require that schools "provide balance and context" for bias and stereotypes about sexual orientation. In other words, although the schools are required to protect student from antigay bias, they are also required to provide school time for explanations for that bias. Criticizing the call for making sexual orientation a special form of protection requiring opponents to homosexuality to have voice in the curriculum, one advocate for sexual minorities argued, "We don't hear people say we need balanced views of racism."[3] Further, changes made to the draft of regulations, now state law, removed a requirement for sexual orientation that is still in place for racial minorities and gender: that curricula "depict individuals of both sexes and from minority groups in 'a broad variety of positive roles.'"[4] In other words, despite the law's intention to make schools proactive against bias, all the sections that publicly denote proactive intervention into curriculum have been removed so that they don't have to be applied to the specific case of sexual orientation.

Maryland and Massachusetts are in the seemingly unusual position of having to grapple with nondiscrimination laws that specifically name sexual orientation as a protected class and school policies that specifically constrain the representation of gay and lesbian issues in curricula. While they improve the school climate for sexual minority students, schools are not encouraged to provide specific instruction on exactly who gay and lesbian people are or why, specifically, they ought not to suffer discrimination. These compromised strategies for bringing sexuality into public schools set up a difficult situation in which the kind of protection afforded by the policy is the same protection that prohibits explicit discussions and lessons on sexual minorities.

Still, much positive work has been done in public schools to protect sexual minority students. Recent court cases, especially the record $900,000 settlement of Jamie Nabozny's suit against his high school for not intervening in the antigay harassment that forced him out of school, have publicized the harassment and assault common for sexual minority youth in public schools. Because the Boy Scouts of America continue to discriminate against gay scout masters and members, school districts have severed their association with BSA in all of Massachusetts and in selected districts in Arizona, California, Florida, Illinois, Minnesota, New Hampshire, New York, North Carolina, and Oregon.[5] Only eight states (California, Connecticut, Massachusetts, Minnesota, New Jersey, Vermont, Washington, and Wisconsin) and the District of Columbia have laws that specifically protect gay and lesbian students from harassment and discrimination.[6] Of those states, only California, Minnesota, and New Jersey protect students from discrimination and harassment based on gender identity.

But while legislatures and schools continue to add sexual orientation to antidiscrimination policies and more infrequently to curricula, schools also continue to be difficult and dangerous environments for sexual minority youth. Two major surveys have found a high rate of harassment against lesbian, gay, bisexual, and transgender students. According to a study by the Human Rights Watch, "nearly every one of the 140 youth we interviewed described incidents of verbal or other nonphysical harassment in school because of their own or other students' perceived sexuality."[7] The Gay Lesbian and Straight Educators Network (GLSEN) 2001 School Climate Report indicates that 94 percent of the 904 students surveyed heard homophobic remarks in school, the majority of them did so "frequently."[8] Not only do almost all sexual minority students in both surveys report harassment, they also note that antigay harassment is also directed at students who are not gay but are perceived to be different in some way, or antigay harassment is just a common way to express dislike. Gender nonconforming students, transgender students, and heterosexual students perceived to be not straight enough all also bear the brunt of homophobic harassment and violence. The GLSEN Report found higher rates of sexual harassment among sexual minority students than other reports had found among public school students as a whole.[9] Further, female students, whether lesbian, bisexual, or heterosexual, experience gender-based harassment laced with homophobic harassment and vice versa. As one lesbian explained, "The boys mess with us [girls] all the time—I don't even think most of the time that I get it worse because I am a lesbian."[10]

Over one-third of students surveyed reported physical harassment (shoved, pushed, etc.) because of their sexuality; one-third also reported physical harassment because of their gender expression; close to 20 percent reported physical harassment because of their gender; and 10 percent reported physical harassment because of their race.[11] Twenty percent indicated physical assault (punched, kicked, injured with a weapon, etc.) because of their sexual orientation, gender expression, gender, or race.[12] Over two-thirds of youth felt unsafe at school because of their sexual orientation, with close to one-third missing classes or days of school because of those feelings.[13] While these forms of discrimination and the resulting alienation from schools might usually be thought to be cause for positive intervention from school staff, many sexual minority students report inattention or dismissive reactions from school authorities. In addition, researchers note that sexual minorities themselves learn to expect harassment as a normal part of their school day.[14]

On a positive note, just over 60 percent of students knew of an lgbt-supportive teacher or staff member. About half said they would be comfortable talking to at least one teacher about lgbt issues, more than half reported comfort with a counselor, about one-third said they'd be comfortable talking to the principal, and one-third were comfortable talking to the nurse.[15] Students who knew of a supportive staff member or teacher were themselves more likely to feel like they belonged in their school. Thirty-five percent with a supportive teacher felt like they belonged (compared to nearly 26 percent who felt like they belonged but did not have a supportive teacher) and 38.5 percent who knew of an "out" lbgt teacher or staff member felt like they belonged (compared to nearly 28 percent who felt like they belonged but did not know an out staff member or teacher). Students were also less likely to feel unsafe if their school had a GSA. Almost 63 percent felt unsafe in schools with a GSA because of their sexual orientation compared to 72 percent who felt unsafe in schools without a GSA.

Unfortunately teachers and other school employees continue to be inadequately prepared to address the needs of sexual minority students. Pre-service teachers still feel unable to address the needs of sexual minority youth or uncomfortable intervening in anti-lgbt harassment.[16] Because in many areas employment rights are not extended to lesbian, gay, bisexual, and transgender school employees, teachers may be reluctant to act as advocates for sexual minority students. In-service training on sexuality issues is not available in all areas, especially not in states where teaching about sexual minorities is illegal or severely constrained. While universities increasingly require at least one course on diversity issues and multicultural education, the leading textbooks continue to be silent on sexuality and some leading advocates of multicultural education continue to vocally maintain sexuality is not a multicultural issue. [17] As Barbara Wallace has argued, the inattention to sexuality (and global and disability issues) in graduate programs in education means that populations in need of sensitive and experienced professionals will continue to be underserved.[18]

This book focuses on a period of time in which sexuality became central to public school curricula and school communities. The extended case study of controversies over sex, AIDS, and gay inclusive multicultural education illuminate instances in which community membership, schooling, and sexuality collided. The controversies help to show the kind of confused tumble of discourses and seemingly nonsensical policy decisions that are born of this fraught relationship. Because this book deals with abstract issues, I have chosen several case studies to examine my points in concrete detail. For instance, when the New York State Board of Regents approved their AIDS education curricular guide in 1986, the Regents cited themselves as an authority describing condom *use* as a high-risk activity. The document noted that the Surgeon General of the United States, nationally recognized medical authorities, and local boards of health all disagreed with the Regents's assessment but, nonetheless, AIDS education in New York State had to abide by their determination that condoms were risky. The decision to define condom use as a risk activity for HIV coincided with New York City's status as one of the national centers of the adolescent and young adult HIV epidemic. Despite evidence that condom use and other safer sex activities would drastically diminish risk for HIV, the policymakers devising AIDS education felt that public schools should instead stress the safety of abstinence, a practice notorious for its high failure rate, over condom use.

I will show how discourses of sexuality education during the AIDS crisis became so closely associated with a variety of risks: risk of HIV, risk to community cohesion, and risk to heterosexuality itself. The controversies I examine are not limited to educational issues, indeed, they often spill over into school board and broader elections. By 1993, disputes over sexuality and public school, including providing access to condoms in high school and beginning antihomophobia lessons in elementary school, led to the firing of the New York City School's Chancellor Joseph Fernandez and eventually contributed to Mayor David Dinkins's defeat in his reelection bid.

The intertwining of sexuality and public school curricula generated public debate over who might be legitimately considered part of the school and broader community. Further, these debates provide a way to examine the competing notions of identity that became part of the culture wars of the late 1980s and 1990s. I bring together poststructural contemporary theory with educational studies to argue that school controversies illuminate social tensions around sexuality and point to the necessity of schools having a broader understanding of sexual meanings, practices, and identities in order to provide support for all students. The school controversies I examine exemplify the tensions between changing discourses around sexuality and public school policies and curricula. I contend that these tensions are exacerbated by liberal and communitarian discourses about identity and the continuing shifts in meaning and practice of sexuality. To examine the tension between theories of identity and actual educational policies, I combine educational philosophy, contemporary social theory, and educational policy studies. School policies attempted to steer a course through potential public dissent, but they did so by ignoring the complexity of meanings of sexuality and the needs of sexual minority students. By setting an impossible standard for normative heterosexuality, schools do a disservice to heterosexual students as well as to sexual minority students.

When, in 1986, the New York State Board of Regents approved a measure that made AIDS curriculum mandatory in all elementary and secondary schools in the state it stimulated a series of controversies in which identity and sexuality entered public discussion about education in ways that had not been previously possible. While the advent of AIDS spurred this discussion on, it was also facilitated by a substantially broadened public discussion of identity informed by discourses of civil rights, feminism, gay rights, and broad demographic shifts in family configurations. Legislation and popular opinion called upon public education to provide some measure of safety to students in an epidemic. However, schools were in reality unable to easily educate about issues concerning a subject so contentious as sexuality. The difficulties schools faced were largely due to an unwillingness or inability to attend to the complexity of meaning in the central concepts in public debate over AIDS. The key terms—community, identity, and sexuality—were all themselves highly debated. Their place and meaning in public education and policy was still being thrashed out among the policymakers, school staff, community at large, and students themselves. Still, AIDS curricular materials attempted to stabilize the meanings of key terms, a move which only served to highlight the contingency of these slippery concepts as public debate continued.

Public conversations about the role of sexuality in public life at least had the effect of undermining the easy presumption of heterosexuality as the "universal subject" of public discourse. By raising public debate over the subject of sex, not only was "sex" disputed, but so too was the very understanding of public subjectivity. The debates over AIDS education were also public discussions over who in the community might rightly call upon the state and education for protection and help in time of crisis. Further, the 1992–1993 debates over gay-inclusive multicultural education, happening just after controversy over the provision of condoms in high schools, turned on defining who the "legitimate minorities" were who might make political claims and have their interests reflected in curricula. That these contentious issues were articulated through education issues and largely around youth only further confounded the discussion over legitimate identities and minorities.

This public conversation on subjectivity and sex was evident during the early years of AIDS education, when curricula and public debates over curricula in the areas of AIDS education, sex education, and gay-inclusive multicultural education collided. In particular, I focus on New York State's *Instructional Guide for AIDS Education K-12*, New York City's "Children of the Rainbow" multicultural curriculum guide, New York City's "Abstinence Oath" for AIDS educators, and the *Sex Respect* curriculum, as well as the development of Gay, Straight, and Questioning Alliances in after-school programs. These debates and the curricula themselves drew a variety of constituencies into both cooperative and contestatory relationships with one another. The debates and controversy represent a strongly contextualized moment where dominant and minority discourses clashed, combined, and rearticulated themselves, challenging and altering key terms, as well as taking up each other's terms. While these moments highlighted the relationality of terms of identity, they also underscored the antagonism in these relations and the central place of sexuality in maintaining that antagonism.

Debate also connected sexuality to citizenship and highlighted the role of public school in maintaining particular notions of proper identity, citizenship, and community membership.[19] The particular notions of identity—liberal and communitarian—most powerful in debate and curricula were insufficiently educative. The clash between liberal and communitarian conceptions of identity is evident, for instance, in the controversy over the provision of condoms to high school students. Where some youth advocates argued for students' individual right to attend to their own protection, other advocates for community-sensitive education argued for parental and community regulation of young people's behavior. The issue of sexuality shows surprising similarities between liberal[20] and communitarian[21] discourses that mark out what is normal and acceptable identity for public subjectivity. The normalizing tendencies of these competing and prevalent understandings of identity create problems for sexual minority students and sexual majority students alike as they constrain curricula in ways that limit not only access to basic information but also limit student ability to critically engage with that information.

Underlying all of these debates is an inherently uneducational belief in "normal" identity and behavior. School policy, curricula, and public debates over education, while purportedly committed to democratic practice and community formation, instead constrained student negotiations with identity and with strategies for avoiding risk in sexual activity.[22] For example, when New York City policy makers withdrew references to gay teens negotiating safer sex from curricula, they missed a crucial opportunity to directly address how to minimize risk for HIV in adolescent males engaged in potentially risky unprotected sex with males. In so doing, they limited information and critical skills available to students confronting a world in which, as always, sexual practices, meanings, pleasures, and dangers are never stable, and are always shifting. Liberals and conservatives, individualists and communitarians all appeared to be more than willing to trade away students' critical examination of sexual identity and practice in the hopes of maintaining stable community support of schools.

A claim to a preexisting and perfectly legible "heterosexual tradition" on which to base curricular and policy decisions is dubious.[23] Especially problematic is the degree to which policymakers, parents, and community members neglected to examine new formations of identity formed out of the mix of the new context and the old contradictions in preceding discourses of identity. Many participants in debates over AIDS education, sex education, and gay inclusive multicultural education inclined toward a cultivation of "traditional" heterosexual notions of student sexual identity and practice. By continually extolling the virtues of waiting until marriage in order to have risk-free sexual relations, curricula made marriage itself unproblematically safe, despite warnings from public health experts that activities, not identities or forms of relationship, put one at risk for HIV. In addition, by positing heterosexual marriage as safe, curricula left no reasonable way for sexual minority students or sexually active students to conceive of themselves as capable of safer practices outside of traditional married heterosexuality.

Accordingly, I argue that the very need for AIDS education and gay-inclusive multiculturalism indicates that meanings and practices comprising sexuality have changed. Without a concern that students might be engaging in risk activities, including unprotected homosexual anal intercourse, for instance, there would be no particular need to educate students about the potential risk of that behavior. In addition, the particular contours of the AIDS epidemic in the United States necessitated a more public discussion, albeit not always progressive, on homosexuality and the increasingly public face of gay and lesbian families reminded school policymakers and practitioners that their constituency was shifting.

Identity, Sexuality, and Theory

In my first two chapters, I summarize liberal, communitarian, and poststructural conceptions of identity. Sex, gender, sexuality, and sexual identity, because their meanings are at once so various and so taken for granted, pose particular difficulties for liberal and communitarian theories and practice. Examining these theories and their influences in public school policy illuminates the tendency in liberal and communitarian theory and practice to relegate disruptive forms of subjectivity, like sexual identity, to the private sphere. As I show in later chapters, liberal and communitarian notions of identity have exerted significant weight in informing responses to specific public school curricular controversies. For liberals, many aspects of identity are properly conceived as private matters. Identity may give particular meaning to private life but ought not to impinge on the individual's ability to interact in public. For communitarians, identity may be more central to the experience of life in public and in private, but the limits to forms of identity in both areas may be strictly limited by tradition or practice. Poststructuralist conceptions of identity find flaws with foundations of liberal and communitarian identity theories. Poststructuralists contend, in contrast to liberals, that identity concerns are deeply infused in both spheres, indeed, that the distinction between the two spheres only serves to cover over the penetration of power in both. To limit the discussion of identity in the public sphere or to deny that diversity of identity exists within communities, furthermore, is *not* to not speak of it. As Foucault contends, silences are a part of discourse, a way of speaking about something without saying anything or a way of marking an absence as correct.[24] Poststructural theories of identity, in contrast to communitarian discourse, point to the play of power in defining the limits of membership in a community or tradition and so take to task even the more nuanced communitarian understandings of identity and community.

In chapter 2, I turn to poststructural work on power, subjectivity and sexuality. I examine the interplay between the three terms that helps to problematize liberal and communitarian conceptions of identity. Because social constructionism places sexuality within specific discursive and historical contexts it is better able to attend to the complexity of sexual identity, practice, and meaning. For example, social constructionist work examines the historical shifts in meaning of homosexual activity into gay identity and argues that changes in context greatly alter the meaning of sexual identities and practices. Therefore, social constructionism challenges claims that some versions of sexuality are not "natural" and are thus improper by examining sexual identities and practices as socially, politically, and historically negotiated. While this may not convince conservatives, it does make explicit the workings of power, resistance, and gender in sexual identities.

Social constructionism's attention to the interplay of identity, activity, and social context that constitute sexuality provides educators with a fuller understanding of the range of sexual meanings and definitions. I argue that this complex understanding of sexuality can better address the ways students experience and act on their sexuality and provide a fuller sense of sexuality's potential importance to self-concept and relationships with others. I then turn to the relationship between identity, pluralization, and maintenance of a space for new conceptions of identity that may further multiply the ability for educators to address concerns about safety and tolerance.[25] Poststructural concerns about identity provide complications to the view of identity represented in school controversies by liberal and communitarian discourses.[26] While I will trouble the foundations of liberalism and communitarianism in the opening chapter, I will rely on elements of both throughout as the basis for criticism of public school curricula.

Curricular Definitions of "Community" and "Sex"

In chapters 3 and 4, I look at concrete examples of curricula, examining the controversy they generated and the repercussions they still have for our understanding the subject of sex. The text and implementation of New York State's AIDS curriculum attempt to carve out a particular notion of responsible community membership based on abstinence and heterosexuality. In so doing, the curriculum positions students who do not conform to these norms as outsiders, both through the text of the curriculum guide and lessons and through the processes by which the curriculum is tailored to local tastes. As outsiders, then, the particular needs of sexually active students of all sexual orientations and practices are left largely unaddressed, leaving these students at a loss. The students most in need of information to protect themselves from HIV infection are in effect discriminated against by policies developed to avoid offending local community values. A sense of situatedness in a community is crucial to enable students to make considered decisions about sexual activity, but when students are unable to place themselves within an exclusionary community or are actively kept out, this sense of connectedness with others is disrupted.

By neglecting the diversity of student sexuality, curricula not only limit participation in the community but also attempt to constrain the understanding of what it means to be properly sexual, indeed, what "sex" means at all. I examine the text of the New York State guide and show how the language of liberal impartiality seemingly keeps the definition of sex and gender fairly open. But as my analysis of the text will show, "sex" comes to mean "heterosexual intercourse" and specifically gendered concerns about sexual relationships are left out. In addition, students are addressed as atomistic sexual decisionmakers and discouraged from viewing sexual relationships as ethical. The curriculum suggests students can maintain "respect" only by avoiding all forms of sexuality. In so doing, AIDS education misses an opportunity to encourage students to consider their relationships with one another as deserving respect, which can also be expressed through engaging in sexual activities that minimize risk for HIV. Especially crucial for my analysis, the curriculum neglects to consider how adolescents themselves arrange and understand their own sexual lives, information that could provide the kind of embedded understanding that supposedly underwrites community involvement in curricular decisions.

The intention of chapters 3 and 4 is to show the institutional limitations on identity expressed through specific curricula. These limitations do not prevent students from reading against the text of the lessons and forming their own responses. Nor do the provisions for community involvement fully constrain the meanings of proper community membership. As chapters 5 and 6 will show, the public engagement with these issues complicates the boundaries of identity in ways that policymakers, whose work reflects attempts to maintain these boundaries, did not expect.

Complex Identity and
Curricular Debates

While chapters 3 and 4 focused on the curricular limitations of key concepts in AIDS education, chapters 5 and 6 focus on the complications to identity and sexuality that spin off debates and policy addressing homosexuality, AIDS, and adolescent sexual activity. In chapter 5, I analyze the public controversy generated by New York City's attempt to revise its multicultural curriculum to include sexual orientation. My contention here is that public debate over the issue affected a shift in the meaning of heterosexuality. By addressing homosexuality, an identity previously unspoken or silenced, conservatives linked their own identities to a firmer relation with homosexuality. I examine the shifts in conservative discourse about homosexuality to point to the instability of heterosexuality (and thus homosexuality) and to the reliance of each term of identity upon the other for its meaning. I also examine conservative attempts to whiten homosexuality and heterosexualize race. In addition, I contend that the public nature of the debate alters the way that homosexuality can be considered, as once out of the closet and part of the language of identity, it is much harder to ignore. School policy changes and debate, then, are as educative to the public as they might be to students.

In chapter 6, I analyze other curricula, like *Sex Respect*, where sexuality is given an explicit and public form. Here I point to complications that this new "public sex" brings to education. New York City's insistence that AIDS educators themselves take an "Abstinence Oath" was intended to prevent educators from deviating from approved curriculum, even if students asked specific questions about safer sex practices. Where the oath was meant to be a clear statement of policy and obligation, educators faced with taking the oath found it made teaching difficult and felt the oath continued to centralize sexuality as the missing, censored topic behind their lessons. Thus, although the intention of the oath was to limit the discussion of sexuality, the public declaration and debate over the oath continued the process of publicizing sexual identity and activity. The "Abstinence Oath" follows in the tradition of "just say no" campaigns and contains the same potential for shifting spaces of sexuality as other public declarations of sexual identity or intention.

Like the "Abstinence Oath," "secondary virginity" complicates identities and spaces of sexuality. "Secondary Virginity" is a concept that *Sex Respect*, an abstinence-only curriculum, that advocates that young women rededicate themselves to virgin status after they have already had sex. The effect of this curricular concept means that a refusal of sexual activity can be reconceived as an identity category. Young girls who embrace secondary virginity appear to centralize their sexuality, rather than simply repress it. The continued requirement that secondary virgins check on one another's status and publicly testify to their sexual inactivity has the side effect of sexualizing the interactions of these young virgins. The public prohibition of speaking about sex broadens the spaces of its consideration and discussion. Both oaths examined in this chapter, one for teachers and the other for students, attempt to use a simple pledge to stem the tide of the complex sexual meanings and practices, but in doing so open public spaces for sexual identity.

Conclusion

In the conclusion, "Curious Alliance," I examine the growth of Gay Straight Alliances as public school extracurricular activities. This chapter shows how the interaction among new political and social formations of identity interact with school policy, as well as how student negotiations of policy help create new kinds of identity. Policies provide possibility for identity negotiation, albeit often unintentionally. But conceptions of identity are no more stable than the people they attempt to bring together and so are themselves continually shifting. Even as new identity formations serve as critiques of what has come before they are also in conversation with earlier formations. In the case of sexual identity, new kinds of identity help to expand who is considered and named as part of the school—and wider—community and they chart the relationship among sexual identities.[27] As critiques of identity politics, where the defining features of identity are clear, consistent, and agreed upon, these groups chart new associations. These alliances also remind us that student resistance to silences in the curricula are themselves an important part of curricula. In other words, these student alliances are responding to what is ambivalent, confused, and/or missing and actually do something themselves to fill in the blanks. GSQA's also remind us of the contradictory messages students get about sexuality and thus are marbled throughout with the complications of the discourses that help form them. Because these groups are formed with the twin projects of addressing discrimination against sexual minorities and providing students with space to interrogate their own identities and desires, the groups encourage students to see themselves as responsible to one another and responsible to themselves. Further, because gay straight alliances so often run into barriers of homophobia at the local or even state level, they provide students with laboratories for democracy. These student groups remind us of the complexity of education and the importance of student activity in reshaping identity and spaces for education.

All of the issues examined here serve as reminders that sexuality is always a part of school and broader community issues. But sexuality is also interlocked with other aspects of identity and community. I hope this book will provide a model for interrogating these deeper connections and the persistence of anxiety about sexuality, particularly the relationship between sexuality and schooling. While there is reason to be hopeful that students are working hard to improve conditions for sexual minority youth, it remains striking that few states provide specific protections for transgender youth and few states are willing to have sexual minority issues become part of school curricula.

Notes

1. Stephanie Desmond, "School Board Defers Vote on Policy to Protect Gay Students: Some Believe Measure Could Allow Teaching about Homosexuality," *Baltimore Sun*, 27 June 2002.

2. John Gehring,, "Mass. Stance on Anti-gay Bias in Schools Stirring Debate," *Education Week*, 17 May 2000, 23.

3. David LaFontaine quoted in Gehring, "Mass. Stance on Anti-gay Bias," 23.

4. Gehring, "Mass. Stance," 23.

5. "Updated: School Districts That Have Disassociated from the Discriminatory BSA," www.glsen.org/templates/resources/record. html? section=115 & record=409, 10 December 2001, [cited 4 September 2002].

6. Allison F. Bauer, *State of the States 2002: Gay, Lesbian, and Straight Educators Network (GLSEN) Policy Analysis of Lesbian, Gay, Bisexual, and Transgender (LGBT) Safer Schools Issues*. Rhode Island's Department of Education provides statewide protection for gay and lesbian students.

7. Michael Bochenek and A. Widney Brown, *Hatred in the Hallways: Violence and Discrimination against Lesbian, Gay, Bisexual, and Transgender Students in U.S. Schools* (New York: Human Rights Watch, 2001), 33.

8. Joseph G. Kosciw and M. K. Cullen, *The GLSEN 2001 National School Climate Survey: The School-Related Experiences of Our Nation's Lesbian, Gay, Bisexual, and Transgender Youth* (New York: GLSEN, 2001), 6.

9. Kosciw and Cullen, *GLSEN 2001 School Climate Survey*, 14–16.

10. Sabrina L. quoted in Bochenek and Brown, *Hatred in the Hallways*, 52.

11. Kosciw and Cullen, *GLSEN 2001 School Climate Survey*, 14.

12. Kosciw and Cullen, *GLSEN 2001 School Climate Survey*, 14.

13. Kosciw and Cullen, *GLSEN 2001 School Climate Survey*, 12.

14. Bochenek and Brown, *Hatred in the Hallways*, 33.

15. Kosciw and Cullen, *GLSEN 2001 School Climate Survey,* 32–33.

16. See Cris Mayo, "Education by Association: The Shortcomings of Discourses of Privacy and Civility in Anti-homophobia Education," in *Getting Ready for Benjamin* ed. Rita Kissen (Boulder, Colo.: Rowman and Littlefield, 2002), 81–90.

17. See for instance, James A. Banks and Cherry A. McGee Banks, *Multicultural Education: Issues and Perspective,* 4th ed. (New York: John Wiley & Sons, 2001), and Sonia Nieto, *Affirming Diversity: The Sociopolitical Context of Multicultural Education,* 3rd ed. (New York: Longman, 2000). The lack of attention to sexuality should not be taken to indicate homophobia but rather that "culture" in these texts means race, religion, and ethnicity.

18. Barbara Wallace, "A Call for Change in Multicultural Training at Graduate Schools of Education: Educating to End Oppression and for Social Justice," *Teachers College Record* 102, no. 6 (2000): 1093–1111. Interestingly, Wallace article is indexed under "Race and Ethnicity," not "Sexuality" (or "Language" or "Disability"), a choice which seems to reinforce her point.

19. See, for instance, Cindy Patton, *Fatal Advice: How Safe-Sex Education Went Wrong* (Durham, N.C.: Duke University Press, 1996); James T. Sears, "Dilemmas and Possibilities of Sexuality Education: Reproducing the Body Politic," in *Sexuality and the Curriculum: The Politics and Practices of Sexuality Education*, ed. James T. Sears (New York: Teachers College Press. 1992); Simon Watney, "School's Out," in *Inside/out: Lesbian Theories, Gay Theories,*

ed. D. Fuss, (New York: Routledge, 1992), 387–404; Bonnie Trudell and Mariamne Whatley, "Sex Respect: A Problematic Public School Sexuality Curriculum," *Journal of Sex Education and Therapy* 17, no. 2 (1991): 125–140; Amy Gutmann, *Democratic Education* (Princeton, N.J.: Princeton University Press, 1987).

20. For the purposes of this project, I will be using liberal and communitarian theorists attempting to find balance between individual rights and community membership. See Will Kymlicka, *Multicultural Citizenship: A Liberal Theory of Minority Rights* (Oxford: Clarendon Press, 1995), and *Liberalism, Community, and Culture* (Oxford: Clarendon Press, 1989); also see Charles Taylor, *Multiculturalism and "The Politics of Recognition"* (Princeton, N.J.: Princeton University Press, 1992).

21. Seyla Benhabib, *Situating the Self: Gender, Community, and Postmodernism in Contemporary Ethics* (New York: Routledge, 1992); Michael Walzer, "Comment," in *Multiculturalism and "The Politics of Recognition,"* edited by Amy Gutmann (Princeton, N.J.: Princeton University Press, 1992), 99–103; Michael Sandel, *Liberalism and the Limits of Justice* (Cambridge: Cambridge University Press, 1982).

22. For other critiques of sex education and safer sex education see Andrew McKay, *Sexual Ideology and Schooling: Towards Democractic Sexuality Education* (Albany, N.Y.: State University of New York Press, 1999); Jonathan G. Silin, *Sex, Death, and the Education of Children: Our Passion for Ignorance in the Age of AIDS* (New York: Teachers College Press, 1995).

23. Eve Kosofsky Sedgwick, *Epistemology of the Closet* (Berkeley: University of California Press, 1990); Judith Butler, *Gender Trouble: Feminism and the Subversion of Identity* (New York: Routledge, 1989); Michel Foucault, *History of Sexuality, Volume One: An Introduction* (New York: Vintage, 1978).

24. Foucault, *History of Sexuality, Volume One,* 101.

25. William Connolly, *The Ethos of Pluralization* (Minneapolis: University of Minnesota Press, 1995).

26. William Pinar, ed., *Queer Theory in Education* (Mahwah, N.J.: Lawrence Erlbaum, 1998).

Part I: Identity, Sexuality, and Theory

1

Sexuality and Theory

Controversies over sexuality and education give us a clear view of the complex and competing ways people understand what sexuality is, how it is related to education, and who is a valued member of the community based on their sexual identity. Because the ideas circulating through these controversies are so varied and changing, it is something of a challenge to untangle them. The next two chapters attempt to show at least three of the main versions of sexuality's relationship to education and community life: liberal, communitarian, and poststructural. I choose this particular way of splitting up the issues because these are discourses that are common in controversies over sexuality and they are therefore quite familiar, even if not always explicitly labeled. People seem comfortable saying things like, "I don't care what she does, as long as she does it in private," which is a version of the liberal right to privacy. Others might respond with "well, it may be her right, but it goes against our community's values and I don't want that around here," which is a version of communitarian arguments. Even people who don't approve of the changes in practices of sexuality can easily point to the shifts in sexual meanings and understandings by saying, "it didn't used to be like this." The rest of the book will show the more nuanced and complicated way these discourses weave through debates. While I think the theoretical chapters are worth the time, if only to give the reader a fuller sense of the deeper meanings of each discourse, it is also possible to read the case study chapters first and return to the theoretical chapters for clarification of terms and definitions.

In pulling apart the main competing discourses in sexuality and education controversies, I am outlining very common ways we have of discussing, challenging, and protecting sexuality. While I will point to problems in the theory and practice of liberal and communitarian ideals, both approaches bring much that is good and useful to our understandings of sexuality. Arguments for gay rights are deeply indebted to liberal theory's insistence that individuals are bearers of rights and that their participation in political processes requires the protection of their autonomy and freedom. Gay, lesbian, bisexual, and transgender community members well understand communitarianism's stress on the importance of membership and belonging, even if their particular traditions are more variable and their community boundaries more permeable than traditional communities.

Nonetheless, despite debts to liberalism and communitarianism, sexual minorities may also find key theoretical blind spots in each that show that rigid ideas about gender, sexuality, and tradition permeate both discourses. I will later show that social constructionist and poststructural theories of sexuality provide better accounts of the variation and shifts in the meaning and practice of sexuality. But for now, I will examine the problems procedural and substantive liberalism pose for advocates of sexual minorities. Then I turn to an examination of the conservative tendency of communitarian theory to turn community dissenters into outsiders.

Liberalism is a political theory intent on preserving individual freedom, political equality, and social stability. To ensure each of these, liberalism purports to maintain neutrality on the particular identities and commitments of its political actors, essentially welcoming them into political processes as bearers of rights and framing their particularities as private matters. While over the course of time liberal governments have had to specifically address inequalities in property ownership, race, and gender, and have done so by recognizing that distinctions of class, race, and gender do make a difference, liberalism has largely continued to view sexuality as a matter of private freedom. The "rights" one has to be a sexual minority, then, are very often interpreted to be the right to privacy. Unfortunately, during the period covered by this book, the right to privacy was not been particularly helpful to gays and lesbians either as, until 2003, the Supreme Court has held that states may make private consensual homosexual sexual activity illegal. While principles of liberalism keep much of private life protected from state interference, nonetheless in practice the rights and privileges of heterosexuality are fully protected through marriage, benefits, inheritance laws, insurance, and public school curricula, to name only a few. In other words, although liberalism may claim that all citizens are equal and that their particularities are best protected through their private exercise of liberty and public exercise of equal political rights, heterosexuality manages to receive both public and private protections. Indeed much of the political wrangling over sexuality in recent years has been a variety of "no promo homo" laws in which Congress and state legislatures have legally defined marriage as between a man and a woman. These laws are designed to ensure that gay and lesbian relationships are unable to enjoy the protections and benefits of heterosexual relationships. While liberalism may, then, give us all a discourse of rights, in practice, political rights and private liberties belong most often to heterosexuals.

A right to privacy may also not be much help to a sexual minority youth harassed at a public school. Many such students report that school administrators, teachers, and other students criticize them for being too overt.[1] If only they would be more subtle and quiet about their sexual orientation, the argument goes, people would leave them alone. Taken together with the statistic that disproportionate numbers of gay and lesbian youth contemplate and commit suicide, often because they feel isolated or have been the victims of harassment and violence, being left alone is hardly the finest experience of freedom and privacy.[2] Being alone or staying hidden means that sexual minority youth have no support and are not receiving an adequate education. In short, they have the "right" to be neglected.

Still, because rights discourse is central to how we understand what it means to be a citizen and a person, sexual minorities continue to attempt to expand recognition and protection of their rights. By adding protections to nondiscrimination laws at state and local levels, lesbians, gay men, bisexuals, and, in fewer areas, transgender people have proven successful in protecting their ability to work and live without hiding who they are. Notice that in order to have one's rights protected, one must have a degree of recognition from others and from the state. In other words, the seemingly neutral citizen of liberal theory does have an identity, potentially has a partner, a community, and a variety of differences from other actors that will also require some form of recognition from others in order to receive equal rights and equal protection. Equality does not mean sameness. We do not expect people with disabilities to endure difficulties accessing public buildings. We do not think it fair and equal to teach all students in exactly the same way because we know students have different learning styles and interests. But in order to understand how people may need different things from their fellow citizens, we also need to recognize differences in identity, culture, and practices that may help us to better understand that being treated equally may not be exactly the same thing for everyone. While opponents of gay rights have argued that sexual minorities want "special rights," in fact, gay rights activists have organized for the right to be protected from discrimination on the grounds of sexual orientation, in other words, to be treated with the same respect as heterosexual citizens are treated.

Protection from discrimination is well in keeping with liberalism's purpose, which is to enable the flourishing of every individual by giving each an opportunity to choose how they best want to live. Liberalism also has a substantial commitment to particular ideas about what that best life will entail. For liberals, the purpose of autonomy and freedom is to enable individuals to reflect on a variety of good ways to live and choose well. Further, because freedoms are fragile, liberalism also requires citizens to commit themselves to nourishing those abilities in others in a context that provides stability for their choices. To a certain extent, liberalism requires recognition of those choices in order to ensure that they exist as possibilities. This recognition may be minimal, where all agree to recognize and respect surface-level differences, or recognition may be robust, where differences are understood to be deeper and more in need of substantial accommodation.[3] Liberal theorists are cautious on the question of robust recognition, fearing that cultures demand too much from their members or may encourage practices that diminish the abilities of their members to critically examine cultural practices. But at the same time, liberals stress the importance of group membership for providing a full and rich context for individual choice. Liberals continue to be critical of the idea of group rights, especially when groups want the right to have institutions like schools provide substantial support for their members to flourish in their traditions and practices that may be at odds with liberal emphasis on individual rights. Indeed because of their emphasis on the individual, liberals tend to value cultures instrumentally for the context they may provide for individual flourishing, not because cultures are particularly valuable things in and of themselves.[4]

Liberal Proceduralism, Democratic Education, and the Failure to Recognize Sexual Minorities

Two different forms of liberalism have similar difficulties protecting the rights of sexual minority students. Proceduralist liberals who stress the importance of maintaining the procedures of liberal discussion over any particular substantial commitments attempt to keep public discussion thin, in the hopes of keeping more people engaged. Democratic theorists believe that the substance of people's commitment to liberalism is stronger than just agreeing to talk. They argue, for instance, that commitment to liberalism and democracy require agreement on key ideas and practices that cannot be removed just to allow seemingly liberal conversations to continue. I will show in the following section that both proceduralist and democratic theorists have neglected sexual minority youth in their attempts to forestall controversy over public school policies.

Fearing the fracturing of public life, liberal proceduralists attempt to emphasize commonalities and areas of agreement in civic discussions. For proceduralist liberals, strong disagreement or differences ought to become private issues. Differences can still flourish in private, argue proceduralists, but they cannot be brought into areas of public dispute because they will damage liberal conversations by importing ideas contrary to liberalism. When applied to public school curricula, liberal proceduralism argues that although some ideas will have to be sacrificed, the broadest range of people must be included in decision-making processes. In practice this has meant that conservatives are brought into the decision-making process to ensure that they will not be offended by curricula. Sexuality-related curricula are more likely to be the site of this negotiation than other areas of curriculum, even though conservative religious people may have as strong a stake in seeing other issues addressed in public school, for instance, advocating prayer in school or removal of "secular humanist" textbooks. While conservatives challenge school policy on other curricular issues, they are most successful in challenging sexuality-related curricula.

Liberal proceduralists have argued that conservative input on AIDS education, even if it removed controversial information directed at sexual minorities, could be acceptable as long as democratic procedures were followed. Ken Howe, for instance, argues that AIDS education ought to be open to local control and that communities ought to be able to remove information they find offensive. This may sometimes result in "questionable programmes," but democratization of the curriculum is necessary because parents and teachers share the responsibility for educating children.[5] Howe worries that without this stress on democratic decision making in the area of public health, curricular decisions will be turned over to experts and their "technocratic rationality."[6] He misses, however, the discriminatory potential for limits on offensive materials. What constitutes offensiveness to a community becomes defined as outside of that community—minorities within communities come to be viewed as outsiders even if they live within its physical boundaries. Though he specifically notes that "morally abhorrent view—such as 'AIDS victims ought to be cast off to some far away island' ought to be met head on," he neglects to consider the cost of omission of information from the perspective of sexual minority youth (or, for that matter, all students). Parents may well find adolescent sexual behavior offensive or homosexual behavior offensive, but by removing information that might help those students to engage in less risky activities parents may unwittingly compound the risks these adolescents face. While conservatives are welcomed into decision-making processes, no one represents students in need of information and strategies that can help them minimize their risk for contracting HIV.

The proceduralist liberal strategy produces a dilemma—how can controversy over authority and offensiveness be avoided at the same time school curricula address the broadest array of concerns? As Bruce Ackerman argues:

> When you and I learn that we disagree with one or another dimension of the moral truth, we should not search for some common value that will trump this disagreement. . . . We should simply say nothing at all about this disagreement and try to solve our problem by invoking premises that we do agree on. In restraining ourselves in this way, we need not lose the chance to talk to one another about our deepest, moral disagreements in countless other, more private, contexts.[7]

As an ideal, the notion that public conversation should be constrained to principles interlocutors can agree on, as opposed to endlessly coming to loggerheads on questions of faith and morality, appears to protect diversity as well as to encourage communication across differences. Indeed, Ackerman protects diversity and equality by insisting that one can participate in a liberal conversation only if one does not consider one's own version of the good intrinsically superior to another's or one does not consider oneself intrinsically superior to another. These are basic premises for any negotiation in a liberal state. However, in practice, interlocutors may not share common premises or may find those basic premises insufficient to reach a mutually agreed upon decision, even within a context in which one might expect liberal procedures to rule the day. Thus, those who cannot articulate a right to engage in certain proscribed behaviors, even in private, may find entering the liberal conversation difficult.[8]

When advocates of liberal proceduralism minimize conflict by minimizing difference they begin to form an exclusionary political community. As "local control" and "community involvement" are terms used to create a political community based on agreement, the minority is not merely cast as a dissenting voice, but actually removed from what comes to be considered the community. The liberal proceduralist intention is to encourage a diversity of conceptions of the good to flourish by not allowing the state to set out a particular notion of the good, in this case, to avoid state mandates on the particular form that sensitive curricular issues take in local communities. But within those communities that procedurally decide on a limited notion of the good in terms of a particular version of sex, adolescence, and the family, this strategy for insuring plural notions of the good is undermined. The local community that comes to be represented by the very decisions regarding limits on sex and AIDS education includes what might be considered sexual outsiders, whose interests by definition are no longer the interests of the community. Proceduralist liberals, in attempting to maintain a civil public, may mistakenly help to create a climate in which some people are unwelcome because they themselves are the bearers of what is offensive to local values.

Even Amy Gutmann, critical of liberals for insufficiently democratizing their approach to nourishing plural notions of the good, is willing to trade away controversial issues in sex education in order to encourage conservative parents to keep their children in public school. Gutmann argues for the centrality of nondiscrimination and nonrepression for guaranteeing that public schools prepare students for their future participation in democratic society by encouraging students to critically reflect on plural notions of the good life. As Gutmann argues, schools have a responsibility to conform to local values, but not when those values are discriminatory or repressive.[9] Gutmann contends that critical deliberation among good lives is central to democratic education. As such:

> Adults must be free to deliberate and disagree but constrained to secure the intellectual grounds for deliberation and disagreement among children. Adults must therefore be prevented from using their present deliberative freedom to undermine the future deliberative freedom of children.[10]

Though parents have a strong stake in the education and future of their children, Gutmann argues that educational decisions ought not to be made with the parents' freedom in mind, but rather with an eye to cultivating future freedoms for children. These freedoms are particularly crucial when children may not share all aspects of their parents' identity and thus may not be able to access information about parts of their own lives or future lives. Schools have the responsibility to educate children into the capacities that will prepare them for critical citizenship in a democracy in a way that balances their identities as family members, state members, and individuals. Education needs to recognize that students will become participants in a democracy and needs to expose children to the greatest possible range of good lives from which to choose.[11]

But Gutmann does not apply these principles to the issue of mandatory sex education. Concerned that mandatory sex education may drive some parents from public education and thus further limit their children's ability to deliberate freely, she advocates allowing parents to opt out of curricula they find offensive. Their children, Gutmann opines, are likely to get information about sex from their friends anyway.[12] Since she notes the heavy burden that this lack of information places, particularly on young girls, it is unclear why, in the case of sex education, the parents' right to have their values respected by the schools trumps the students' right to potentially crucial information. Contending that democratic decisions may not always have the best outcome, Gutmann suggests they will be more enlightened thanks to their respect for the variety of communities that make up a democracy.[13] But her account of the communities involved in the decision over sex education leaves out the children of conservative parents and supports the exclusion of information that a community may find offensive. Thus, despite her attempts to have diverse communities involved in democracy, she removes their voices from decisions over sex education.

Part of the liberal and democratic willingness to allow controversial curricular issues to be removed by local communities follows from a liberal presumption that heterosexual families encourage the commitment and order necessary for a smoothly functioning society, as well as an interest base from which to act.[14] While theories may not be specifically at the back of the minds of those liberals who are unwilling to take on conservative revolts against sex and AIDS education, nonetheless, liberals appear to be most comfortable supporting gay-inclusivity and sexual freedom as private expressions, not as family-like relationships whose interests are articulated in public.

In response to the problems faced by minorities in liberal states Will Kymlicka sets out principles that would protect minorities from state interference, as long as they do not engage in domination of other minorities and also could guarantee members of minorities safety from illiberal intra-group coercion.[15] While he contends that his ideas should apply to gender and sexual minorities, religion and sexuality both appear to be muddier than some of the issues of multinationality he addresses. He assumes that minorities of any stripe except national minorities are fighting to be included in the national culture.[16] Thus he misses the potential external criticism gays might lodge against the presumed naturalness of heterosexual relations and gender norms. Gays and other sexual dissenters may want representation without fully wanting to conform to the heterosexual norm.

Feminist and queer theorists contend that liberalism's unquestioning embrace of marriage only shows the extent to which liberalism emphasizes reflection in the public sphere but discourages it in the private. As feminists have long argued, the personal is political. Liberalism, they argue, depends on a too-ready split between public and private. Further, the distinction between public and private always privileges male power and maintains traditional gender roles. Susan Moller Okin also notes that some liberals and communitarians stress participation in the family as being so integral to social and political participation that they would like to see divorce made more difficult. This, they argue, would encourage family stability and foster the kind of commitment to the family they would like to see reflected in a commitment to politics.[17] They tie the disintegration of the family to an inability of people to commit to one another rather than to the gender inequality upon which the "traditional" family relies. The trouble with this reading is that it ignores how rising divorce rates can also be attributed to women's (and men's) dissatisfaction with an institution that requires too much gender role conformity in an economic and cultural world that opens up more possibilities for independence and alteration in gender relations. Here liberals do not attend to possible power differentials in the kind of traditional practices they advocate but do not interrogate.[18] By explicitly or implicitly arguing that heterosexual relations are the stable base for political life, liberal theory maintains a rigidity of gender norms and relationships that not only makes it shortsighted with regard to heterosexual relationships but potentially disconnects homosexual relationships from political participation and protection. This heterosexual bias is not necessarily intrinsic to liberalism, despite its reliance on the public/private split that appears to energize most of liberalism's heterosexist bias. So the problem may not be so much that liberals absolutely must analogize political stability with heterosexual familial stability, but rather that even liberals intent on minimizing outside influences on political processes are heavily influenced by their own social norms. As Justice Kennedy argued in his majority opinion in *Romer v. Evans,* much of the legal reasoning behind anti-gay rights laws appears to be motivated only by animus.

Communitarians, Membership, and Boundaries

In contrast to liberals who stress the rights of individuals, communitarians argue that community membership makes meaningful life possible. According to communitarians, individuals do not make the kind of abstract, reflective choices that liberals claim because no one can think from nowhere. They argue that the autonomous liberal citizen does not make abstract choices but rather deliberates from within a deep cultural understanding. In other words, everyone has a view from somewhere.[19] The exact location of this "somewhere" of community or tradition varies greatly among communitarian theorists. Tradition may be local custom and practice, national attitude and history, a particular religious or ethnic practice, a school of thought, or any number of other kinds of practices and beliefs ranging in size and duration.[20]   But communitarians point out that whatever the particular definition of tradition or community, people are inevitably already participating and continually drawn back to their roots. Even an archetypical liberal individualist culture, such as that of the white, middle-class, U.S. citizen, longs for the connections of community-based life[21] and constantly re-creates tradition, even as it seems to desire new practices.[22]

While liberals stress the need for citizens to make considered choices about their lives, communitarians emphasize that choice is meaningless without a context and without others who care about the kinds of choices that might be made. To talk about oneself is also to talk about the traditions from whence one comes and the people with whom one is connected. While sometimes communitarians appear to desire a nostalgic homogeneous community, others explain community and tradition as processes of change and shift. In the controversies over sexuality and education, competing forms of communitarianism have vied for ownership of the concept of "community values." Religious conservatives argued that sexual minorities had no place in traditional communities and were, by definition, outsiders. Conservatives argued that the heterosexual family had always been at the base of organized society and that sexual minorities were selfish individualists only caring for their own pleasures, not the responsibilities of family life and community membership.[23]   Advocates for sexual minority youth also argued for the importance of community membership, criticizing school policy that cast sexual minority youth as outsiders and thus made school an uncomfortable and threatening place to be.[24] Gay activists argued that the development of strong and committed gay communities enabled the growth of gay AIDS services organization and enabled the creation of safer sex education using the language of the gay communities.[25] Without the bonds of community, all of these groups argued, people's lives and actions would be meaningless.

In this section, I will summarize some of the communitarian correctives to liberal neutrality and then move to a criticism of communitarianism for its inability to address dissent and diversity within its conceptions of community and tradition, with particular regard to gender and sexuality. The degree to which communitarian theorists acknowledge the shifting boundaries of community is crucial to their ability to address a complex vision of sexuality and sexual identity, but as the following will show, communitarians all too often draw problematic, exclusionary boundaries even when they appear to initially advocate for hazy conceptions of community and tradition.

In contrast to liberal proceduralists who want to maintain neutrality in the public sphere, communitarians contend that biases and context provide the grounds from which understanding can proceed. They question the degree to which the liberal emphasis on rational revision of one's ends is possible. While communitarians hold the ability to reflect on one's position in very high esteem, they question the degree to which one can and should abstract oneself from one's position. In terms of providing a meaningful context for identities, deliberation, and justice, communitarian corrective to potentially alienating versions of liberal neutrality is useful. But when communitarians carve out areas of life they hold to be beyond reflection (or they believe ought to be considered beyond reflection) in order to safeguard their meaning, they begin to raise concerns among liberals and others that they do not always hold strongly to deliberation and revisability of ends. In addition, the communitarian tendency to draw boundaries around communities while at the same time holding to ambiguous definitions of the traditions that constitute those communities is a troubling example of the exclusionary potential of identity.

Not all communitarians stress conformity, but in setting out how criticism within a community takes place, some communitarians begin to hazily draw boundaries between membership and nonmembership. Michael Walzer, for instance, argues that the strongest criticism of a tradition comes from within that tradition because insiders have a stronger sense of what the tradition, cultural identity, or community means. Walzer points to the importance of intuition and social grounding in moral philosophy because it requires

> a reflection upon the familiar, a reinvention of our own homes. This is, however, a critical reflection, reinvention with a purpose: we are to correct our intuitions by reference to the model we construct out of those same intuitions, or we are to correct our more groping intuitions by reference to a model we construct out of our more confident intuitions. We move back and forth in either case between moral immediacy and moral abstraction, between an intuitive and a reflective understanding. . . . Our focus is on ourselves, our own principles and values—otherwise, intuition would be of no help.[26]

That our embeddedness is the source of our ability to reflect and even conceive of identity is a concept that communitarians share with social constructionists and poststructuralist theorists, which is addressed later in this chapter. But whereas the latter two also explore the disjunctions and resistances to embeddedness, communitarians tend to be more certain about the boundaries they draw around community and tradition. Some recognize the potential problems in this and attempt to circumvent the repressive potential of drawing boundaries too firmly. As Walzer notes, "The community is itself a good—conceivably the most important good—that gets distributed."[27] He has difficulty in balancing his descriptions of community between the embattled minority fighting for group self-determination and the close-minded, boundary-drawing in-group intent on keeping outsiders away. He contends that "admission and exclusion are at the core of communal independence, they suggest the deepest meaning or self-determination."[28] But he also notes: "The denial of membership is always the first in a long train of abuses."[29] Though he firmly holds to a notion that the internal critic has a privileged access to an understanding of his or her culture, he also holds that there are "no clear cut definitions or boundaries between members and strangers."[30] Furthermore, "common understandings [are] . . . always subject to dispute."[31] Yet somehow, according to Walzer, "to override [common understandings] is (always) to act unjustly."[32] The key issue for a dissenter in a community would be to figure out when one has overstepped a boundary in one's criticism that then places one outside of one's original community. Communitarians are hazy on this point and despite their emphasis on intersubjectivity, which liberals may neglect, what constitutes membership in a community appears to be an intersubjective concern. But how differences in interpretation of insider/outsider are adjudicated remains unclear in many communitarian writings.

Charles Taylor contends that as long as people are engaged in a conversation that disputes the meaning of something, potentially including membership in a community, they do in fact occupy common ground. Indeed, Taylor argues that it is this recognition of the plurality of interpretations about tradition that binds people into a common tradition. It is a common object of dispute that forms the bond, not a common set of principles and beliefs.[33] This rather contentious picture of tradition's place in maintaining a sort of social cohesion is also reflected in Michael Oakeshott's characterization of tradition as a conversation about "intimations" of the world. This conversation is also not settled with regard to who may participate and what may be said. He argues that "no traditional way of behavior, no traditional skill ever remains fixed; its history is one of continuous change."[34] Indeed, change may be integral to a tradition, coming from the "freedom and inventiveness at the heart of every traditional way of life."[35] The potential for inventiveness pushes tradition past what may even be recognizable by most of its participants. In describing how the Christian tradition undergoes change, Oakeshott contends that "an idea or practice may be properly Christian which, in part at least, runs counter to much that had been previously regarded as Christian."[36] As long as these changes don't "[disturb] the unity or [break] down [the tradition's] consistency" they are not threatening.[37]

The difficult task for those participating in a tradition is to be able to determine the consistency throughout this process of change:

> A tradition of behavior is a tricky thing to get to know. Indeed, it may even appear to be essentially unintelligible. It is neither fixed nor finished; it has no changeless center to which understanding can anchor itself; there is no sovereign purpose to be perceived or invariable direction to be detected; there is no model to be copied, idea to be realized, or rule to be followed. Some parts of it may change more slowly than others, but none is immune from change. Everything is temporary. Nevertheless, though a tradition of behavior is flimsy and elusive, it is not without identity, and what makes it a possible object of knowledge is the fact that all its parts do not change at the same time and that the changes it undergoes are potential within it. Its principle is a principle of continuity: authority is diffused between past, present, and future.[38]

As long as the picture of community, tradition, or culture remains hazy one would think dissenters could not be easily dismissed. But community, in practice, often comes to have a circular definition in which diversity is defined as outside of community. As we will see in later chapters, for instance, the Christian Right, in its attempt to have information about sexuality and particularly homosexuality removed from public school curricula, cites "community values" as its ground for action. Even where open and active gay community members were present within the geographical community, conservative activists have claimed that gay people were outsiders.

But where conservative communitarians may desire a homogeneous community, poststructuralists describe communities as places of difference. As Jeffrey Weeks puts it, "To care for difference becomes an affirmation of our limits, and our need for others."[39] The next chapter will outline poststructural conceptions of identity and community that help reconceive these central concepts in light of sexuality and difference. While liberalism and communitarianism provide some helpful ideals, in practice their difficult relations with sexuality mean they are unable to theoretically grapple with the complexities of sexuality and the range of communities that do exist but do not often find representation in policy decisions.

Notes

1. See Michael Bochenek and A. Widney Brown, *Hatred in the Hallways: Violence and Discrimination against Lesbian, Gay, Bisexual, and Transgender Students in U.S. Schools* (New York: Human Rights Watch, 2001) and Joseph G. Kosciw and M. K. Cullen, *The GLSEN 2001 National School Climate Survey: The School–Related Experiences of Our Nation's Lesbian, Gay, Bisexual, and Transgender Youth* (New York: Gay, Lesbian, and Straight Educators Network, 2001).

2. Gary Remafedi, "Introduction: The State of Knowledge on Gay, Lesbian, and Bisexual Youth Suicide," *Death by Denial: Studies of Suicide in Gay and Lesbian Teenagers*, ed. Gary Remafedi (Boston: Alyson, 1994), 7–14.

3. Walter Feinberg, *Common Schools, Uncommon Identities: National Unity and Cultural Differences* (New Haven, Conn.: Yale University Press, 1998), 167–171.

4. Charles Taylor, *Multiculturalism: Examining the Politics of Recognition*, ed. Amy Gutmann (Princeton, N.J.: Princeton University Press, 1994), 72–73.

5. Kenneth R. Howe, "AIDS Education in the Public Schools: Old Wine in New Bottles?" *Journal of Moral Education* 19, no. 2 (May 1990): 114–123.

6. Howe, "AIDS Education," 120.

7. Bruce Ackerman, "Why Dialogue?" *Journal of Philosophy* 86 (January 1989): 8.

8. Liberalism also appears to encourage a moral power vacuum that allows conservative traditionalism to step in when it lacks the courage of its own convictions with regard to freedom. For instance, in the decision in *Bowers v. Hardwick* (overturned by the 2003 decision in *Lawrence v. Texas*), the principles invoked by the Supreme Court to let stand the state of Georgia's antisodomy law were those of "our Judeo–Christian tradition" and not those of the liberal state. In this context, the freedom potentially afforded by privacy was not a strong enough concern to override the strength of tradition. This tendency may not at base be a fault with liberalism as an ideal, but rather with some liberal theory and practice on the issue of sexuality. Sometimes, in other words, liberal neutrality does not live up to its promise because it has not interrogated foundational concepts for bias and particularity. Thus, some liberal attempts to maintain diversity by evoking a relatively neutral public sphere of political interaction often do have the effect of removing sexuality from view, especially in public school policy decisions to remove controversial information about homosexuality, abortion, birth control, and masturbation.

9. Amy Gutmann, *Democratic Education* (Princeton, N.J.: Princeton University Press: 1987), 44–45.

10. Gutmann, *Democratic Education*, 45.

11. Gutmann, *Democratic Education*, 44.

12. Gutmann, *Democratic Education*, 110.

13. Gutmann, *Democratic Education*, 11.

14. John Rawls, *A Theory of Justice* (Cambridge, Mass.: Harvard University Press, 1971), 7.

15. Will Kymlicka, *Multicultural Citizenship: A Liberal Theory of Minority Rights* (Oxford: Clarendon Press, 1995), 152.

16. Kymlicka, *Multicultural Citizenship*, 180–181.

17. Susan Moller Okin, *Justice, Gender and the Family* (New York: Basic Books, 1989). See Daniel Bell, *Communitarianism and Its Critics* (Oxford: Oxford University Press, 1994) for more on the argument to make divorce difficult.

18. Okin, *Justice, Gender, and the Family*, 93.

19. See, for instance, Michael Walzer, *Interpretation and Social Criticism*. (Cambridge, Mass.: Harvard University Press, 1987), 5–6.

20. In keeping with the communitarian tendency toward seeing culture, community, and tradition as largely interchangeable concepts, I will also be using them interchangeably.

21. Robert N. Bellah, *Habits of the Heart: Individualism and Commitment in American Life* (Berkeley: University of California Press, 1996).

22. Judith Martin, *Star–Spangled Manners: In Which Miss Manners® Defends American Etiquette (For a Change)* (New York: W.W. Norton, 2002), 35–36.

23. This particular outlook is clearly schematized in a chart comparing "Family" to "Lifestyles," Janet G. Hunt and Larry L. Hunt, "Here to Play: Families to Lifestyles," *Journal of Family Issues* vol 8, no. 4 (December, 1987): 440–443.

24. See N'Tanya Lee et al., "Whose Kids? Our Kids! Race, Sexuality and the Right in New York City's Curriculum Battles," *Radical America* 25, no. 1 (March 1993).

25. Douglas Crimp, "How to Have Promiscuity in an Epidemic," in *AIDS: Cultural Analysis/Cultural Activism* (Cambridge: Massachusetts Institute of Technology Press, 1988), 265.

26. Michael Walzer, *Interpretation and Social Criticism* (Cambridge, Mass.: Harvard University Press, 1987), 17–18.

27. Michael Walzer, *Spheres of Justice: A Defense of Pluralism and Equality* (New York: Basic Books, 1983), 29.

28. Walzer, *Spheres of Justice*, 62.

29. Walzer, *Spheres of Justice*, 62.

30. Walzer, *Spheres of Justice*, 150–151.

31. Walzer, *Spheres of Justice*, 182.

32. Walzer, *Spheres of Justice*, 314.

33. Charles Taylor, "Interpretation and the Sciences of Man," in *Knowledge and Values in Social and Educational Research*, ed. Eric Bredo and Walter Feinberg (Philadelphia: Temple University Press, 1982), 176.

34. Michael Oakeshott, "The Tower of Babel," in *Rationalism in Politics and Other Essays* (Indianapolis: Liberty Press, 1991), 64.

35. Oakeshott, "The Tower of Babel," 65.

36. Michael Oakeshott quoted in Timothy Fuller, "Introduction," in *Religion, Politics and the Moral Life*, ed. Timothy Fuller (New Haven, Conn.: Yale University Press, 1993), 15.

37. Oakeshott quoted in Fuller, *Religion, Politics and the Moral Life*, 15.

38. Oakeshott, "Political Education," in *The Voice of Liberal Learning: Michael Oakeshott on Education*, ed. Timothy Fuller (New Haven, Conn.: Yale University Press, 1989), 151.

39. Jeffrey Weeks, *Inventing Moralities: Sexual Values in an Age of Uncertainty* (New York: Columbia University Press, 1995), 76.

2

Cautions on the Subject

As the previous chapter argued, liberal and communitarian theories of identity do not adequately address the complications of identity manifested in public controversies over sexuality. Liberals, by limiting discussions of identity to the private sphere, neglect the extent to which identities are present in public as well as private relations. Communitarians, by firmly drawing boundaries around even their hazier conceptions of community, neglect to address dissenting members and complications of identity adequately. Neither theory adequately attends to the role of normalizing power in producing a range of identity positions nor the complications of specific context to the meaning of identity. Both of these complications need to be addressed by curricula seeking to help students negotiate their own identities, especially in the contentious areas of sexuality the following chapters explore.

The discontinuities, contradictions, and multiplicities of beliefs and practices within a culture or community are not the focus of liberal and communitarian theorists. I will foreground these very entangled problems of community and identity in public school controversies in later chapters. For now, I turn to poststructural theories that, with their concerns with the competing, overlapping, and clashing discourses that play themselves out in cultural debates over meaning and membership, bring a helpful understanding of identity in the controversies I examine. Liberalism and communitarianism, in contrast, hold foundational concepts, for instance, gender and sexuality, steady and neglect to notice that these key concepts are shifting all the while. In addition, by limiting the scope of their analysis they tend to overlook their own foundational concepts and therefore aspects of identity that may be central to controversies that arise. In contrast, poststructuralism examines the social relations that produce "foundations" and shows how discourses that rely on unquestioned foundations are used to justify relations as they are. For poststructuralism, the recourse to unquestioned or unquestionable foundations covers over the strategic use of "foundational" claims. Because they see social categories by which subjectivities are defined are themselves potentially problematic, poststructuralists look upon the uninterrogated continuation of identity categories with suspicion. This happens on at least three levels: one, a recognition that subjects are themselves divided and complex, and two, a concern that members of identity categories will too readily police their own boundaries and remove dissenters rather than realizing that categories are too constricting, and finally, a concern that conformity to categories serves the interests of institutions to maintain control over categories of people through normalizing power. A suspicion of the potential for the abuse of power is behind all of these concerns, though power itself is inevitably part of relations between subjects.

Poststructural theories of identity and subjectivity have been of particular use to AIDS educators troubled by the simplistic and oppressive curricula supported by public education and other institutions. Their experiences with the inefficacy of risk group-directed education and the disjunctures of identity and activity categories highlighted the shortcomings of using identity categories in stable and certain ways. Similarly, educators have noted the tension in a definition of childhood as innocence, and adolescence as abstinence. By examining the construction of forms of subjectivity within and through power, educators may help to explain not only more educative approaches to sexuality but more complex approaches to understanding the relations among self and community.

First, I will address the workings of power in the constitution of the subject, with particular reference to sexuality. I will then turn to the promise of social constructionist genealogies in order to expand the range of what might be considered sexuality, identity, and adolescence. In conclusion I will explore a number of strategies advocating post-identity practices that avoid the problematics of normalizing and foundational identity. An emphasis on contingency allows students a broader range of strategies to negotiate their relationships with each other, as well as their relationship to identity.

The Subject and Subjectification

Foucault argues that subjectivity can be seen in a twofold sense, namely, that of being a subject and that of being subjected to.[1] In other words, a subject may be thought of as an agent of itself, but the process whereby that subject understands its agency, through institutionally controlled identity categories or institutionally monitored forms of introspection, tie that subject more closely to practices that control, rather than free, the subject. Subjects are created as the purported sites of agency, but, according to Foucault, agency lies in the constant interplay between strategies of power and resistance, not in the self-consciousness of the subject. Thus the Foucauldian concerns about identity include both an overarching criticism of the concept of the individual subject as independent agent and a criticism of the various categories used to organize types of individuals into recognizable groups. Because his theories attempt to trace the discourses that have made sexuality and the responses that attempt to wrest control from these discourses central, his method of genealogy is helpful for disentangling the competing discourses and resistances that attend contemporary school controversies over sexuality.

Sexuality has a central place in the constitution of what it is to be a modern subject. Tracing the configuration of power from that of the sovereign to modern bio-power, Foucault notes that the subject of power has changed, as have the ways power works. Power ought not to be conceived as solely juridical, coming from the prohibitive force of law, but as productive. Power does not act as repression, but rather produces responses to discourse that may conform or resist. Foucault argues that new methods of power are "not ensured by right but by technique, not by law but by normalization, not by punishment but by control, methods that are deployed on all levels and in forms that go beyond the state and its apparatus."[2] Modern bio-power is concerned with the intensification of bodies and populations as sites of normalization.

To this end, modern power is a power "bent on generating forces, making them grow, and ordering them, rather than one dedicated to impeding them, making them submit, or destroying them."[3] This is not simple repressive power or, in the case of the deployment of sexuality, a singular discourse, but rather multiple discourses.[4] The growth of these discourses also affected "a dispersion of centers from which discourses emanated, a diversification of their forms, and the complex deployment of the network connecting them."[5] This process of normalization extends power from the sovereignty of the king into micropractices of the self, relations, and the body. Thus much that other conceptions of identity take for granted as natural substrates are, in Foucault's view, highly infused with power and have increasingly become the object of knowledge. He argues that an increased emphasis on sovereignty is not the antidote to this normalizing power. Both sovereignty and normalizing power are closely related to one another.[6] The individual who is the supposed bearer of sovereignty is the product of normalizing power: "The individual is an effect of power, and at the same time, or precisely to the extent to which it is that effect, it is the element of its articulation. The individual which power has constituted is at the same time its vehicle."[7]

But while power has increased the extent to which it penetrates subjects, resistance always accompanies power, but is not "in a position of exteriority in relation to power."[8] Power is relational, its "existence depends on a multiplicity of points of resistance: these play the role of adversary, target, support or handle in power relations."[9] These resistances are capable of "producing cleavages in a society that shift about, fracturing unities and effecting regroupings, furrowing across individuals themselves, cutting them up and remolding them, marking off irreducible regions in them, in their bodies and minds."[10] Resistances effective on one level may also fail at another level. The relations of power and resistance that Foucault draws underscore the unpredictability of power and the extent to which there are multiple relations of power and resistance. This difficulty in understanding and altering power relations need not lead to apathy but rather "to a hyper- and pessimistic activism."[11]

Foucault contends that bio-power's concern with populations and disciplinary power's attention to individuation and normalization dovetail together to deploy sexuality as the purported key to the modern subject's self-understanding. According to Foucault, "[Sex] became the stamp of individuality—at the same time what enabled one to analyze the latter and what made it possible to master it."[12] This deployment of sexuality, rather than providing a way out of power, has "its reason for being, not in reproducing itself, but in proliferating, innovating, annexing, creating, and penetrating bodies in an increasingly detailed way, and in controlling populations in an increasingly comprehensive way."[13] Part of the extension of power into bodies has the function of making "it possible to group together, in an artificial unity, anatomical elements, biological functions, conducts, sensations, and pleasures, and it enabled one to make use of this fictitious unity as a causal principle, an omnipresent meaning, a secret to be discovered everywhere."[14]

The deployment of sexuality thus has the effect of extending and deepening notions of what it would mean to have an identity and define specific places on the body as integral to that identity. As subjects become more introspective they also come under the watch of experts to help them understand their motivations and drives. These drives and desires are themselves aspects of power, both the constructions of power and the now indispensable elements of self-understanding. Indeed, Foucault explains that his original intention in doing a genealogy of sexuality had been to study desire, but that the trail of desire led to a concern with the interior workings of the individual or "a hermeneutics of the self."[15] His intention was to "learn to what extent the effort to think one's own history can free thought from what it silently thinks, and so enable it to think differently."[16] Genealogy is useful for students negotiating their own identities because "it disturbs what was considered immobile; it fragments what was thought unified; it shows the heterogeneity of what was imagined consistent with itself."[17] By doing a genealogy of identity, students can be encouraged to examine power relations and uses, and disjunctures of identity. They can ask questions about the ambivalent uses of identity and the relationship of identity to exclusion and limitation.

Contingent Contexts

In a move that seeks to push beyond normalized identity, Foucault argues that "the rallying point for the counterattack against the deployment of sexuality ought not to be sex-desire, but bodies and pleasures."[18] Social constructionism studies the varieties of "bodies and pleasures" that arise in different times, contexts, and relations. Just as Foucault was not attempting to find a way out of our contemporary state by studying the Greeks, but finding a way to think differently, social constructionist studies of sexuality trouble the foundations of commonly held assumptions about the naturalness and continuity of sexuality. For social constructionists, the foundation of concepts like sexuality shift over time so that it becomes difficult to even define what is considered sexuality, if anything. In addition, social constructionists look for resistances to dominant conceptions of sexuality and gender, local knowledges, and challenges to accepted practices.

This acceptance of the shifting foundations of categories makes social constructionism a particularly useful ally for notions of identity that also stress contingency. Indeed, the concept "sexuality," because it is so reliant on a variety of meanings, may not even from some perspectives appear to be sexual acts. Desire, definition of gender, and the very materiality of bodies are all historically and contextually contingent categories. The point then is not to uncover a natural sexuality but to examine relations in context that form particular sexualities and define particular relations as problems.

Social constructionists warn that we should not presume the continuity of sexuality from one time period to another. As Carole Vance has argued:

[To] the extent that social construction theory grants that sexual acts, identities and even desire are mediated by cultural and historical factors, the object of study—sexuality—becomes evanescent and threatens to disappear. If sexuality is constructed differently at each time and place, can we use the term in a comparatively meaningful way? . . . Is there an "it" to study?[19]

The difficulties of defining what is meant by sexuality or the place of sexuality in meaning systems vary and this has implications for how we understand the interplay of identity and activity. These understandings are particularly crucial for safer sex education. For instance, the globalization of Western, most specifically, American gayness has altered the ways that local forms of homosexuality negotiate themselves. Katie King distinguishes between the globalized "gay" and the localized "homosexual" noting that even "homosexual" may not be the pertinent term in many local concepts.[20] As the concept "gay" gains more recognition, other forms that may or may not have been related to it are subsumed under it. The differences of social dynamics and meanings change with the newer understanding of what "gay" has come to mean. King explains the shift this causes in northern Mexican understandings of homosexuality, where, like in other areas of the Americas, the "passive" or receptive partner in anal intercourse is understood as homosexual whereas the active partner is not.[21] Globalized understandings of "gay," however, disrupt this and also implicate the active partner in a gay identity and the discourse of gay rights. This shift tended to occur among men who had been to the United States. and were thus receptive to educational programs directed at gay men. But local understandings persist as well and resistance to the globalized "gay" brings into play the resistance to Americanization and the separation of same-gender activity from the realm of heterosexuality. In other words, the separation of sexual identity into homosexual and heterosexual disrupted the social relations of men involved in same gender sexual behavior. Where local understandings of sexuality held that a man could penetrate a partner of either gender without his masculinity being in question, the "international" definition of "gay" challenged his ability to do so. This same "global gay" definition also challenged the social approbation placed on this perceived loss of masculinity as well as the partially negative valuation of the passive partner, who had been in a role akin to that of "other woman." For safer sex educators, understanding these complications of identity enable educational programs to address themselves to local identities that may be closely interwoven with global understandings.

These same complications of local meanings and global meanings play out in young people's understandings of their sexual feelings and experiences. Indeed, what an outsider might view as a sexual relationship might not be viewed by the participants as such. That young boys masturbate together is not often considered to be an expression of their homosexual desires, but rather a group form of competition or amusement. But what is the interaction between these social forms and more globalized meanings of gayness? For some, engagement in these activities will figure as founding moments in their development of a gay identity, for others memories of these experiences may either fade or be denied because they do not form a founding or even important moment in their definition of their sexuality. Because of the interplay between identity and experience, then, experiences are not central to memory or identity in the same way as when they are viewed as crucial. This is not simply a case of repression (although it may be), but also a marker of how meanings coalesce and those experiences peripheral to identity sometimes are not understood as "there" in the first place or recede from memory sooner than they would if they had been central to self-understanding. These situations raise questions about how identity structures experience and how experience alters identity. Social constructionist methodology enables one to ask questions of these situations to attempt to decipher how they might function as problems, what their place is in defining sexuality, according to whom and why, among others. By being attentive to the disjuncture among identity, activity, and commonly held definitions, social constructionism allows a greater understanding of the shifts and contradictions in localized and contextual sexual practices.

The identity category of "adolescent" needs to be put to the same scrutiny as the concept of sexual identity. Adolescence is at once defined as irresponsibility and recklessness. In some instances, the expected recklessness of adolescence becomes an approval of adolescent male behavior that may place adolescent females at risk for sexual coercion or disproportionately burden them with the consequences of sexual activity. Boys will be boys and girls must learn to protect themselves. In this gendered version of adolescence, girls are strongly encouraged to protect or reclaim their virginity while few messages are directed toward curbing male sexuality. These gender dynamics affect not only how adolescents are perceived but what is deemed appropriate for them to learn. Curricula address adolescents considering sexual activity as individuals who simply need to learn refusal skills, not people involved in a relationship with one another with complex reasons for engaging or not engaging in sexual relationships. When educational materials directed at protecting young people from HIV presume a natural adolescent rebellion that will naturally result in unsafe sexual activity they neglect to interrogate the place of sexuality in adolescent lives. Curricula that warn teachers that adolescents are especially unable to plan for safer sex and thus should be encouraged to remain abstinent position young people in ways that encourage self-fulfilling prophecies with differential outcomes by gender. Condom usage has been on the rise among some adolescents though consistent use is still quite low. But to suggest that these rates are due to the particular inability of the adolescent sex drive to control itself or adolescent feelings of immortality covers over the ambivalent position of adolescents. The period described as adolescence has lengthened considerably since its relatively recent solidification around the turn of the twentieth century. It is increasingly unreasonable to assume that people in the adolescent category can be expected to remain abstinent.[22] As a liminal identity, adolescence is subject to ambivalent messages—on the one hand, a strong message about the need for responsibility and, as in some sex education curricula that encourage abstinence pledges and oath-taking; on the other hand, adolescents are equally constructed as immature and unable to handle the responsibility of sexual activity. These ambivalences show through in adolescent response to surveys on sexual activity. More report engaging in sexual activity because they associate sexual activity with adult status than report doing so for pleasure. And adolescent girls report not planning ahead for sex or having condoms available because they know as adolescents they are not supposed to be having sex.[23]

School curricular decisions attempt to represent particular ideas about sex, not limited to simple understandings of heterosexuality. As I will show in more detail in a later chapter, the meanings of sex are represented by the inclusion of certain topics, the exclusion of others, and through using particular definitions of sex. Accordingly, curricula reflect dominant understandings of where sex occurs, which gendered bodies have which particular experiences of sex, how certain sexual concerns are racialized, and how certain identities and activities are represented as inappropriate. The sexual body as described by curricula reflects gendered roles in reproduction and in the gendered and raced meanings of sexuality. Michelle Fine has noted that curricula and policies fail to acknowledge that adolescents engage in a range of sexual behaviors and that positioning adolescents as victims of sexuality or as interested only in penile-vaginal intercourse does a disservice to sexually active adolescents. These curricula limit the potential for sex education to encourage adolescents girls to develop what Fine calls "female sexual subjectivity."[24] Fine argues adolescent girls ought to be taught more than just that sex will lead to disease and pregnancy. Fine points to the theme of victimization in sex education directed at young females and argues that this theme obscures both female sexual desire and the broad victimization of females that occurs within our social structure.

According to Fine, a discourse of sexual victimization paradoxically disempowers young women by portraying them as at risk from male sexuality while it encourages young women to see marriage as a haven from this victimization.[25] Fine argues that "the absence of a discourse of desire, combined with the lack of analysis of the language of victimization" may slow the ability of adolescents to take responsibility for their sexual activity, especially female students and nonheterosexual male students.[26] One serious consequence of this discourse of sexual victimization is that it fosters negative attitudes toward sex in women. A recent study shows that sex-negative attitudes are negatively correlated with contraception use. Apparently, according to Fisher, Byrne, and White, this is because "teens who believe sexual involvement is wrong deny responsibility for contraception."[27] In other words, there is a clear cost to, in particular, young girls when sex education reflects gendered meanings of sexual responsibility and sexual victimization.

In addition, sex and AIDS curricula are rife with heterosexist and racist assumptions, both in theory and in practice. The realm of the sexual is circumscribed by sex and AIDS education curricula that define particular sexual activities, usually vaginal-penile intercourse as "sex" and suggest other sexual activities, mutual masturbation, for instance, as alternatives to sex. Students are thus encouraged to see themselves as having to miss out on real sex in order to avoid HIV, other sexually transmitted diseases, and/or pregnancy. There is a clear hierarchy of sexually significant parts of the body that at once limit possibilities for sexual experience and reinforce gender roles and heterosexuality. Another aspect of assumptions made about the sexual body is reflected in the relatively lower scores on sexual knowledge tests administered to students of color, with Native American students scoring the lowest. Part of the reason for the disparity in scores appears to be the presumption on the part of teachers that students of color are by nature sexual and thus do not need to be taught about sex. This same presumption fuels the representation of teenage pregnancy as overwhelmingly a problem of African-American girls. Similarly, a suspicion about exotic sexual practices among people of color is reflected in the suggestion that AIDS has its origin in Africa and that HIV is more common among heterosexuals in Africa because of their different sexual practices. Paula Treichler notes that accounts of the AIDS epidemic in Africa draw parallels between heterosexual Africans and homosexual American men, parallels that seem to attempt to maintain the deviance of each group.[28]

The complications of these representations of risk becomes clear in a comparison between "risk groups" as described by curricula and rate of infection as represented by statistics. "Risk groups" is a problematic term in that it conflates identity with activity and is most often used to single out sexual minorities from the "general" population. The disproportionate effect of HIV on communities of color is neglected in this schema, as HIV continues to become a disease associated with poverty and lack of access to information and health. This racial and class aspect of HIV infection is another aspect of the AIDS epidemic that strongly raises challenges to public school AIDS curricula on the grounds of discrimination. According to the Centers for Disease Control (CDC), the number of AIDS cases among "white, not Hispanic" people is 268, 856; among "black, not Hispanic" 203,189, and among "Hispanic" 103,023.[29] In addition, AIDS is the leading cause of death among black women, aged 15 to 44 in New Jersey and New York.[30] But the AIDS curriculum in New York State still refers to risk groups as bisexual men, homosexuals, and intravenous drug users. Even while young women of all races, especially women of color, are experiencing the most dramatic increase in rates of seropositivity, women are not considered by curricula to be at a specifically high level of risk. According to the CDC, the proportion of females among adolescent cases of HIV infection has more than doubled since 1987, rising from 13 percent in 1987 to 34 percent in 1991.[31] Alexander observes that women are a "forgotten group" largely regarded "primarily as vectors of transmission to their children and as a male's sexual partner, rather than as people with AIDS/HIV."[32] Nor do curricula address the issue of men's reluctance to use condoms and women's greater likelihood of HIV infection from men than vice versa. The disproportionate risk in sexual activity for heterosexual women remains unchallenged by curricula, even in the midst of the curricula centering its definition of the sexual on heterosexuality.

Schools play a role in demarcating proper from improper identity and inscribing boundaries around particular identities and activities. When curricula limit their discussions of "sex" to heterosexual intercourse they mark out for students what ought to properly be considered sex, thus denying the safer potential of nonpenetrative sex and denying the existence of same-gender sexual activity. Heterosexuality, most likely its abstinent form, becomes the unquestioned identity of all students. This is particularly problematic for AIDS and sex education curricula whose version of identity constrain in advance students' abilities to negotiate safer sex and conceive of a range of possibilities for sexuality not limited to abstinent heterosexuality. Students need to be more critical of identity and cautious about how they understand themselves through categories. A more contingent, contextual sense of identity would encourage them to understand themselves not through a category but through a series of relations, to view identity as a process.

Cultivating Possibilities

To solidify itself identity requires an origin, whether in a tradition, biological base, or other foundational claim. This origin or foundation becomes the justification for the identity's coherence. But identities are not as pure and uncomplicated as some theories take them to be. Even at the founding moments purity eludes them: "What is found at the historical beginning of things is not the inviolable identity of their origin; it is the dissension of other things. It is disparity."[33] But to cover over this disparity identities project disparity onto others. Because identity requires a sense of its own solidity and because that sense is derived from the projection of difference onto others, identity is inherently insecure. Identities thus must negate parts of their complexity and negate their relations to others, even while both are integral to the possibility of the boundaries of identity. The loss is twofold, internal in complexity and external in ability to form connections and identifications with presumed outsiders.

To overcome these losses identity needs to be conceived as contingent, relational, and political. In *Identity/Difference*, William Connolly advocates for contingency in identity to overcome the fundamentalism that attends other conceptions of identity. He contends that the solidification of identity categories or personal identities requires the creation of an other whose difference enables the stability of identity. Identities clash because, when based on foundational claims to truth, they cannot accommodate each other's existence. Rather than accepting other identity possibilities as valid, identity categories relegate outsiders to the status of other or radical difference.

Theories stressing contingency in identity suggest that democratic pluralism insufficiently cultivates possibilities for identity because pluralism requires that identities already have a certain permanence and organization in order to be recognized by others. In addition, the process of recognition is not without its difficulties, and some already constituted identity categories have difficulty in achieving recognition. For instance, the critique of natural and stable sexual identity inherent in a radical gay identity is lost when homosexuality is recognized only as a discrete and naturally occurring minority. Thus the recognition afforded to identity by democratic pluralism is insufficient in that it is unable to recognize or cultivate care for ways of living that do not take the form of understandable identity categories, possibilities that exceed current understandings of identity. Rather than emphasizing a pluralism that predetermines the categories it will embrace, Connolly advocates for pluralization, a care for identities and formations even prior to their concretizing into forms that would demand recognition.[34] In other words, a care for the abundance of possibilities that does not require that these protoidentities conform to what has previously been required of identities—that they organize, that they follow certain protocols and forms for recognition from the broader society. Instead of creating the normalized individual, Connolly argues that pluralization would have greater care for new forms of identity rather than limit the possibilities open to each person or group.[35]

The point is not to do without identity altogether, but to try to find ways to minimize the potentially problematic effects of identity. The consequences of identity formations and practices need to be questioned, even at the most basic level. Judith Butler examines how the institutional structuring of heterosexuality has created and bolstered certain views of gender difference. Butler takes one of the aspects of this hierarchy and challenges its status as natural, examining how gender is constructed through the matrix of heterosexuality. Her contention is to show that identity, the presumed site of origin of ethical action, is already produced by institutions and practices that predetermine the range of actions that can be taken. In terms of gender, Butler argues that, rather than it being a natural category, it is the effect of prohibitions and meanings that attempt to construct heterosexuality's status as natural. She contends that agency without identity is a possibility, indeed, that there is more room for agency once the fiction of gender has been challenged because feminists then do not need to fashion their political claims around or in challenge to the makeup of the essential woman and her participation in the institution of heterosexuality.

Butler undertakes a genealogy of gender in order to investigate "the political stakes in designating as an origin and cause those identity categories that are in fact the effects of institutions, practices and discourses with multiple and diffuse points of origin."[36] Because of the limits to the possibilities for gender, new and politically engaged conceptions of identity are "foreclose[d] in advance."[37] Gender, rather than being a foregone conclusion that we ought to argue on behalf of, is rather "performatively produced . . . always a doing, though not by a subject who might be said to pre-exist the deed."[38] Focusing on the productive power that Foucault posits, Butler argues that productions of gender "swerve from their original purposes and inadvertently mobilize possibilities of 'subjects' that do not merely exceed the bounds of cultural intelligibility" but even expand those boundaries.[39] Butler sees subversive potential in performativity because it variously brings gender into action, challenging commonly held assumptions about what it means to be gendered. Gender, conceived as performative, expands the range of possibilities and confounds previously held limits of intelligibility.

The performative and process-oriented aspect of identity, which I address in more detail in chapters 5 and 6, underscores the importance of context and intersubjective relations to identity. Identities are constantly negotiated and altered, and some aspects of identity may recede in certain contexts and others come to the fore. But these negotiations need to be undertaken in a democratic context, in which one identity is not able to maintain hegemony over others and in which the claims of identities and proto-identities can be made in ways that do not threaten the existence of identities or identities yet to come (or not to come, as identities as such).

Because we come to expect identity to identify us, we relinquish those parts of ourselves that are not contained by the explanation a category affords us. To counter these problems, Cindy Patton emphasizes the need for "ob-scene" identity and education. Patton contends that "safe sex activists overemphasized the power of a given text, while disregarding its uses in myriad place and its interpretation by multiple publics."[40] To encourage multiple readings and multiple identity position possibilities, Patton turns to the promise of obscenity. She explains:

> Broken down into its original Latin components, ob-scene adds a prefix indication priority to scene, a root word meaning stage or theatrical place. Thus ob-scene mean something like *before staged* or indicates something before the moment of spatial visibility in official space . . . [O]b-scenity is the abjected, the meaningless, the thing that does not try to recover meaning but tries to secure the space *prior to visibility*, prior to information.[41]

Obscenity, like pluralization, attempts to account for possibilities prior to their becoming normalized and concretized. The use of "obscenity" to describe an identity that tries to remain unnormalized underscores the difficulty of pushing limits of intelligibility. Pushing these limits of intelligibility may give more options to students trying to negotiate their way through the contingencies of identity. But there is also a discomfort with the obscene. Recognizable identity has a strong role in normalizing the subject and nonconforming groups or individuals are unsettling. However, education that attempts to address the complications of sexuality, students, and HIV needs to be open to the use of the obscene. Too often curricula have stepped away from sexual activity among adolescents or neglected to address same-gender sexual activity for fear of offending. The result has been the exclusion of students' concerns from the curricula, which is considerably more offensive.

The next chapter will focus on the formation of an exclusionary community encouraged by AIDS/HIV educational policy in New York

State. This example will show the limitations placed on education by such monolithic definitions of who may properly belong to the school community. Had the AIDS education policy looked to the poststructural concerns outlined above, the problems of limiting students access to knowledge and forms of identity would have been clearer. Curricula, through constraining identity possibilities for students and community alike, were unable to adequately address the range of student activities and identities and were thus limited in their ability to provide students with a full range of strategies by which to protect themselves from HIV and to envision strategies for survival if students became HIV positive. Instead of encouraging the development of a caring and pluralistic community, AIDS/HIV policy and the ensuing debate over its contents mirrored the failings of communitarianism and encouraged the development of a heterosexual community intent on excluding the concerns of sexual minority students.

Notes

An earlier version of this chapter was published as "Foucauldian Cautions on the Subject and the Educative Implications of Contingent Identity." *Philosophy of Education 1997*, edited by Susan Laird, (Urbana, IL: Philosophy of Education Society, 1998), 115-123.

1. Michel Foucault, *Power/Knowledge: Selected Interviews and Other Writings 1972–1977* (New York: Pantheon Books, 1977), 98.
2. Michel Foucault, *History of Sexuality, Volume One: An Introduction* (New York: Vintage Books, 1990), 89.
3. Foucault, *History of Sexuality, Volume One*, 136.
4. Foucault, *History of Sexuality, Volume One*, 33.
5. Foucault, *History of Sexuality, Volume One*, 34.
6. Foucault, *Power/Knowledge*, 108.
7. Foucault, *Power/Knowledge*, 98.
8. Foucault, *History of Sexuality, Volume One*, 95.
9. Foucault, *History of Sexuality, Volume One*, 95.
10. Foucault, *History of Sexuality, Volume One*, 96.
11. Interview with Michel Foucault, "On the Genealogy of Ethics," in *Michel Foucault: Beyond Structuralism and Hermeneutics*, ed. Hubert L. Dreyfus and Paul Rabinow (Chicago: University of Chicago Press, 1983), 232.
12. Foucault, *History of Sexuality, Volume One*, 146.
13. Foucault, *History of Sexuality, Volume One*, 106.
14. Foucault, *History of Sexuality, Volume One*, 154.
15. Michel Foucault, *The Use of Pleasure: Volume Two of the History of Sexuality* (New York: Vintage Books, 1990), 6.
16. Foucault, *The Use of Pleasure*, 9.

17. Foucault, "Nietzsche, Genealogy, History," in *Language, Counter –Memory, Practice: Selected Essays and Interviews by Michel Foucault*, ed. Donald F. Bouchard (Ithaca, N.Y.: Cornell University Press, 1977), 147.

18. Foucault, *History of Sexuality, Volume One*, 157.

19. Carole Vance quoted in Martin Duberman, Martin, Martha Vicinus, and George Chauncey, Jr., "Introduction," in *Hidden from History: Reclaiming the Gay and Lesbian Past* (New York: Meridian, 1989), 6.

20. Katie King, "Local and Global: AIDS Activism and Feminist Theory," *Camera Obscura* (Janurary 1989): 80.

21. King, "Local and Global," 89.

22. Ronald William Morris, *Values in Sexuality Education: A Philosophical Study* (Lanham, Md.: University Press of America, 1994), 17.

23. W. Fisher, D. Byrne, and L. White, "Emotional Barriers to Contraception," in *Adolescents, Sex, and Contraception*, ed. D. Byrne and W. Fisher (Hillsdale, N.J.: Lawrence Erlbaum, 1983), 207–239.

24. Michelle Fine, "Sexuality, Schooling, and Adolescent Females: The Missing Discourse of Desire," *Harvard Educational Review* (February 1988): 34. See also Joseph A. Diorio, "Contraception, Copulation Domination, and the Theoretical Barrenness of Sex Education Literature," *Educational Theory* (Summer 1985): 239–254.

25. Fine, "Sexuality, Schooling, and Adolescent Females," 32.

26. Fine, "Sexuality, Schooling, and Adolescent Females," 50.

27. Fisher et al. quoted in Fine, "The Missing Discourse of Desire," 31. See W. Fisher, D. Byrne, and L. White, "Emotional Barriers to Contraception," in *Adolescents, Sex, and Contraception*, ed. D. Byrne and W. Fisher (Hillsdale, N.J.: Lawrence Erlbaum, 1983), 207–239. Paul Epstein also points to other outcomes from programs that presume adolescents to be sexually active and encourage them to use condoms—researchers at Johns Hopkins found that students who had participated in a sex education program that included information on condom usage had an increased rate of abstention from sex and a delay in onset of sexual activity. In Paul Epstein "Condoms in Schools: The Right Lesson," *New York Times*, 19 January 1991, 31.

28. Paula A. Treichler, "AIDS and HIV Infection in the Third World: A First World Chronicle" in *Remaking History*, ed. Barbara Kruger and Phil Mariani (Seattle: Bay Press, 1989), 35.

29. Center for Disease Control, "HIV/AIDS Surveillance Report," Centers for Disease Control Page, <www.ede.gov/nchstp/hivaids/stats.htm> December 1996 [cited 3 May 1997].

30. Vicki Alexander, "Black Women and HIV/AIDS," *SIECUS Report* (December 1990/January 1991): 8.

31. U.S. Department of Health and Human Services, *Centers for Disease Control HIV/AIDS Prevention Newsletter* (October 1992): 1.

32. Alexander, "Black Women and HIV/AIDS," 9.

33. Foucault, "Nietzsche, Genealogy, History," 142.

34. William Connolly, *The Ethos of Pluralization* (Minneapolis: University of Minnesota Press, 1995), xiv.

35. For an examination of the educational dilemma concerning "newness" see Natasha Levinson, "Teaching in the Midst of Belatedness: The Paradox of Natality in Hannah Arendt's Educational Thought," *Educational Theory* 47, no. 4 (Fall 1997): 435–451.

36. Judith Butler, *Gender Trouble: Feminism and the Subversion of Gender* (New York: Routledge, 1990), xi.

37. Butler, *Gender Trouble*, 15.

38. Butler, *Gender Trouble*, 24–25.

39. Butler, *Gender Trouble*, 29.

40. Cindy Patton, *Fatal Advice: How Safe–Sex Education Went Wrong* (Durham, N.C.: Duke University Press, 1996), 139.

41. Patton, *Fatal Advice*, 141.

Part II: Curricular Definitions of "Community" and "Sex"

3

Identity and the Monolithic Community

In this chapter I will problematize definitions of community that are explicitly and implicitly mobilized in discussions and controversies over HIV and homosexuality. I begin with competing notions of community membership derived from *Romer v. Evans*, in which liberal values protected gays and lesbians from exclusion from full participation in Colorado politics. I then turn to the debates over community membership in the early years of the AIDS epidemic as background to the kinds of community expressed in AIDS curricula. Next, I analyze New York State's AIDS policy as reflective of the development of an exclusionary community. In particular I focus on the place of community advisory boards in the development of state and local HIV education in the public schools and the messages about community reflected in the text of the *Instructional Guide*. My main contention is that "community" in this context comes to mean a very specific, homogeneous, inherently safe collection of heterosexual families. Consequently, difference and risk are outside of the community.

In his majority opinion in *Romer v. Evans*, which overturned Colorado's Amendment 2 (an amendment passed by popular referendum outlawing laws against discrimination on the basis of sexual orientation), Justice Kennedy argued that no state can "deem a class of persons strangers to its laws."[1] Amendment 2 prohibited antidiscrimination policies in the state of Colorado from including sexual orientation as a protected category. What the majority of Colorado voters took to be their right to articulate the character of their state, the Supreme Court found to violate the rights of the gay and lesbian minority in that state. Writing for the majority, Kennedy argued that no compelling state interest appeared to be behind the removal of antidiscrimination laws and instead that the

voters' decision "seems inexplicable by anything but animus."[2] The State
of Colorado had attempted to argue, among other points, that by protecting gay and lesbian citizens the rights to free association of other citizens were violated. Antidiscrimination laws might force Christian land-
lords who found homosexuality repugnant to rent to homosexuals
because their rights to freedom from discrimination in housing would
otherwise be violated. In short, Colorado argued that the right of citizens
to determine the character of their homes and communities was hampered by antidiscrimination laws that protected people whose practices or
identity constituted a challenge to the beliefs of the majority.

A similar dynamic occurs in decisions over public school sex education when community advisory boards decide to tailor sex and
HIV/AIDS education to suit the character of their communities. Information about homosexuality is among the most common controversial
topics to be removed by such communities.[3] In this respect, curricular
decisions make groups of students strangers to their schools. Decisions
that exclude information on homosexuality and other sexual minorities
do so on the grounds that local districts have the right to have their particular community values reflected in their curricula. But this raises the
question as to whether local values, even if derived through democratic
means, should trump the plurality that is also valued in public schools.
Proceduralist liberals argue that locally and democratically derived curricular decisions do reflect the ideals and practice of democracy by ensuring that communities have a distinctive voice in their children's education and that school decisions encourage local democratic procedures.[4]
But when these local democratic procedures are undertaken to disadvantage minorities they run counter to democratic ideals of tolerance, nondiscrimination, and pluralism. What some local communities may find to
be distasteful information, some students within those communities may
find to be crucial for their self-preservation and safety. Specifically,
when communities decide to omit references to homosexuality or to limit
the range of information about any sexual activity to their students, they
diminish students' ability to safely and responsibly conduct their sexual
activity and discourage those students from examining the diverse range
of identities and behaviors that comprise sexuality. Students are neither
encouraged to respect sexual minorities nor encouraged to fully interrogate their own sexualities. Locally approved curricular materials may
appear to be democratically developed, but they may have embedded
within them antipluralist practices that position some students as outsiders to the community.

While the broad principles undergirding the two situations are similar, there are crucial differences between the issue of community control
of information in school and the issues in Amendment 2. The relation-

ship between parent and child is different from the relationship between dominant community member and minority community member. But each relationship is a site of negotiation over the meaning of community membership and the contours of community identity. Voters attempt to negotiate the shape of public political rights. Parents as members of curricular advisory boards help their schools to educate their children in the ways that reflect their values, beliefs, and concerns. Schools play a strong role in preparing students for eventual membership in communities and families as adults. In this respect, schools are part of local community building and reproduction. School-related decisions help to build a community by bringing together people in that community, most often concerned parents, to work together on curricular issues that reflect and create the kind of community the parents want. Decision making about curricula and school policy, then, is a moment when community is enacted. It is also a moment when plans are made for how the community will be represented and enacted in the future. This disturbs the usual definition of community as something that is already static and finished, a group of people who have bonds preexisting their action on those bonds. But debates over what constitutes membership and definition of community show that community does not preexist its enactment. Instead, it is constructed through the activity of public debate and engagement. Looking closely at these debates, as I will later in the context of AIDS and multicultural education, it is crucial to understanding how the claim to community is undermined by particular forms of exclusion.

When children differ substantially in identity from their parents, for instance, in the case of children who do not conform to their community's norms regarding sexuality and gender, there may be no one to advocate for them and no one to represent their needs as part of the community. In these cases, parents may not support their children's identity and indeed may actively engage in attempts to change that identity, for instance, through attempts to bring a halt to "Gender Identity Disorder of Childhood" lest those gender nonconforming children turn out to be gay adults.[5] The kind of community enacted in situations where information about homosexuality and other sexual minorities is removed or avoided is a community that actively undertakes the project of defining itself and its children as heterosexual, whether this is actively and explicitly recognized or not. In other words, even communities that would not be inclined to define themselves as heteronormative do in fact privilege heterosexuality through their unwillingness to actively advocate for sexual minorities. The decision to avoid mention of homosexuality or sexual activity among young people positions these young people as outsiders to the community. Outsider status is confirmed when curricula neglect information that could potentially help these students to see themselves as connected to caring communities. By neglecting the concerns of sexual minority students a community hinders their ability to negotiate their way through sexual experiences in greater safety. In other words, a community's preference for heterosexual identity in its children may undermine their children's ability to engage in ethical behaviors that the community might hold more dear, such as caring, the ability to be honest, and the ability to form close, committed relationships.

While I will largely concentrate on sexual orientation as a criterion for overt and covert exclusionary policy decisions, many of the same issues of exclusion are applicable to other sexually nonconforming students. All students have limited access to information on negotiating sexual relationships, information on birth control, and protection against sexually transmitted diseases (STDs). The reluctance of schools to address sexuality outside the context of reproduction and disease neglects student concerns about more positive aspects of sexuality, such as relationship dynamics, passion, pleasure, and a host of other concerns.

Practices and beliefs regarding sexuality are part of school experience whether in lessons addressing relationships or hallway interactions between couples, but "sexuality" defined as such is placed within the context of health or family life education. The placement of the subject of sexuality in health classes emphasizes messages about sexual activity as a physical/biological concern, in terms of disease or reproduction, a topic I address in chapter 4. As such, sexuality is a collection of facts about how organs, hormones, and STDs frame the realm of the sexual. When the subject of sexuality is only addressed directly in the family life curricula, sexual activity is placed within the context of the married family. A tension is then set up between the health problems associated with sexuality and the eventual role of sexuality within a married relationship. The problem of this complicated message is not lost on curricula developers, who, at one point in the New York State *AIDS Instructional Guide*, wonder how students will be able to switch from conceptualizing sex as dangerous prior to marriage to conceptualizing sex as pleasurable within marriage. This concern illuminates the extreme attempts to demonize sexual activity itself without explaining that many of the dangers of sexual activity are preventable.

Public schools that provide sex and HIV/AIDS education are often under pressure from conservative parents to avoid giving students information that would make sexual activity less dangerous because these parents argue that community and religious values embrace abstinence as the only safe and morally acceptable alternative for young people. Deemed inappropriate to local community values, information that would potentially help a variety of sexually active young people avoid the consequences of unprotected sexual activity is kept from students in a circular attempt to have them avoid these activities for fear of the dangers associated with them. However, despite the values of local communities, rates of sexual activity among young people show that a substantial proportion of them do not avoid sexual activity. In addition, a substantial proportion of young people also do not engage in the kinds of activities that would minimize their risk of pregnancy, HIV, or other sexually transmitted infections. Though condom use among teens has doubled since the 1980s, there are still considerable numbers of teens who do not consistently use condoms during sexual intercourse, whether heterosexual or homosexual. One reason for the relatively low consistent use of condoms and lack of knowledge about and use of other safer sex techniques derives from the restrictive definition of community articulated in curricular materials and controversies over those curricula. The curricular embrace of a narrow definition of sexuality, then, has far reaching implications for all students.

Contagion and Homosexuality: Precursors to Exclusions in Curricula

From the beginning of the AIDS pandemic in the United States, AIDS and gayness have been closely linked in medical accounts, media representations, and in public school AIDS curricula. Early accounts of the syndrome called it the "Gay Plague," "Gay Cancer," and "Gay-Related Immune Disorder (GRID)." Initially assumed by many to be the result of or the symptoms justifying the unnaturalness of homosexual sex, AIDS and homosexuality have shared many images in the public mind, each image reinforcing popular ideas about sex, contagion, and fear of difference. Representations of AIDS reinforced a definition of homosexuals as outsiders. Health and Human Services Secretary Margaret Heckler urged in 1985 "an all out war on the HTLV III virus" to "stop the spread of AIDS before it hits the heterosexual community."[6] The populations already affected by AIDS, by implication, were not sufficient reason for funding to be stepped up or for the "heterosexual community" to be concerned. In short, Heckler's words confirmed what other representations had made clear: AIDS was only a problem insofar as it affected heterosexuals. To Heckler, there was nothing inherently problematic in a "disease" that affected persons already presumed by their sexuality to be in some sense "diseased."

Because in the United States AIDS first affected gay men, intravenous drug users, and Haitians it was considered by many to be a disease of outsiders. Cindy Patton notes that had there not been an identifiable gay community, AIDS might not have been recognizable as anything other than a series of disconnected immune system deficiency-related cases. That in 1981 a group of "previously healthy gay men" were diagnosed with a rare pneumonia indicated a potentially widespread problem.[7] Patton points out that were it not for the removal of homosexuality from the *Diagnostic and Statistical Manual III* in 1973, it would not have been likely that "healthy" would have been linked with gay men. That is to say, gayness itself would have been presumed in some part to have been the reason for their illness (an assumption that was certainly not once and for all a thing of the past but had died down enough so that the possibility that some physicians might consider that gay men were healthy was not inconceivable). Indeed, Patton and others have suggested that AIDS had affected people in the United States some time before the 1981 diagnoses. In 1978, "junky pneumonia" reportedly killed a number of New York intravenous drug users, but, according to Patton, since the idea of junkies getting sick and dying seemed to be unremarkable, this pneumonia did not raise any alarms.[8] The point here is that there has to be at least a partial presumption of health in order for illness to be visible. Ironically, the ways in which representations of AIDS were mobilized in the media involved attempts to reintegrate homosexuality with illness, an association that had only briefly been broken.

The scare tactics of early AIDS public service announcements[9] (as well as the obfuscations of more recent campaigns)[10] strongly suggest that sexual behavior is out of control and AIDS is the consequence. Simon Watney points to a New York City public education campaign featuring posters in the subway challenging riders, "You Don't Have AIDS, Now Prove It."[11] The campaign plays off most people's denial of risk and fear of AIDS in others, while encouraging them to test for HIV, if for no other reason than to prove that they were not at risk in the first place. Rather than providing information for risk avoidance, campaigns like this encourage the sorting of persons at risk and persons not at risk. The continued emphasis on testing and contact tracing over emphasis on prevention and education reflects a perennial shortcoming in public health education.

Watney also notes that media representations of AIDS pit images of sexualized gay men against images of the family. In these accounts, gay men are irresponsible, disconnected from family and community structures, and their behavior is represented as a threat to those families and communities. In a program about the potential for bisexual men to spread HIV to the family, Watney notes that gay men are positioned at the bottom of the screen as a line of "boogying disco dancers." Above this image is a "typical family." Watney argues that images like these encourage the viewer to "imagine some absolute divide between the two domains of 'gay life' and 'the family,' as if gay men grew up, were educated, worked and lived our lives in total isolation from the rest of society."[12]

Media accounts of AIDS, like similar educational videos produced recently by the New Right to promote the passage of Amendment 2 in Colorado, portray gays as promiscuous leathermen only out for a good time. But viewers of these images of gay men in dark and smoky bars are not informed, for instance, that the titleholder in the Mr. Leather competition spends the year of his reign doing education for safer sex in leather bars—a task which reflects a strong dedication to community service. Viewers are discouraged from viewing leathermen, bars, or gay ghettos as sites of *alternative* communities, places where people help one another. Instead, images of hedonism gone wild attempt to encourage the presumably not-at-risk viewer to see gay men as people to be feared and kept under lock and key. The stylistic differences that mark out these particular gay people are used to indicate their difference from dominant society. In other words, taken against the backdrop of the conservative heterosexual community, gay people look different and isolated. Viewed from within the gay community, they are the source of organizing health campaigns and centers providing care to people with HIV.

Representations of people with AIDS encourage viewers to accept the idea of quarantine and separation by showing the person with AIDS as distant and isolated—single gay men fighting a losing battle without a social support system, a person with AIDS surrounded by masked and gowned medical professionals. Sander Gilman argues that in these common images of a person with AIDS "the sense of physical distance is palpable" and that distance corresponds to the anxiety of the "general public."[13] These images of gayness, coming at a time when mandatory testing and quarantine was part of public and political discussions about AIDS, were a mechanism by which the not-at-risk viewers could distance themselves from gays, at the same time as these images legitimated the idea that the confinement of gays might be reasonable. Images that attempt to sort gay people into individual isolation begin to suggest that the viewing public is connected by their presumed heterosexual identity.

Margaret Heckler's concern that the risk of HIV might spread to "the heterosexual community" and, I will argue later, educational materials developed to address the AIDS crisis posit that there is actually something called a heterosexual community. This transformation of heterosexuals into what can be considered a community has complex consequences. On the one hand, the suggestion that the "heterosexual community" is the one community that ought to be the object of concern marks out other communities as less worthy of concern. If AIDS had remained outside "the heterosexual community," worry would not be as great. On the other hand, it also inextricably links these other, less worthy communities to the "heterosexual community" since without these others there would be no reason to create a particular "heterosexual community," a point I return to in more detail in chapter 5.

Clearly, Heckler's presumption is that her listeners will share her concern and agree that the spread of AIDS into the "heterosexual community" warrants stepped up work against AIDS. Indeed, her comments were made at about the time of the inception of AIDS education in the public schools. The discovery of HIV and the development of HIV blood tests ushered in a concerted effort to ensure that children and youth in public schools would be educated about AIDS. The discovery of HIV and the development of blood tests for HIV meant, at the same time, that people with HIV could be diagnosed, categorized, and potentially separated from everyone else. The only problem was that people could not be discovered to have HIV unless they were tested. Indeed, the focus on HIV testing and the fear of contracting HIV through casual contact all emphasize the ways in which HIV sets off what Cindy Patton calls a "contagion and containment panic: identify the germ, the people who have it, and then figure out the most efficient method of staying away from them."[14] In setting out to identify either people with HIV or people at risk, the boundaries of who has a right to a safe and healthy community are set. Thus the panic over AIDS makes distinctions not only between infected and uninfected but also between who is considered part of the "community" and who is considered part of the "risk" to that community. I will show that this issue of testing, marking out difference, and making sure that those who are presumed to be heterosexual and/or innocent are kept from infection are all key components of AIDS/HIV education in the public schools.

As the "heterosexual community" becomes consolidated in popular representation and imaginary, an attendant consolidation does not always happen to the "gay community." Studies of representation of AIDS in the media have shown the ways AIDS "victims" were presumed to be rootless, disconnected from community and family.[15] These disconnections reinforce particular definitions of community and family in which both are defined in traditional and heterosexual terms. The irony and, indeed, tragedy of the disconnection from family and community that people with AIDS have experienced is that it is the traditional family and community that refuses them. People with AIDS are not alone, of course; but the kinds of communities that surround them are largely ignored in mass representations and curricula. Gay relationships and gay communities are often present in the lives of people with AIDS, but when "family" and "community" take on specifically heterosexual meanings, the presence of nontraditional family and community go unremarked. Representations of isolated outcast people with AIDS appear to act as reassurance that alternative forms of community, outside of the heterosexual community, cannot flourish. That the gay community took responsibility for caring for people with AIDS, developing social service organizations, activism, and safer sex, was for the first few years of the epidemic largely ignored by mainstream representations of the AIDS epidemic.

The omission of information on the gay community's response to AIDS from school curricula has the effect of emphasizing a definition of gayness that links gayness with individual activity and lack of responsibility. Students are only encouraged to see heterosexual families and heterosexual communities responding to the epidemic with care and concern for those affected. But they are not encouraged to see that those most frequently affected by AIDS are also responsible and caring people who often had to create their own social services when the "heterosexual community" was less inclined to be concerned. Images of heterosexual caring, then, cover over the exclusions attendant upon the construction of community as necessarily heterosexual.

The Helms Amendment to AIDS educational funding, eventually part of the Health Omnibus Programs Extension Act of 1988, went one step further in ignoring the work of the gay community in the face of AIDS by attempting to prevent its work.[16] The Helms Amendment, passed by the Senate 94 to 2, prohibited the use of federal funds for local AIDS educational programs that "promote homosexuality" and required "federally financed educational materials about AIDS to stress sexual abstinence."[17] In short, the federal government, in the midst of claiming to fund AIDS education for targeted at-risk populations on the local level, prohibited groups receiving federal funds from directing their information to the gay community in any way that would not attack gayness itself. That Congress suggested homosexuality *could* be promoted is interesting on a number of levels, not the least of which is the parallel between "promotion" and "contagion" in the context of AIDS. Homosexuality, so closely related to AIDS according to Helms, is the same sort of a disease that can be passed to unwitting persons who haven't taken proper precautions. In an attempt to prohibit the promotion of homosexuality, Helms's logic appears to be that, though most people are heterosexual, their heterosexuality is perpetually at risk of conversion to homosexuality, a process that can be stopped by curtailing information that makes homosexual activities less risky for the contraction of HIV. Helms, in his own way, articulates gay and heterosexual identity as relational. With enough information, an individual might find him or herself "promoted" into homosexuality. The threat of AIDS is thus as an incentive for those potential dissidents to remain within the heterosexual fold. Those who choose to leave, despite the danger, are literally on their own.

His policy cuts off their connection to funding from the federal government, disconnecting them from a sort of official sexual citizenship.

Policies about AIDS and representations of AIDS show that fear of
HIV infection mingles with fear of homosexuality. Homosexuality and
HIV both threaten the traditional community and family. Homosexuality
threatens the unquestioned acceptance of heterosexual norms, HIV
threatens the confidence the community has in its members' adherence to
those norms.

The 1988 *Report of the Presidential Commission on the Human Immunodeficiency Virus Epidemic* describes "distinct populations" at risk
for HIV, including homosexual men, blacks, Hispanics, students, runaways, and homeless youth, among others. Though these distinct populations might appear to be communities unto themselves, the commission
does not give them community status, but it does argue that it is up to
"local communities" to decide how to address the needs of these "distinct
populations."[18] Thus, those who are at risk for HIV are positioned as not
communities themselves, but rather populations whose needs should be
determined by the broader structure that they live under, that is, the "heterosexual" community. Groups at risk are thus not sufficiently "community" like in their own organization, nor are individuals at risk quite fully
community members. They can be separated into distinct populations,
but they are not themselves to be in control of their own educational or
service needs. That control should be in the hands of "community leaders."[19] In short, whereas the word "community" may mobilize notions of
caring and authority, "population" lacks such connotations.

The segmentation of people into "populations," as opposed to
"communities," signals that people who are at risk are already in some
way split off from "community" life. At the same time people at risk are
not full community members, but rather "populations," they nonetheless
exist, unidentified within communities. In other words, risk groups pass
as community members. For instance, the *New York State Instructional
Guide* places homosexual and bisexual men under the category "Major
Risk Factors."[20] When specific populations can be distinguished as risk
factors in and of themselves, HIV becomes sufficient reason to search
out and separate those people. There is at once a confidence that the
threat will turn out to be people whom the community does not want and
a fear that these outsiders may be lurking within. But there is an uneasy
confidence that even these outsiders within are sufficiently different from
upstanding members of the community to be recognizable as different.
On the one hand, bisexual and homosexual men, particularly as represented in the popular media, seem to be sufficiently different as to be
recognizable. But, as New York State's *AIDS Instructional Guide:*

Grades K-12 points out in "Appendix D: Current Information on AIDS," "Most infected people have no signs or symptoms of illness."[21]

The problem of HIV becomes one of attempting to make the invisible HIV visible and to make the invisibility of sexuality visible—both HIV and gayness are invisible and part of their threat lies in their ability to pass. Calls for mandatory testing and representations in the media of gayness as excessive and as constituting overt sexuality are attempts to render the potentially invisible visible. But the presumption is still that these invisibilities are not within the community or the family. It seems that parents confidently assume that their children are not gay but still argue against inclusion of gay-related material in public schools because it might easily sway their children to adopt such a lifestyle. Though the possibility of difference within communities and even families is raised by issues surrounding sexuality and AIDS, this difference is often ignored.

New York State and the Construction of the Heterosexual Community

New York State's *AIDS Instructional Guide: Grades K-12* contributes to the creation of a normative heterosexual community and thus hampers the ability of some public school students to minimize their risk for Human Immunodeficiency Virus (HIV). The document restricts the meaning of community in two ways. First, an exclusionary conception of community operates through the *Guide*'s provision for community involvement in revising lessons to reflect local values and, second, there is a restrictive notion of community written into the text of the lessons themselves. The suggested list of participants on community review boards does not include gay groups or people with HIV. Advocates for any of the risk groups are not considered experts or community resources. No specific mention of concerns of homosexual, bisexual, any sexually active, or IV drug-using students are addressed in the *Guide*.

Though there was an attempt to maintain a unified heterosexual community in response to the AIDS epidemic, the development of AIDS educational policy in the public schools shows how fractured and contentious this "community" can be. A concern that "community values" not be offended by New York State's mandate to provide AIDS education in the public schools can be seen by tracing the New York State Board of Regents' deliberations. On September 19, 1987, the Regents approved a measure that made AIDS curricula mandatory in all elementary and secondary schools in the state. They could not, however, reach an agreement on an instructional guide for teachers. The main concern raised by the Regents was that the *Instructional Guide* contained "descriptions of sexual activity [that] would lead to more, not less, sexual activity, as well as to earlier activity among students."[22] An additional concern raised by a number of Regents was over "the tone" of the *Instructional Guide*, that it turned the course "into a 'how-to' manual on methods of avoidance."[23] The Regents maintained that abstinence should have been stressed as the only way to avoid HIV. An initial draft of the *Instructional Guide* had included information on condom usage and was sent out to selected areas for testing. After feedback from the schools was reviewed, the draft was rejected by the Regents in part because of its inclusion of information on condoms and in part because of its lack of provision for a parental opt-out whereby parents could have their children excused from lessons the parents found offensive.[24]

The next draft of the *Instructional Guide* met with more approval. Though not the final approved draft, it stressed abstinence and included a parental opt-out provision for "certain lessons dealing with how to prevent the disease (including use of condoms)."[25] Reviewing the same draft, Dr. Hugh Carroll, superintendent of schools for the diocese of Rockville Center, also approved of its "stress that abstinence is the best form of prevention" in contrast to the earlier draft in which "almost on every page, the alternative of condom use is brought up. We want to emphasize, as the church does, that sexual intercourse should be kept to marriage."[26] Regent Floyd Linton, agreeing with Catholic concerns about the *Guide*, said he "anticipated further changes in the tone of the document, with more emphasis placed on sexual abstinence as the only risk-free way to avoid AIDS."[27] A staff member contended a strong desire to avoid controversy at all costs was instrumental in the development of the *Guide*. The Regents met most of the demands of the religious participants, either agreeing with them or hoping that agreement on the AIDS curriculum guide would demonstrate cooperation between public schools and religious authority.[28]

Late in October 1987, the Regents approved the final draft of the *Instructional Guide*. Though the Regents had attempted to forestall controversy by catering to religious concerns, the *Guide* was immediately criticized on its public health shortcomings by New York City's health commissioner Stephen C. Joseph because it "does not advocate the use of condoms to slow transmission of the deadly virus."[29] However, the Regents chose not to alter their abstinence-based curriculum. Thomas Sobol, the state commissioner of education, said that the *Guide*, which cites the use of condoms as "extremely high-risk behavior," "was a compromise to reconcile various points of view."[30] Sobol explained:

We are trying to deal with a large and a very diverse state. It was not easy to gain agreement of the majority of the Board of Regents on any guide at all, and it was under discussion for some months. I think, from a political point of view, it's a very wise and fair compromise. And from an educational standpoint, it goes a long way toward meeting the needs of the kids of this state.[31]

In addition to its position on condoms, the Regents also drew criticism for their requirement that community review boards develop community-specific AIDS curricula and that these boards include clergy. Sally Storm, member of the Dobbs Ferry Board of Education and chairwoman of the district's Family Living and Human Sexuality Advisory Committee (the area of the curriculum where the new AIDS instruction was to be situated), said that when the district began a community review of its curriculum, "out of the woodwork came fundamentalist Catholic and fundamentalist other people."[32] Opponents of the new AIDS curriculum, and later of the already existing family life curriculum, formed a group called the Concerned Parents and Citizens of Dobbs Ferry. They complained that "the curriculum had been written by teachers and administrators instead of being developed by all the members of the advisory committee."[33] This one example raises a number of important points about the attempt to involve the community in decisions about AIDS education. First, as Storm argued, the policy had brought "into the school system as advisory committee members, people who are naturally suspicious of public schools."[34] Storm claimed this suspicion was grounded in religious concerns, that the main objections to the entire family life curriculum, including the new sections on AIDS they were supposed to be reviewing, were that the curriculum "tried to show students how difficult it is to be a parent" and that because of its teaching about those difficulties it encouraged abortion.[35] Storm predicted that "many schools are going to run into [this problem] as soon as state rules requiring an advisory committee and mandating clergy on that committee" are enforced.[36] For Storm, then, the issue is not just religion but also the involvement of school outsiders in curricular decisions.

That parents and members of the community were considered by some school authorities to be outsiders points to the uncertainty in the use of the term "community." Storm's position closely parallels that of the experts insensitive to the concerns of parents criticized by Dorothy Nelkin and Stephen Hilgartner. AIDS does bring public health concerns to public schools, but that alone is an insufficient justification for neglecting to consider the potential areas of discomfort the curriculum changes may raise. Nelkin and Hilgartner found a similar reaction to outside authority in their study of the controversy in Queens over news that children with AIDS were attending New York City schools. They argue

that the very way in which the School Board removed the issue from discussion and relied on expert opinion added fuel to parental reaction, to
parental feelings of frustration and fear.[37] The expert opinions included
those of school officials, public health experts, and the parents themselves, all using different language and different standards when assess-
ing risk, but often not in contexts where they could speak to each other's
concerns. Nelkin and Hilgartner were not arguing that children with
AIDS ought not to be allowed in the schools but that the decisions need
to be made in public and need to address genuine parental concerns about
the safety of their children. Parental rights or religious rights may not, in
the end, trump the rights of students to information to help them in their
process of decision making. But there appeared to be no concerted effort
to find a compromise that explicitly balanced each concern. That consensus on the issue of AIDS education is not possible in a diverse society is
not a reason to sidestep attempts at engaging the issues of parental rights,
students' rights, and the needs of people faced with an epidemic. School
policy decisions can become educative sites, but the sides in this case
quickly polarized.

The battle over AIDS instruction came to involve authority as well as
values, religion as well as science, though participants did not always
acknowledge all these dimensions. For instance, one member of the Concerned Parents and Citizens of Dobbs Ferry told the *New York Times*,
"This is not a religious issue, this is an issue of parents' rights versus
teachers' rights."[38] But a strong religious agenda fueled the claim that
New York State's family life curriculum approved of abortion because it
recognized the difficulties of parenthood. The curriculum's intention is to
discourage students from having intercourse before marriage, not to
promote abortion as a contraceptive. But the criticism of the Dobbs Ferry
district's community advisory committee also clearly raises the important
issue of authority in schooling.

James Hottois and Neal A. Milner's mid-1970s study of sex education programs in the public schools found that controversy was most often avoided if sex education curricula were opened to inspection and alteration by parents.[39] Concluding that the struggle over authority was
often more important than the question of whether sex education ought to
be taught or not, the authors argue that "the professionalization of school
policy makers and their ability convincingly to define an issue as being
within their own professional sphere of competence are techniques and
processes that limit the participation of active minorities."[40] Hottois and
Milner suggest that policy makers grant more participation to community
members to prevent controversy.[41] Yet they also found that the topics
most often deleted by parents were abortion and homosexuality.[42] Kenneth Howe's discussion of AIDS education closely follows Hottois and

Milner's findings in that Howe argues that AIDS education ought to be open to local control and that communities ought to be able to remove information they find offensive.[43] However, these procedural attempts to avoid controversy by opening curricula to local values have the potential to encourage intolerance. On the one hand, a guarantee of parental rights and community involvement does seem to engender support for sex education's place in the public schools. But, on the other hand, opening up the curricula to parental authority potentially limits the range of consensus—sometimes challenging or eliminating topics that ultimately exclude the concerns of unheard constituencies within the community. In the case of decisions about sex education, information about homosexuality or contraception is prohibited by parents whose children may well be gay or sexually active and have a strong interest in having the schools address the very topics their parents often unwittingly prohibit.

This raises the question: Who gets to decide whether minority interests within a community will be addressed by that community's school? What constitutes offensiveness to a community becomes defined as outside of that community—those minorities within communities come to be viewed as outsiders even if they live within its physical boundaries. All of this leads to a dilemma for democratic education, namely, a desire to avoid controversy over the issue of authority and encourage local communities to be involved in curricular decisions reflecting their values, but also a pluralist concern to have school curricula prepare students for participation in a diverse society. When local control and community involvement come to justify the imposition of the majority on the minority, the minority is not merely cast as a dissenting voice but actually removed from what comes to be considered the community.

The intention of the Regents in making sure that the reviewers of the *AIDS Instructional Guide*'s development included religious representatives was to avoid religious controversy. The Regents similarly provided for inclusion of clergy on the local advisory boards to help avoid controversy. Community advisory boards are, from the perspective of school administrators, supposed to alter the *Guide* to suit perceived local needs. They are not supposed to call into question the entire curriculum and whether it should exist in the first place. However, in Dobbs Ferry, the community advisory committee for the AIDS curriculum broadened its review to include the entire family life curriculum. They also contended that even then their scope was not broad enough because teachers and administrators had already written the family life curriculum without their input. This claim was not entirely accurate; the Bureau of Curriculum Development for New York State had written it, local teachers and administrators made changes to it and then submitted it to the advisory board for review. This was not exactly the proper procedure; teachers,

administrators, and community members were all supposed to work together to make the curriculum locally specific. On the one hand, the advisory committee did not go far enough in allowing community involvement, no doubt precipitating the controversy. On the other hand, the
community members had no jurisdiction to overhaul the entire curriculum.

In Valley Stream, the community advisory board attempted to go
further than merely attempting to make the AIDS guide locally specific.
They attempted to claim that New York State did not have the authority
to mandate the teaching of AIDS prevention and that such teaching violated the right to religious freedom. In *Ware v. Valley Stream* (1989),[44]
the New York State Court of Appeals ruled that the state commissioner
of education does have the power to mandate AIDS education.[45] In addition, "the courts have repeatedly placed the State's educational interest
above the exercise of unbridled religious freedom."[46]

The particular decision to make clergy part of the defined community, but not to include representatives of what the *Guide* refers to as risk
groups, seems intended to stave off controversy rather than to provide
insights into what the epidemic means and how it is experienced by the
very people whom the *Guide* has labeled as intrinsically caught up with
the epidemic. The specific inclusion of clergy reinforced the view that
AIDS is a moral epidemic as much as a health problem. This duality is
reflected in "Teacher Notes for Lesson 26," a lesson designed to help
students identify school and community resources for information about
AIDS. "[R]eligious groups" are listed above "regional AIDS centers" as
potential sources of information on AIDS.[47] In the *Guide*'s chapter on
"Planning, Implementing, and Evaluating AIDS Instruction," "religious
organizations" are second on a list of seven possible community resources for AIDS instruction; the other six are all health-related agencies
and organizations.[48] While it is not possible nor desirable to cleanly separate public health issues from moral issues, the inclusion of clergy to fulfill the requirement for moral engagement with AIDS issues creates a
particular version of what the moral community is. By creating a moral
community in which religious teachings are given an equal say about
public health concerns, the ability of the curriculum to reach students
engaging in activities that put them at risk for HIV is diminished.

The Regents also distance themselves from public health authorities
through their attempt to avoid controversy over contraceptives and premarital sex that would follow from educating on condom use. We see
this in "Appendix C: Information on Condoms" in which the Regents
state:

Abstinence from sexual activity is the only sure protection against HIV transmission. The Surgeon General of the United States, the Centers for Disease Control, and State and local Health departments have included condom use as one of the strategies for further preventing the spread of HIV. The Board of Regents view the use of condoms as extremely high risk behavior. The view that condoms should or can be used as a way to reduce the risk of transmission of AIDS should not be supported.[49]

It is difficult to pit the failure rate for condoms against the failure rate for abstinence. The effectiveness of condoms jumps dramatically if they are used consistently and correctly. The effectiveness of abstinence depends on a definitional circularity, though planning for abstinence does have a high failure rate since many sexually active persons claim they had planned to be abstinent. In other words, the effectiveness of absti-nence is measured by the presumption that it is achieved, the rate of "human failure" is usually not calculated. Studies of condom effective-ness do take into account the rate of "human failure." The failure rate for condoms typically cited by opponents is about 12 percent, a figure that includes the number of times couples failed to even use condoms. It is estimated that the failure rate for condoms would drop to 2 to 3 percent if couples used condoms "consistently and correctly."[50]

But in addition to fears about the safety of condoms, the Regents's policy is tied to the condom's potential ability to displace marriage as a practice of safety. Condoms, by making possible sexual relations that do not require marriage, in turn, displace the safety and presumed homoge-neity of the community. Condoms have the potential of making those who do not have the option of marriage, for instance, gays and lesbians, safer from the threat of HIV infection. Following the Regents' logic here, there is no possibility for safe sex outside of marriage though the Regents should not have presumed that there was necessarily safety within mar-riage from HIV infection. Furthermore, the agenda that posits marriage as a place of safety and as a building block of community clearly has to ignore child sexual abuse, domestic violence, and all sorts of coercive community practices to be able to posit those structures, in and of them-selves, as safe.[51] But according to the *Guide*'s logic, the boundaries of community replace the boundary created by the condom—the threat stays outside of the community, the marriages stay safe, HIV does not enter. Condoms, ironically, do not provide a safe boundary for commu-nities because they indicate behaviors that communities do not want to acknowledge that their members engage in. Condoms, thus, are a threat to the boundaries of communities. In addition, condoms are risky be-cause bringing them into public school policy causes controversy. In short, condoms pose a risk to the Regents's ability to maintain order in public schools.[52]

Paralleling their firm policy on condoms, the Regents are very specific about which other issues in the *AIDS Instructional Guide* are not to be changed by advisory groups. For example, concerning the context and tone of AIDS education:

> The Regents and the commissioner intend that any teaching about AIDS be conducted only within a comprehensive program of instruction in positive health values and habits. Pupils should be taught self-respect and respect for others. They should learn to act in ways which promote their own healthy growth and development and to avoid acts which may bring harm or injury. They should learn to be responsible for their own behavior and for the consequences it may have on themselves and other people. They should learn to appreciate the value of the nurturing relationships that occur within stable families. They should be taught to abstain from sex. They should be led to understand that postponing sexual activity until adulthood increases one's positive life choices for career and marriage. Only within such a context of positive teaching about health and personal responsibility should instruction about AIDS be provided.[53]

The first four sentences are broad statements about the importance of general sorts of ethical behavior. It seems unlikely that many would disagree that health is a good thing, that people should be respectful of themselves and others, and even though the notion that "actions have consequences" is sometimes problematically deployed in AIDS information to mean that people should be abstinent, clearly actions do have consequences. The moral community represented by the first four sentences, then, does not seem to be a specific, exclusive one. However, the next four sentences do specify a very particular view of what this moral community is to consist of. Stable families can be a good thing, provided that stability is not achieved through coercion and that "families" can be broadened to mean a variety of relationships. But it is clear from the call to avoid sexual activity before marriage that the stable family advocated by this passage is the married, heterosexual family.

It is participation in this specific version of family, then, that the *Guide* and the Regents hope to have AIDS education facilitate. Though community advisory boards are charged with being certain that their programs are "consistent with community values," "those charged with developing local programs should be certain that such programs include these values."[54] Very clearly, then, the policies are directed at a presumed heterosexual community intent on having its presumed heterosexual children avoid AIDS by adhering to specific heterosexual values and practices. This first set of context requirements clearly outline the Regents's intention to have the curriculum situated within a context that emphasizes health, responsibility to the community, and sexuality within marriage. Each of these elements goes into the makeup of what the Regents and the writers of the *Guide* define as community—a healthy, heterosexual, community of families.

According to the mandate of the "Commissioner's Regulations Subchapter G, Part 135," AIDS education in both elementary and secondary schools shall: "provide accurate information to pupils concerning the nature of the disease, methods of transmission, and methods of prevention; shall stress abstinence as the most appropriate and effective premarital protection against AIDS; shall be age appropriate and consistent with community values. "[55]

The advisory council can make changes in the specifics of how this is taught but the basic information about transmission, prevention, and the stress on abstinence are not negotiable. That abstinence is described as the "most appropriate and effective premarital protection against AIDS" is clear evidence that the audience for the *Guide* is presumed to be heterosexual. The *Guide* makes no attempt to suggest what might be effective protection for students not eventually planning on marrying nor does the *Guide* explain what it is about marriage, per se, that gives it the status of safety that the *Guide* bestows upon it. In its combined message of the safety of marriage and students' responsibility to the community, students are also encouraged to see "community" as meaning a gathering of safe, responsible married heterosexuals, who, because of their adherence to social norms, have managed to stave off an epidemic that has apparently chosen other people who are not part of this safe, heterosexual community. Indeed, this safe community does not even need to know about condoms because all they have to do is wait and safety will come to them in the form of marriage.

The mandate for AIDS education in New York public schools strongly suggests that such instruction take place in the context of "A Family Life Approach to AIDS."[56] The mandate for AIDS education also supplies an occasion to push for a family life education component for health education. In the absence of an already existing family life education program, schools are directed to use the *AIDS Instructional Guide* as a tool for providing one, as "some of the program objectives and learner outcomes of a family life education program have been partially integrated into this guide."[57] Thus AIDS quite clearly becomes an issue that can be used to mobilize particular moral lessons, not just about the ways in which AIDS should be confronted or avoided but about the ways in which the family should be structured. To that end the *Guide* provides lessons that explore "family structure, roles and responsibilities of family members, responsibilities for exploring sound interpersonal relationships, characteristics of nurturing relationships, and sexual relationships."[58] As we will see from the lessons in the *Guide*, the families described are quite clearly heterosexual and ostensibly form a seamless continuum with heterosexualized conceptions of community.

Community and Family in the Lessons of the *Guide*

Public school AIDS/HIV education in the *Guide* emphasizes abstinence until marriage. This message assumes a number of things. First, it assumes that there is something inherently dangerous in sex itself that precludes any sort of precautions, condoms, and/or nonpenetrative sex from preventing HIV infection. In addition, the message of abstinence until marriage presumes that all students will one day marry or, failing that, will remain abstinent for their entire lives. Furthermore, abstinence curricula assume that abstinence and marriage, without additional information about the vagaries of human relationships, such as the possibility that one's partner will be dishonest in recounting his/her previous sex partners, will be sufficient to protect students from HIV. By addressing the message of the curricula to students presumed to be abstinent, abstinence curricula also assume that students have not yet been exposed to HIV. In terms of the creation of community through abstinence curricula, placing sex only within the context of family life sends the message that the only possible way to have a family and be part of a community is to be heterosexual and married. In other words, the curriculum's construction of the abstinent individual is intertwined with a specific, exclusionary, and simplistic conception of community. Combined with the curriculum's representation and construction of people with AIDS, this conception of community has serious consequences for people with AIDS and for gay students and community members; their needs are not addressed and students are encouraged to view these populations as outsiders.

Only the family is presumed to be safe in connection with AIDS. There is more ambivalence about the family when it is addressed on its own in the *Guide* than when it is addressed in connection with AIDS. Thus the lessons in the *Guide* that deal with specific non-AIDS issues, such as descriptions of family structures, roles, and responsibilities, caution teachers to be aware of the possibility of sensitive topics, like child sexual abuse, different family practices, violence, alcoholism, among others, being raised by the lessons. Teachers are warned that lesson 7, which has as its learner outcome to "describe how family members show care and help one another," may require "special sensitivity."[59] Teachers should watch for students discussing problems such as "alcoholism, incest, abuse, etc. Should such situations arise in the class it is best to thank the student for sharing such information but refocus the student as quickly as possible on positive ways the family shows care."[60] The teacher is directed to follow up with the student on an individual basis and to report suspected abuse. The instructions suggest that publicly discussing one student's family problems would be traumatic for other students. The *Guide* does helpfully suggest individual attention for the troubled student. But the larger construction of families as safe, happy places in the curriculum makes the discussion of family problems doubly disturbing for students. That those dysfunctional families come to be indicative of individual, private family failings rather than part of structural problems with families tends to put a further burden on students from families with problems.

In the context of discussions of AIDS, the family is represented as a place of safety and understanding. It appears that family can be mobilized much in the same way as heterosexual community can be mobilized—it is something that only appears solid and safe in reference to something which appears to be a greater threat, like the threat of AIDS. Family and community can be places of warmth and compassion, but to avoid discussing potential problems within either means that lessons reflect only the ideal versions of the two. Students whose lives do not measure up to the ideal or whose families or identities are not reflected in the curricula are held at a distance. Where curricula might attend to the complexities and stress of family and community life to prepare students for both, teachers are directed to treat problems as individual concerns.

Other lessons in the *Guide* teach students to link family and community as "those who are able to provide assistance." Lesson 8, for example, has students construct "a booklet of health resources" and suggests that students list the health resources in the "home, school, community, and religious organization."[61] In addition, students are to learn about and use "the appropriate health resources, such as: family, teacher, school nurse, principal, police officer, pharmacist, and religious leader."[62] Though clearly this lesson is intended to encourage students to view their community as full of a variety of people concerned about their health and willing to help, it does not seem that either police officer or religious leader will provide health-related assistance, least of all to gay youth.[63] This is not to diminish the good work that police and clergy may do for their communities or to suggest that all police and all clergy would be inappropriate resources, even for gay youth. However, by construing community resources as including clergy, but not including specific gay-supportive organizations and agencies, the isolation felt by gay students is undoubtedly increased. By definition, in the *Guide*, community resources do not include specifically gay-friendly resources; therefore, by definition as well, gay-friendly resources are outsiders. By teaching students to think of these authorities as people they might reasonably turn to with health concerns, students are subtly taught what sorts of health concerns are appropriate. Students may be discouraged from seeking help from health resources at all as they begin to decipher more clearly the norms they should be following.

To its credit, the *Guide* does encourage compassion toward those who are ill and emphasizes that students need be aware of how the AIDS virus is transmitted and how it is not.[64] Lesson 21 asks students how they would respond to the problem, "My friend has AIDS. Should I go to dinner at her/his home?"[65] Students are encouraged to identify the alternatives (to go or not to go) and identify their concerns. The *Guide* provides sample concerns that involve fear of AIDS, fear of getting AIDS from eating with a person with AIDS, embarrassment at the friend's condition, uncertainty as to how the friend got AIDS (homosexuality, IV drug use, or sexual intercourse with an infected partner).[66] The teacher notes for the lesson warn that students may be misinformed about transmission factors and may "associate AIDS with certain groups of people (drug abusers, the sexually promiscuous, homosexuals) and fear them. [Students] think they can get AIDS in a situation in which they cannot and that it is transmitted in a casual way."[67] Teachers are directed to "clarify misinformation and fears so students may demonstrate respect for others and show care, understanding, and compassion."[68] These are very good qualities to encourage in students, but ultimately the decision on whether to actually go to dinner at the friend's house is left open-ended. The point of the lesson is not necessarily to make students decide that they would, indeed, overcome their fears and show compassion. Rather, the lesson seeks to give them an opportunity to sort it out for themselves. We will see in a later chapter that the *Guide* does not use the same open-ended approach when dealing with the issue of abstinence. In the lessons on abstinence, students negotiate *how* they will be abstinent, not *whether* they will be abstinent. As we have seen in this lesson on compassion, students are given the option to explore the issue of compassion for a person with AIDS, but they are not required to actually claim that they would be compassionate.

Lesson 24 brings the issue of AIDS closer to home by having students respond to a letter: "My sister was just diagnosed as having AIDS. She will be home from the hospital next week. I am 13 years old. What can my family do to help her?"[69] While the previous lesson raised the issue of fear of the person with AIDS because of the possibility that they were members of risk groups or that transmission of AIDS could occur through casual contact, this lesson brushes all of those concerns away. Instead, the central feature of this letter is that the person with AIDS is a member of a family and is returning home from the hospital to be with that family. All questions of how she got AIDS or who she is are displaced by her situatedness within a family. It is interesting that the person with AIDS in this case is not only ageless—we could assume she had pediatric AIDS—but also that she is female. In 1987, when the *Guide* was released, most women with AIDS contracted HIV through either intravenous drug use or heterosexual contact with an intravenous drug user or bisexual man. Thus women's contraction of HIV is in some sense normalized by its transmission through heterosexual means (unless contracted through intravenous drug use). This sister, then, is positioned as not homosexual, not as deviant as she could have been had she been a male. She is distanced from outsider status both by her gender and by her return to the family.

While I have already argued that it is not appropriate for the *Guide* to have students interrogate the identity of the people with AIDS for whom they are supposed to show compassion, the *Guide* already positions people with AIDS as outsiders in its reference to intravenous drug users, those who are sexually promiscuous, and homosexuals. Students are not encouraged to take AIDS as the occasion to overcome their prejudices against people in the "risk groups" for AIDS but are rather encouraged to take the family membership status of a person with AIDS as the occasion to develop compassion toward that person. People with AIDS, then, come to deserve compassion only as part of a family or community, when they remain outsiders they are not "sisters" but "risk groups."

The final lesson in the *Guide* is a class debate designed to have students explore the "balance between the individual's right and society's right" and to have students recognize the "dual responsibility . . . to protect oneself form becoming infected by the AIDS virus and to prevent communication of the AIDS virus to others."[70] The teachers notes on this lesson pose the issue of individual rights as prevailing in instances such as "random drug testing and nondiscrimination in housing, education, employment."[71] Civil rights or minority rights are here described as "individual rights" in contrast to the broader "society's rights." This move emphasizes the way in which the *Guide* has represented "risk groups" in that what may be considered minority practices, like homosexuality, are not given the same social weight as majority practices, such as heterosexual marriage. Homosexuality and the right to nondiscrimination both become individualized concerns, separated from the concerns of the community and from society as a whole. When rendered as "individual" concerns, minority rights sound voluntaristic and isolated from social groupings, similar to the *Guide*'s rendering of homosexuals as not part of a community and potentially a risk to the community because of their separateness. Situating minority concerns as an issue of individual rights reinforces the *Guide*'s active neglect of the gay community's response to the AIDS epidemic. According to the *Guide*'s lessons, the family and the community are the structures that respond to health crises and that protect one from "risk groups." These "risk groups" are never described as having the same sense of responsibility or similar abilities to provide care for people with AIDS. They remain, in the *Guide*, a collection of individuals, occasionally asserting their rights as individuals but not responsible enough to organize or to make claims on any other basis than their own individual rights.

On the Need to Express Community

James F. Childress argues that the call for mandatory HIV testing is an attempt to "impose" community through coercive measures. He argues there should be an attempt to "express community through protection against such negative consequences" because of the clear negative consequences including discrimination that people may face for testing positive for HIV.[72] Childress is here using the sense of community that emphasizes its relational quality. To express community is, then, to care for the needs of a potential variety of people who are all then part of community. The New York State policy on AIDS education works against this "expression of community" in a number of ways. The call for community involvement includes clergy as a special concern, but it does not specifically call for public health professionals or members of "risk groups." With notable exceptions, clergy have not been outspoken defenders of gay youth. Given the emphasis on their inclusion in the process of determining the local tone of AIDS education, one can only assume that they would not be the likely advocates for the needs of gay youth, or for that matter, any sexually active youth.

Public health organization representatives and local AIDS project members may be an additional choice for inclusion who would address these concerns, but, according to New York State, their presence is not necessary. The presence of clergy determines that a community advisory board does represent the "community" and suggests that "community" would not be represented by members of "risk groups" or people who work with them. Controversy is staved off by inclusion of clergy, but controversy would be courted by inviting these outsiders to the advisory board. Thus, through its policies, New York State reflects prevalent attitudes about who should rightly be considered to be part of the community and who is a controversial outsider. They become an inseparable part of community while "risk group" members become expendable.

The lessons of the *Instructional Guide* reinforce the message of this normative, exclusive community. Whereas religious organizations are community resources, gay people are not represented as having any sense of community or responsibility—they only embody risk. Similarly, students are encouraged to act with compassion toward people with AIDS, but largely in the context of family relations. The family is represented as the site of safety from HIV or the place where a person with HIV can return. Certainly one would want students to be confident that their families would care for them if they became ill. But what is missing from this account is an accurate representation of how other social forms and structures can provide the same responsible caring and support. When a high percentage of runaways report having to leave home because of their homosexuality, holding out the family as a haven is not helpful. What would be more helpful is to express community by broadening its membership to include people who are not in traditional families, rather than keeping them out from fear of contagion.

Notes

1. Justice Kennedy in *Romer, Governor of Colorado, et al. v. Evans et al.* (1996) no. 94–1039: 14.
2. Kennedy, *Romer v. Evans*, 14.
3. See James Hottois and Neal A. Milner, *The Sex Education Controversy: A Study of Politics, Education, and Morality* (Lexington, Mass.: Lexington Books, 1975) and D. Kirby, *Sexuality Education: An Evaluation of Programs* (Santa Cruz, Calif.: Network Publications, 1984).
4. See Kenneth R. Howe, "AIDS Education in the Public Schools: Old Wine in New Bottles?" *Journal of Moral Education* 19, no. 2 (May 1990): 114–123.
5. Eve Kosofsky Sedgwick, "How to Bring Your Kids up Gay," *Social Text* 29 (1991): 23.
6. Margaret Heckler quoted in Cindy Patton, *Sex and Germs: The Politics of AIDS* (Boston: South End Press, 1985), 38.
7. Patton, *Sex and Germs*, 22.
8. Cindy Patton, *Inventing AIDS* (New York: Routledge, 1990), 27–28.
9. See B. R. Simon Rosser, *Male Homosexual Behavior and the Effects of AIDS Education: A Study of Behavior and Safer Sex in New Zealand and South Australia* (New York: Prager, 1991). The Grim Reaper Campaign in Britain he describes is one example: ads featured pictures of Death and his scythe ready to cut down people with AIDS. Reactions to the campaign, including high rates of denial, learned helplessness, and disempowerment, are documented in his study (187). Rosser's study indicates that the campaign scared people into feelings of helplessness and fatalism rather than encouraging them to take active steps to avoid HIV. They report feeling it was inevitable so it did not matter whether they took precautions.
10. For instance, the "AIDS: Get the Facts" campaign on television which tells viewers to "get the facts," but never does actually supply the full "facts."

11. Simon Watney, *Policing Desire: Pornography, AIDS, and the Media* (Minneapolis: University of Minneapolis Press, 1987), 151.

12. Watney, *Policing Desire*, 103.

13. Sander L. Gilman, "AIDS and Syphilis: The Iconography of Disease," in *AIDS: Cultural Analysis/Cultural Activism*, ed. Douglas Crimp (Cambridge: Massachusetts Institute of Technology Press, 1988), 98.

14. Patton, *Sex and Germs*, 7.

15. See Watney's *Policing Desire*, particularly 58–98; also see Watney's "The Spectacle of AIDS," in *AIDS: Cultural Analysis/Cultural Activism*, ed. Douglas Crimp (Cambridge: Massachusetts Institute of Technology Press, 1988), 71–86.

16. The bill to which the amendment was attached was eventually enveloped into S2889, which in turn became the Health Omnibus Programs Extension Act of 1988 § 2–2500–102 STAT. 3093 (1988). The specific part of the law that the Helms Amendment formed is Title XV, sec. 2500.

17. "Senate Votes." *New York Times*, 15 October 1987, II, 12.

18. Presidential Commission on the Human Immunodeficiency Virus Epidemic, *Report of the Presidential Commission on the Human Immunodeficiency Virus Epidemic* (Washington, D.C.: U.S. Government Printing Office, June 1988), 86.

19. Presidential Commission on the HIV Epidemic, *Report*, 86.

20. University of the State of New York State Department of Education, Bureau of Curriculum Development, *AIDS Instructional Guide: Grades K–12* (Albany: New York State Education Department, 1987), 165. Hereafter referred to as USNY SED.

21. USNY SED, *AIDS Instructional Guide*, 166.

22. Deirdre Carmody, "Regents Require AIDS Instruction for Elementary and High Schools," *New York Times*, 19 September 1987, 1, 34.

23. Carmody, "Regents Require," 34.

24. Carmody, "Regents Require," 34.

25. Michael Kornfield, "Schools Welcome AIDS Teaching," *New York Times*, 11 October 1987, 12.

26. Kornfield, "Schools Welcome," 12.

27. Kornfield, "Schools Welcome," 12.

28. Anonymous interview with author, Albany, N.Y., 7 June 1991.

29. Jane Gross, "New York State's Curriculum on AIDS Criticized," *New York Times*, 2 November 1987, 19.

30. Gross, "New York State's Curriculum," 19.

31. Gross, "New York State's Curriculum," 19.

32. Patrick Keegan, "Sex Education Raises New Concern for Schools," *New York Times*, 21 October 1987, 1.

33. Keegan, "Sex Education," 1.

34. Keegan, "Sex Education," 1.

35. Keegan, "Sex Education," 1.

36. Keegan, "Sex Education," 1.

37. Dorothy Nelkin and Stephen Hilgartner, "Disputed Dimensions of Risk: A Public School Controversy over AIDS," *The Milbank Quarterly* 64, supplement 1 (1986): 118–142.

38. Nelkin and Hilgartner, "Disputed Dimensions," 140.

39. James Hottois and Neal A. Milner, *The Sex Education Controversy: A Study of Politics, Education, and Morality* (Lexington, Mass.: Lexington Books, 1975).

40. Hottois and Milner, *The Sex Education Controversy*, xix.

41. Hottois and Milner, *The Sex Education Controversy*, 95.

42. Hottois and Milner, *The Sex Education Controversy*, 97.

43. Kenneth R. Howe, "AIDS Education in the Public Schools: Old Wine in New Bottles?" *Journal of Moral Education* 19, no. 2 (May 1990): 114–123.

44. *Ware v. Valley Stream High School District*, 545 N.Y.S. 2d 316 (1989).

45. Dennis L. Carlson, "Ideological Conflict and Change in the Sexuality Curriculum" in *Sexuality and the Curriculum: The Politics and Practices of Sexuality Education*, ed. James T. Sears (New York: Teachers College Press, 1992), 51.

46. Carlson, "Ideological Conflict," 51.

47. USNY SED, *AIDS Instructional Guide*, 100.

48. USNY SED, *AIDS Instructional Guide*, 9. The other resources are: community AIDS organizations/specialists, public health agencies, health care organizations, family planning agencies, local chapters of the American Red Cross, substance abuse agencies, and physicians.

49. USNY SED, *AIDS Instructional Guide*, 162.

50. "Consumer Reports: How Reliable are Condoms?" reprint of *Consumer Reports* May 1995, Consumers Union of U.S., Inc. Page, www.tezcat.com/~alan/html/condoms/html, n. d., [cited 3 May 1997].

51. The *AIDS Instructional Guide* does contain a justification for AIDS education in grades K–6 that acknowledges child sexual abuse and that students K–6 are at risk for AIDS through this abuse (10). Certainly educators are aware of the dangers within family relationships and do address these concerns in the school. My point here is only that in the context of AIDS education the married family is uncritically assumed to be a relationship of safety.

52. This is not meant to suggest that condoms are a panacea. In a later chapter, I will argue that AIDS educational controversy all too often falls into anti–condom/pro–condom camps, both of which define sexual activity as penetrative, and thus miss an opportunity to interrogate the range of possible sexual activity or refigure the meaning of sexuality.

53. USNY SED, *AIDS Instructional Guide*, vii.

54. USNY SED, *AIDS Instructional Guide*, 17.

55. USNY SED, *AIDS Instructional Guide*, 159.

56. USNY SED, *AIDS Instructional Guide*, 15.

57. USNY SED, *AIDS Instructional Guide*, 15.

58. USNY SED, *AIDS Instructional Guide*, 15.

59. USNY SED, *AIDS Instructional Guide*, 36.

60. USNY SED, *AIDS Instructional Guide*, 36.

61. USNY SED, *AIDS Instructional Guide*, 39.

62. USNY SED, *AIDS Instructional Guide*, 40.

63. A later lesson that builds on this one and encourages students to identify sources of health information drop religious leader and police officer from the list (60). But religious representative shows up on later lists, too (70).

64. Technically, of course, there is no such thing as an AIDS virus, but "AIDS virus" is the term the *AIDS Instructional Guide*, most frequently uses for HIV.

65. USNY SED, *AIDS Instructional Guide,* 83.

66. USNY SED, *AIDS Instructional Guide*, 83. Clearly there is something amiss with this list—being gay is singled out as a risk for AIDS that is equivalent to having sex with a partner infected with HIV. That the guide separates out gayness as a risk equivalent to sex with an infected partner does indicate a clear bias against homosexuality. I will return to this issue at length in my next chapter.

67. USNY SED, *AIDS Instructional Guide*, 83.

68. USNY SED, *AIDS Instructional Guide*, 83.

69. USNY SED, *AIDS Instructional Guide*, 95.

70. USNY SED, *AIDS Instructional Guide*, 152.

71. USNY SED, *AIDS Instructional Guide*, 152.

72. James F. Childress, "Mandatory HIV Screening and Testing," in *AIDS and Ethics*, ed. Frederic G. Reamer (New York: Columbia University Press, 1991), 54.

4

The Adolescent as Abstinent Heterosexual

This chapter will examine the meanings attached to sex, bodies, and ethics in New York State's public school AIDS education. When addressing issues related to sex and bodies, liberals and communitarians presume sex and the resultant gender relations to be largely natural. Both theories are reluctant to critically examine the importance of how sex is defined. However, sex and AIDS education impart clear and specific messages about properly gendered behavior and proper sexual behavior, not all of which are explicitly stated by curricula. Indeed, as an analysis of the *AIDS Instructional Guide* for New York State will show, even gender neutral language and purportedly general definitions of "sex" have embedded within them normative assumptions about the properly sexual body and sexual ethics. These assumptions discriminate against students who are or may become sexually active or who are sexual minorities by omitting information that they could use to minimize their risk for HIV, other STDs, and pregnancy. I first examine the construction of the "proper" adolescent body through an analysis of the *Guide*. In addition, curricula tightly circumscribe the realm of sexuality, defining only vaginal-penile intercourse as "sex" and the correct context for "sex" as "marriage." Further through inattention to problematic gender dynamics in sexual decisionmaking among adolescents, curricula actively engage in creating the understandings of sex and gender that lead young women to bear disproportionate risks for sexual activity. In short, despite the curricular assumption of equality regardless of gender or bodily difference, difference does sometimes make a difference. At the same time, curricula also neglect to address the alternatives to vaginal-penile intercourse or encourage young women and men to consider a broader range of sexual activities as pleasurable and potentially less risky.

Curricula also define students who engage in proscribed activities as outside of the school community. Thus, the communitarian practice of drawing exclusionary lines of membership continues in the very definition of who is properly sexual. In particular, strong messages against anal intercourse and the admonition to defer sexual activity until marriage act together to position gay and lesbian, and other sexually active students, as deviant outsiders. Then I draw out the implications of this restrictive definition of "sex" and the isolated sexual decision makers of the curriculum in shortcomings in the *Guide*'s lessons on ethical behavior. When ethical behavior is linked only to marriage and not to premarital sexual practices, the AIDS/HIV education misses out on an opportunity to stress the intersubjective capacities and practices necessary for responsible sexual relationships. Pleasure could be part of a definition of sex that might stress intersubjectivity and encourage students to view their sexual experiences as positive and worthy of care. By positioning the desiring student as a monadic decision maker, the *Guide* reinscribes the very lack of responsibility to others that its overall message tries to work against. Abstinence-based curricula diminish the ability of students to confront, assess, and challenge the risks they may face from sexual activity by limiting the definition of sex and limiting the scope of sexual ethics.

With regard to a restrictive definition of sex, New York State is not unique in its policy. As of May 1989, twenty-eight states and the District of Columbia had mandated HIV/AIDS education.[1] Of these, eighteen states require that abstinence be stressed as the only certain way of avoiding HIV.[2] New York is one of fourteen states with an abstinence-based curriculum that does not require information on contraception be included along with abstinence.[3] Only four states discuss condoms and, of those, only Rhode Island presents them in a relatively positive light, suggesting that abstinence is preferred, but condom use is also an option. New York, Utah, and Washington (state) all stress the riskiness of condoms (and birth control devices in general).[4] The effect of all of this is to at once prevent students from seeing within the formal school curriculum any possibility of safely engaging in sexual activity outside of marriage and to link such behavior with a fatal contagion. But much of these curricula construe adolescence as a time prior to sexual behavior and as a stage in human development when individuals are likely to be pressured by authority into remaining celibate.

There is little in statistics on adolescent sexual behavior to suggest that either of these assumptions is reasonable.[5] Studies on abstinence-only curricula have found them to have no impact on students' decision to initiate sexual intercourse.[6] Zelnick and Shah report that the average age for first intercourse (heterosexual, penetrative) is 16.2 years of age for girls and 15.7 years of age for boys, with the majority of them reporting the activity to have been "spontaneous."[7] By the age of 18, 56 percent of young women and 73 percent of young men have had intercourse.[8] Problematically, only 25 percent of 15 to 24 year olds use contraception and of those, only 21 percent use condoms.[9] The continued insistence on adolescent abstinence only serves to make condom use and other measures for preventing infection less and less likely, as adolescents are not encouraged to view themselves as sexual and thus take precautions. Failure to plan for intercourse, so that condoms are not even present, and use of drugs and/or alcohol are both factors common to the misuse or nonuse of condoms.[10] In addition, "commitment to sex," a recognition that one accepts the fact of one's sexual activity, is correlated with adolescents' concerted effort at contraception use.[11] Other studies indicate a six-month lag between the onset of an adolescent's sexual activity and his or her understanding of their identity as sexually active.[12] Each of these, taken together, indicate the potential problem of insisting upon an abstinent identity for adolescents, many of whom are likely to become sexually active. Planning to be abstinent means, clearly, that adolescents are not planning for the possibility of sexual activity. This lack of planning for sexual activity means that they will be less likely to engage in safer sex behaviors. Abstinence, in other words, may fail in more than one way. First, an adolescent may simply fail at his or her attempt at abstinence. But the fact of having planned to be abstinent may also mean that either for lack of planning, guilt, or lack of recognition of oneself as engaged in sexual activity an individual will be less likely to practice safer sex.

These are not the only complications to sexual activity among young people. Particularly for young girls, lack of consent to sexual activity is a problem. Though studies of rape indicate that 1 in 6 women will be the victim of sexual assault in her lifetime, the rate is higher for younger women: "7 in 10 women who had sex before age 14, and 6 in 10 of those who had sex before age 15, report having had sex involuntarily."[13] The complications for gay youth appears to be entirely different, as young men who had engaged in sexual activity with another male were at a significantly lower risk for attempting suicide. One study reported that 46.1 percent of celibate homosexual male youth reported attempting suicide, in contrast to reported attempts by 9.4 percent of sexually active homosexual male youth.[14]

Although "adolescents 13-19 years of age comprise less than 1 percent of the total number of AIDS cases," Walter Dowdle of the Centers for Disease Control argues that there are a number of reasons to be particularly concerned with educating adolescents about HIV. He notes that with the long incubation period of AIDS many of the people with AIDS aged 20 to 29 were probably infected with HIV as adolescents. Furthermore, Dowdle argues, behavior that may put a person at risk for HIV infection is developed during adolescence. In addition, he points out that there are 2.5 million cases of other sexually transmitted diseases and 800,000 unintended pregnancies. He notes that 76 percent of AIDS among adolescents was the result of "sexual contact (homosexual and heterosexual)."[15] In addition, "studies show that 28 percent of persons aged 12 to 17 are currently sexually active" and that "about 70 percent and 80 percent of teenage girls and boys, respectively have had at least one coital experience."[16] In addition, "17 percent of boys aged 16 to 19 report at least one homosexual experience."[17] Additional reasons for concern are the very ways in which information about adolescent sexuality are presented. A small example of how seemingly neutral information makes meanings about sexuality clear is contained in the following excerpt from a survey of adolescent sexual activity and AIDS: "Sexual orientation becomes clarified during adolescence. One study found 1-2 percent of the 16-19 year old boys had had homosexual relationships (Hingson, et al. 1990); 0.5 percent reported bisexual relationships (Strunin and Hingson, 1987). These boys could serve as agents of transmission to subsequent female or male partners."[18]

None of the other information in this survey about adolescent risky sexual behavior indicated a concern about the implications of those risks for other partners. Note that only the behavior of bisexual youth is singled out by this survey as potentially risky for future partners, although anyone's risk behaviors have implications for future partners. The above quote, as well as the lessons of AIDS/HIV education, makes certain, limited meanings of sexuality clear to students. In this case, bisexuality gets special notice for its potential risk to future partners. In the New York State's AIDS/HIV *Instructional Guide*, bisexuals and homosexual men are singled out for attention. These are both examples of subtle and not so subtle hints that certain identities are more problematic than others, without regard to the possible precautions bisexuals or homosexuals might take to minimize their risk of HIV infection. By singling out members of certain identities as risky, curricula attempt to educate against identities rather than risky sexual activities. The problematic implications of this limited view of sexuality are not new, as the next section will show.

"Copulation Domination" and the "Missing Discourse of Desire"

Critics of sex education Michelle Fine and Joseph A. Diorio argue that curricula and policies fail to acknowledge that adolescents engage in a range of sexual behaviors and that representing adolescents as victims of sexuality or as interested only in penile-vaginal intercourse does a disservice to sexually active adolescents. These curricula limit the potential for sex education to encourage adolescents to develop what Fine calls "sexual subjectivity"—the ability of students to actively negotiate meanings and practices of sexual relationships with a full range of information.[19] Fine and Diorio agree that adolescents ought to be taught more than just that sex will lead to disease and pregnancy. They also agree that there is more at stake in this than encouraging students to have fulfilling sex lives.

Fine points to the theme of victimization in sex education directed at young females and argues that this theme obscures both female sexual desire and the broad victimization of females that occurs within social structures. According to Fine, a discourse of sexual victimization paradoxically disempowers young women by portraying them at risk from male sexuality while it encourages young women to see marriage as a haven from this victimization.[20] Fine argues that "the absence of a discourse of desire, combined with the lack of analysis of the language of victimization" may slow the ability of adolescents to take responsibility for their sexual activity, especially female students and nonheterosexual male students.[21] One serious consequence of this discourse of sexual victimization is that it fosters negative attitudes toward sex in women. A recent study shows that sex-negative attitudes are negatively correlated with contraception use. Apparently, according to Fisher, Byrne, and White, this is because "teens who believe sexual involvement is wrong deny responsibility for contraception."[22] In other words, sex-negative sex education impedes the ability of young people to conceive of themselves as sexual and to engage in negotiated, safer relationships.

The second problem with many sex education and AIDS education programs is their tendency to equate penile-vaginal intercourse with "sex." This conflation is the result of sex education having been created to address social problems perceived to stem from vaginal intercourse. The problem with a close link between education and a social problem is that

> any curriculum field which is tied closely to a set of social problems easily can come under the control of those problems, not just in the sense that study within that field is justified as a source of practical so-

lutions, but in the more fundamental sense that the nature of the field itself comes to be defined in terms of the problems which it is expected
to alleviate. . . . This, in turn, inhibits any reconceptualization of the social problems associated with that field.[23]

Diorio traces how the meaning of "sex" becomes solidified as "heterosexual copulation" in sex education literature.[24] He argues that this
slippage encourages adolescents to view sexual activities that are not
heterosexual intercourse as "less 'intimate' than intercourse."[25] Further,
"any sex education program which approaches sex as inherently constituted by heterosexual copulation is likely to contribute to the tendency on
the part of students to see it that way."[26] By seeing sex as copulation,
students are discouraged from defining nonintercourse sex as sex—thus
sexual activities that do not put them at risk for pregnancy or disease are
not defined as safer equivalent practices to intercourse, but rather lesser,
lower-status practices.[27] Sex education, in effect, reinforces the very social problems that it seeks to alleviate in that it removes alternative, safer
expressions of adolescent sexual desire.

Further complicating these problems is the fact that public school
AIDS educators reported that their own "highest levels of discomfort
came with discussing homosexuality and bisexuality."[28] More than half
of those surveyed indicated they needed updated information on homosexuality and bisexuality, risk behaviors for HIV, and safer sex practices.[29] A study by R. J. DiClemente and others noted "that educators
who feel uncomfortable discussing sexual matters that they personally
consider offensive are not likely to facilitate frank, open discussion."
DiClemente et al. suggest that inservice training include "a personal assessment of values and attitudes toward sexuality in general and homosexuality in particular."[30] AIDS education, then, continues the trends described by Fine and Diorio and highlights even more the heterosexual
bias in sex education. Not only does heterosexual intercourse stand in for
"sex" in all its variety but also the discussion of specific sexual variations
like homosexuality and bisexuality cause discomfort in educators.

New York State's AIDS education policy, as we will see, does
nothing to alleviate any of these problems and replicates the shortcomings of the curricula criticized by Fine and Diorio. Indeed it is bound
up in the same anxieties over female, gay, and adolescent sexuality in
general. This is perhaps symptomatic of a greater cultural discomfort
with the relationship among sexuality, gender, and risk in which female
and gay sexuality is unthinkable as positive. Instead, these sexualities are
viewed as threatening to the social order. As Bersani argues, the discom-
forts with female and gay male sexuality are linked to "a fantasy of female sexuality as intrinsically diseased; and promiscuity in this fantasy,

far from merely increasing the risk of infection, is the *sign of infection*."[31] Discourse around AIDS positions women in terms of their potential to infect men and the deviance of female sexuality in general, if women behave in ways contrary to gendered sexual norms. AIDS discourse also reinforces women's sexuality as inextricably tied to reproduction and penetration, especially when the only type of sex conceivable is penile-vaginal intercourse. Women's reproductive role is normalized, argues Paula A. Treichler, through medical representations of the "rugged vagina" able to maintain its integrity, in contrast to the fragile anus.[32] The silence in curricula about the possibility of safe anal intercourse is troubling, as is silence about women's sexual pleasure (and sexual pleasure in general). There are strong cultural meanings embedded in the representations of bodies and forms of sex in curricula. The fragility of the anus intends to highlight the reproductive aspects of sexuality, but there are other, potentially subversive readings of the body. As Bersani argues, the rectum ought to be considered the grave of masculinity, a place where masculinity undoes itself through penetration. Given the relative silence on women's sexual pleasure and safer sex techniques which involve the clitoris, this view of sexuality also appears to resurrect Anne Koedt's classic argument that the clitoris too is a challenge to masculinity. Early hopes that the AIDS epidemic would force sex education to become critical of rigid gender roles, more open to sexual possibilities, and less normalizing was short-lived. AIDS became another justification for constraining the definition of sex to exclude certain bodies, activities, identities, and ethical relationships.

Bennett versus Koop: The Moral Stakes of AIDS Education

The most public indication that AIDS would not force a reconsideration of sex education came in the debate between Surgeon General C. Everett Koop and Secretary of Education William Bennett. In October 1986, Koop issued an AIDS report strongly advocating that sex education in the public schools begin at the elementary level.[33] His vision of "gentle, non-mystifying" sex education for students starting in kindergarten included plans for an animated educational video featuring two condoms "with little eyes on them" . . . "chatting."[34] Between 1986 and the development of public school AIDS education policy, many variables interceded to render the possibility of this frank approach to AIDS education in the public schools unlikely. Bennett, in a thinly veiled attack on Koop, railed against the lack of moral content in public school sex education. Bennett's call for a return to morals in sex education and a stress on abstinence was strongly supported by New York State AIDS education policy makers. Despite Koop's attempt to also claim moral status for his argument for sexually explicit, nonjudgmental sex and AIDS education, Bennett was more successful in claiming the moral high ground for his position. In so doing, Bennett and others who supported his position strongly reinforced the equation of sexuality with immorality—an equation that Koop viewed as inimical to broad and effective AIDS education. Certainly Koop was not a sexual libertine; but, although he did plan on stressing monogamy and abstinence, he made much more explicit allowance for the possibility that many people would find these two options insufficient. Hence, he advocated a plan for getting children used to condoms at an early age and called for frank sex education for all Americans.

Bennett's success forestalled these plans and in their place a broad campaign began to essentially limit the possible definitions of what "sex" could be. The Helms Amendment further added limitations to what AIDS education, at least that funded by federal money, could be. The Helms Amendment prohibited federal funds from being used in any educational campaign that promoted homosexuality or drug use—in other words, anything that mentioned homosexuality or drug use without forbidding it. These policies and definitions of sex reinforced similar ideas already in place. Certainly, none of this is new to American ideas about sex, but they came at a time when Koop and his supporters hoped that the gravity of AIDS would encourage a different approach to sex education, one that, although it had moral content, also reflected what he argued were the needs of public health policy—using as many tactics as possible that would keep people from contracting HIV. His tactical error may have been in too readily acceding to Bennett's claim to the moral argument. Rather than stressing a different vision of what it might mean to be moral, Koop tended to counter that AIDS was a health problem and not a moral problem. Thus traditional conservative morals became the only position that claimed an explicitly "moral" basis in the controversy over AIDS, and other forms of morals and ethics were positioned as health concerns or deviant. At stake in this war of position and definition is how sex comes to be represented in general and in public school AIDS curricula in particular. Sex is not represented as a behavior that is potentially ethical; sexual behavior comes to be atomized, taken out of relationships and responsibility, and vilified; and all of this discourages students from seeing sexual relationships as a site of ethical relationships. In short, AIDS curricula are populated by autonomous subjects whose bodies are the focus of normalizing power and whose ability to negotiate relations with one another are severely hampered by this positioning.

AIDS Education in the *Guide* and the Definition of Sex

To trace out a particular example of restrictive definition of "sex," I examine the impact of the debate between Koop and Bennett—and the largely conservative atmosphere in New York State—on the New York State *AIDS Instructional Guide: Grades K-12*. The first section examines how sex is defined in the *Guide* as "intercourse," an inclusive term for vaginal, oral, and anal intercourse that nevertheless tends to slide into meaning only vaginal intercourse. Sex is also continually referred to as an act that must be deferred until marriage. The second section problematizes the narrow view of sexual ethics given to students when "sex" is defined as an activity whose relational aspects are embodied in marriage; sex outside of marriage is not seen to have these same relational qualities. Students are encouraged to view sexual decisions as those which take place only within their own minds, not in communication with their prospective partners. This encourages an overly atomistic view of how sexual partners might act with one another. Instead of encouraging students to engage in ethical relationships with one another in their sexual behaviors, the *Guide* encourages them to view sexual decisions as entirely individual. Ethical sexual relationships are apparently deferred until marriage. In addition, "sex" in the *Guide* is penetrative sex, a definition which drives the controversy between abstinence curricula and condom advocates. Both parties tend to expend their energies on a debate that presumes sex to be solely a penetrative act and thus both miss out on the possibility of having students come to decisions for themselves on what constitutes sex. In the process, the *Guide* discourages students from positing alternative, safer conceptions of sex.

In his criticism of public school sex education programs, Joseph Diorio argues that schools have engaged in a discourse of "copulation domination" in their definition of the realm of the sexual. Most of sex education, Diorio argues, is directed at preventing teenage pregnancy and to that end, "sex" quickly comes to mean vaginal penetrative intercourse. The New York State *AIDS Instructional Guide: Grades K-12* similarly defines "sex" as vaginal penetration. By defining "sex" as "intercourse" and eventually conflating "intercourse" with "heterosexual vaginal intercourse" the *Guide* constrains what may be considered "sex" by the students. By constraining its definition of sex, the *Guide* misses out on an opportunity to encourage students to consider how they might engage in pleasurable activities with one another while minimizing their risk for HIV, STDs, and pregnancy. The *Guide* appears largely concerned about student sexual activity because of the negative consequences associated with unprotected and unsafe sexual activity. If sex and AIDS education were to address these issues, and the potential for physical and emotional abuse within sexual relationships, students could engage in a wide range of sexual behaviors that enable them to avoid the negative consequences. In addition, students might also decide, when fully informed, that they are not willing or ready for sexual activity. This kind of sex and AIDS education would engage students to consider what sexuality means to them, what the range of activities they consider sexual are and why, and a range of other questions that would help them to make a fully considered decision about how and when they will interact with others sexually. But instead of maintaining a minimal openness to its definition of "sex," the *Guide* quickly limits what is meant by the term.

A number of problems arise because of this constrained definition of sex. If intercourse, an activity which seems to imply penetration—whether vaginal, anal, or oral (as the *Guide* notes, but does not consistently accommodate in its discussion)—then a variety of penetrative acts may be construed to be on the same level as vaginal intercourse. Were the *Guide* to consistently refer to each of these varieties of intercourse as equivalent each might be seen as potentially occupying an equivalent position in what is overall considered to be "sex." Were this to be the case, homosexual anal intercourse would have the potential to be a reasonable or even parallel "sex" alternative to heterosexual intercourse. In this case, homosexual intercourse can be seen as "sex" because it shares the same penetrative element as heterosexual intercourse. Oral intercourse presumably makes the list because of its potentially penetrative element, perhaps positing it as an act performed with a male. The potential for homosexual anal intercourse being construed by students as a sexual practice on a par with heterosexual intercourse is strongly discouraged by lessons and definitions provided in the *Guide*. The *Guide* very clearly instructs students to "avoid anal intercourse." While the *Guide* certainly does strongly argue for abstinence as the only sure means of protection from HIV, its message of avoidance of heterosexual intercourse is much less categorically specific. In a document with the clear purpose of educating students to abstain from sexual activity, anal intercourse gets singled out for particular notice. This singling out indicates that, while certainly adolescents should say no to sex, that is, vaginal intercourse, they must most definitely not ever say yes to anal intercourse. Given that unprotected, receptive anal intercourse is the highest risk activity for HIV, the *Guide* is frighteningly silent on particular ways to avoid risk in this activity. In other words, having singled out the activity most likely to transmit HIV, if one partner has HIV, the *Guide* has given only partial information. Since anal intercourse is a high-risk factor, more attention needs to be given specifically to ways to minimize the risk. Given the higher rates of condom breakage during anal intercourse and the need for water-based lubricants to preserve condom strength, leaving out specific information while pointing out the dangers is insufficient.

The message that there is no way to minimize the risk of anal intercourse is also reinforced in the U.S. Department of Health and Human Services pamphlet, *Understanding AIDS*, risk factors for HIV which includes both anal intercourse without a condom and anal intercourse with a condom, without any explanation that the risk for HIV infection is much diminished with proper use of a condom. The pamphlet's message leaves the reader to imagine that anal intercourse itself, even without the presence of HIV, must be risky.[35] The risk for HIV infection depends upon the presence of HIV, not the inherent dangers of particular sexual acts.

The *Guide*'s description of risk groups further underscores its message that anal intercourse, though a penetrative activity, is not an alternative to vaginal intercourse. Homosexual men and bisexual men are themselves risk groups, presumably because of their supposed favored sexual practice, that is, anal intercourse. So while the *Guide*'s seemingly broad definition of what "sex" might be is initially inclusive, its further definition of "risk" makes the alternatives seem hopelessly dangerous, with no means of minimizing the danger. By positing an inherent danger to certain activities, whether they are engaged in with a condom or even without the presence of HIV, the *Guide* appears to indicate that there is nothing that can be done to minimize the riskiness of the activity. The activity itself, not the activity undertaken without a condom and with the presence of HIV, is a risk. Thus, the *Guide* discourages students from being able to negotiate safer ways to engage in these activities, including how to minimize the risk for condom breakage through use of water-based lubricant or suggesting alternative sexual activities to help students who engage in high-risk activities learn how to minimize their risk. Instead, by its silence on specifics, the *Guide* firmly entrenches homosexual men and bisexual men in the "risk" category. Instead, the *Guide* attempts to educate against both the activity and the identity—even if the bearer of that "risk" identity does not engage in the particular risk activity of anal intercourse. Since the *Guide* largely assumes a heterosexual audience, its ability to educate homosexual and bisexual students is severely limited. As a result, the risk to these students is not fully addressed. The *Guide*'s characterization of these populations as "risk groups" thus becomes a self-fulfilling prophecy.

A further problem with the definition of intercourse revolving around penetrative activities is that other forms of sex that are not risky are defined out of the realm of sex and thus are portrayed as "inferior" to real sex. It would also appear that the model of "intercourse" that can claim an equivalency between anal, oral, and vaginal intercourse has in mind the presence of a penis in each one of the activities. Intercourse appears to presume penetration in these equivalencies. These activities are not equivalent in their "riskiness," however. Nor is the risk equivalent between positions in each category. The *Guide* does not discuss the finer points of these distinctions—for instance, that women are more at risk in vaginal intercourse and more likely to be exposed to HIV through vaginal intercourse than men are likely to be exposed to HIV through intercourse with women.[36] Nor does the *Guide* address forms of oral intercourse that do not entail penetration or exchange of bodily fluids and are therefore not risky. The risks and means of prevention for HIV and other STDs that may be associated with oral sex are also not addressed by the *Guide*. Indeed, risks specific to heterosexual, bisexual, and lesbian women are all missing in the *Guide*.

The *Guide* is not alone in these omissions. By assigning women to categories of transmission defined by only their relationship to men, the Centers for Disease Control (CDC) seemed unable to conceive of women as sexual agents. In the late 1980s and early 1990s, not only did the CDC not keep official records on lesbian transmission but it assigned women to categories of transmission based on what their male partners do—if women contracted HIV through intercourse with intravenous drug-using men then the women are placed in the category of transmission through drug use, rather than in a category of transmission through heterosexual intercourse.[37] Likewise, lesbians have been categorized as exposed to HIV because of intravenous drug use, but little specific evidence regarding lesbian transmission of HIV has been noted—either by the CDC or by medical professionals.[38] Since the CDC makes decisions on what is important transmission information about HIV, by not attending to the complexities of sexual activities, the CDC orders its information based on an overly simplified version of what constitutes sex and how people arrange their lives.

The problematic conceptions of what constitutes risky activity follows from the *Guide*'s narrow definition of "sex." This narrow definition in turn makes it difficult to discuss key student concerns about how to be both sexual and safe. Educators report that they do not feel that they have enough information on sexuality to properly address the issue of sex and AIDS education. The areas they cite as most in need of updated information are homosexuality and bisexuality, sexually transmitted diseases, risk behaviors for HIV transmission, and safer sex practices. In addition, educators reported their highest level of discomfort came from discussing homosexuality.[39] Discussions of when it is right to have sex, when students may be assumed to be sexually active, how to talk about condom use, how to talk about homosexuality are among teachers' greatest concerns that are not addressed by curricula.[40] According to policymakers, whose version of sex is essentially "what one does in a married relationship," these questions do not fall within the scope of "sex." "Sex," at least as defined by educational policy makers, has a very specific meaning, as the lessons and definitions in the New York State *Guide* show.

The *Guide* does not rely on the use of clear exclusionary language to limit the sexual choices that students have. Instead, the *Guide* uses the language of liberal impartiality to suggest that when sexual intercourse is referred to, it includes vaginal, anal, and oral intercourse.[41] But except for two times where teachers are encouraged to warn students who they think may be sexually active to "avoid anal intercourse," the only specific references to sex and possible consequences all assume heterosexual vaginal intercourse.[42] In addition, since the benefits of an abstinent lifestyle include freedom from pregnancy and from worry over contraceptives, it is quite clear that if sex is what one abstains from, and these are among the outcomes, then sex is heterosexual intercourse. Rather than opening possibilities to different meanings and practices of sex, the *Guide* "universalizes" sexual intercourse in all its varied forms into one kind of sex. Other nonpenetrative forms of sex are thus either not sex or not worthy of comment, further underscoring the lack of importance assigned to the clitoris and women's sexuality.

This, then, not only limits the possibility of sexual identity but also limits the areas of the body that might rightfully be considered sexual. Sex, ostensibly because of the threat of contagion, is limited to certain places on the body, which are specifically situated on a body in a certain relationship with another body in marriage. Rather than expand what sex could safely be for adolescents wishing to avoid risk activities, the *Guide* neatly cordons off the limits of sex. In making these limits, the *Guide* then portrays the family as the place where all of this forbidden activity can safely take place and represents marginal groups of people as unsafe conveyors of contagion. Thus, the threat both to the family and to the nation's health are situated outside of the family system, and the solution to this public health problem, as well as many other social problems, is a return to the family. Diorio observes that sex education bases its definition of sex on the social problem the education is trying to alleviate. Thus, sex education programs aimed at eliminating teenage pregnancy only focus their attention on heterosexual intercourse.[43] In a similar manner, the *Instructional Guide* is focused on finding the solution to the AIDS epidemic within the confines of the family. Accordingly, sexual activity that does not take place within the family is also, indirectly or not, being educated against. Consequently, identities or activities that are not part of marriage are also being educated against. Again, this restricted conception of sex does little to foster safer sex practices.

Defining Sex: Just Say No

In a number of places, the *Guide* seems to offer students a range of options about sex practices, but in fact students are taught a range of activities through which to come to the same answer. Through role plays, letter writing activities, and developing public service messages, students are encouraged to examine the many different ways that they can argue for abstinence. They are encouraged to choose their own approach to avoiding HIV infection, as long as that approach is some creative variation on the theme of abstinence. For instance, lesson 23 encourages students in grades 7 and 8 to use all their creativity in a role play to come up with new ways to "just say no," without encouraging them to examine why it is that they must say no or without providing any details on just what it is that they are saying no to. The objective for this lesson is to learn that "there are skills to practice that will lead to a healthful lifestyle," while the learner outcome is the ability to "practice skills in saying no."[44] The values that are supposed to be integrated into this lesson include: "Respect for Self: Behaving in accordance with one's values and beliefs;" "Respect for Others: Acceptance and appreciation for the values and beliefs of others;" Reasoning: Thinking for oneself;" and "Self-discipline: Saying no."[45] The role play regarding sexual activity consists of a scenario in which "your boyfriend or girlfriend is pressuring you to have sex and you don't want to."[46] The possibility that students might be involved in a situation in which they and their partner both want to engage in sexual activity is not addressed. Thus the students are encouraged to view this pressuring boy or girlfriend as the villain in a scenario in which the students themselves have no interest in sexual activity.

"Respect," then, necessitates abstention from sexual behavior. Thus, the *Guide* positions sexually active students as incapable of respectful relationships, either with others or to their own bodies. As the section on sexual ethics will show, students are discouraged from viewing sexuality as a relationship that requires respect and negotiation. The possibility that sexual relationships could help to educate young people on respectful and caring interactions is neglected when they are simply instructed to wait until adulthood and marriage. Even the alternative of masturbation as a safer outlet for adolescent desires is not addressed. While masturbation as a solitary act avoids the exchange of bodily fluids and avoids the interpersonal negotiations of sexual relationships, the *Guide*, by limiting the definition of sex and then setting sex off limits, does not allow the adolescent who engages in masturbation to see that activity as constituting a legitimate exploration of pleasure and relationship to their body. The respectful self is apparently not a self with desires or a self interested in pleasure. Not unlike many sex and AIDS curricula used in the public schools, pleasure hovers about the curriculum but is not explicitly addressed as an aspect of life that might enhance students' relationships and enter into their sexual decision making. Instead, the *Guide* encourages students to choose properly without giving them access to a range of choices.

Lesson 27b uses this limited language of choice: "Respect for Self and Others: Making responsible decisions to abstain from sexual activity."[47] Students are supposed to develop a radio script that will "warn their friends about the sexual transmission of the AIDS virus and communicate the advantages of abstinence."[48] In order to do so, students need to "identify the pressures and situations that might put a person at risk to be sexually active and be exposed to the AIDS virus."[49] Sexual activity has not been defined in the teacher's vocabulary yet, nor are the specifics of which type of sexual activity might be risky discussed. Rather than deciding which types of sexual activity one might want to alter or avoid, students "decide what actions a person could take to promote abstinence and to delay sexual activity."[50] The theme of delaying sexual activity comes up in a number of lessons, but why delay itself will necessarily imply a lack of risk is quite unclear, unless we accept the incorrect premise that sex within marriage is intrinsically safe. Again, the specifics of what "sex" might mean or why students might be intrigued or afraid of sex are not discussed in the lesson. Even if most middle school students are not sexually active, they are entering the years in which many of them will become sexually active. If lessons were to address the range of activities available to students and help them to make considered decisions about sexual activity, they would have a broader range of activities to consider saying "yes" or "no" to.

Lesson 31 for students in grades 9-12 is similarly concerned with getting students to "practice skills in saying no."[51] Among the values to be integrated into this lesson are: "Respect for Self: Refusing to compromise beliefs that one holds as important; avoiding behaviors that put one at risk for infection."[52] This value makes clear the connection between an implied assumed belief that it is important not to engage in sexual activity and that belief is closely tied to a desire to avoid infection. However, by this point in their lives the majority of these students have already engaged in sexual activity and already need protection beyond suggestions of abstinence. They ought not to be written out of the lesson with a suggestion that their sexual activity somehow might mean that they are not concerned with infection. In addition, curricula need to address the differential risks and varied challenges to negotiating safer sex in ways that take into account gender dynamics. The *Guide* maintains gender neutrality throughout its examples and it does not raise the specific concerns of young girls in a direct and detailed manner. By positioning "sex" as a penetrative act, the *Guide* does, however, promote "sex" as an activity centrally reliant on a penis. The *Guide* is silent on sexual activities that would be satisfying and safer for young men and women (of any sexual orientation) that do not involve penetration.

The activity involved in lesson 31 is a skit with a scenario similar to lesson 23: "We've been going together for two years. My boy-/girlfriend wants me to sleep with him/her. I love him/her, and I don't want to lose him/her, but I'm not sure this is what I want to do."[53]

According to the "Positive Health Behavior" students are to "recognize and accept their own values," "feel confident about their beliefs," and "recognize situations when it is appropriate to say no, and will practice how to say no."[54] Based on what they have learned in lesson 30, students should know that the reasons young people might get involved in sexual activity include: "sexual attraction, societal pressures, peer pressure, pressure from a partner, family situation, mistaken beliefs, boredom, low self-esteem, drinking and drugs, loneliness, and influence of soap operas and other media."[55] While this list is not meant to be inclusive of all reasons, it reinforces the idea that most of the pressure to engage in improper sexual behavior would come from outside of the student and the family. The purpose of the rest of the lesson is to pick one of the factors "and discuss how that problem can be dealt with in ways other than sexual activity."[56] But as Michelle Fine has noted, curricula that position girls only as sexual victims encourage passivity. Curricula that do not engage girls in conceiving of themselves as sexual agents not only discourage girls from planning to be sexually active but also discourage girls from considering which activities might suit their desires. To address desire and pleasure in AIDS and sex education, while potentially provocative, encourages students to view sex as a relation that ought not be abusive and coercive. Discussing the positive aspects of sexuality further encourages girls to see their own active part in a sexual relationship and be willing to assert themselves as sexual, instead of acquiescing to the "natural" desires of their male partners. Though the *Guide* uses gender neutral terms, these gendered complications of sexuality remain unexamined.

The *Guide* and Sexual Ethics

Though the values that are supposedly addressed in these lessons include both respect for self and respect for others, students are left with only an abstract notion of a self and an other negotiating from empty positions toward a preconceived outcome of abstinence. These approaches have the effect of tacitly encouraging students to defer ethicality until marriage. In this sense, they contribute to the very negative consequences of sexual behavior, that is, disease and pregnancy, by holding marriage up as the ideal. Other sexual relationships thus become problematic in and of themselves, abstinence becomes the mark of ethicality with regard to sexuality in the *Guide*'s approach to sex and AIDS education. But the negative consequences associated with extramarital or premarital sexuality need not be conceived of as necessarily the result of sexual behavior. Technologically and medically, any of these consequences are preventable. But the *Guide* does not make these distinctions. In its Family Life Approach to AIDS Instruction it reminds students that an abstinent lifestyle will allow them to be: "free from pregnancy and venereal disease, free from the bother and dangers of the pill, IUD, and other contraceptives, . . . free from exploitation by others, free from guilt, doubt, disappointment, worry, rejection, free to be in control of your life, . . . free to enjoy being a teenager."[57]

A number of facets of the *Guide*'s construction of sexuality are quite clear in this passage. The passage suggests that sex outside of marriage causes all of the above-mentioned strife. In spite of this message being situated within a Family Life curriculum, which in New York State and many other states is charged with educating students about avoiding teen pregnancy, this passages invites students to view contraceptive devices as a bother.

The Condom Controversy

As I noted earlier, teachers and students reported that AIDS education had not given them enough information about sex in general, and about condom use and homosexuality in particular. What may be responsible for the disjuncture between what both students and teachers report that they need for adequate AIDS education and what they receive from AIDS educational materials is that the policymakers have one definition of sex in mind and the teachers and students have another. What sex means through policy and what sex may mean in all its variety to students and teachers are very different things. Policies quite literally attempt to define sex out of adolescence, which the opening of this chapter shows, is not the case.

The Centers for Disease Control complained early on in their attempts to study adolescent sexual behavior that local districts and state officials were unwilling to cooperate with their survey for fear of parental outcry at the CDC's findings.[58] Eighty percent of the recipients of CDC funds did not administer CDC surveys to their students, although the funds were supposed to be contingent upon the surveys being done.[59]

In short, schools did not want to be blamed by parents for their children's sexual behavior. By forcing sexuality out of the conversation, these curricula have added to the difficulties in even collecting data on students' sexual activities. Many of the schools failed to cooperate with the CDC by limiting their surveys to asking students about their knowledge of the transmission routes of HIV, but they would not ask students if any of the students' activities put them at risk for HIV.

This is not to imply that the solution to the spread of HIV is simply to provide condoms and hope for the best. Ultimately, this overly individualistic solution put the burden of negotiating use of condoms on each person, rather than emphasizing the relational nature of sexual activity. The widespread provision of condoms, without any education on how to use them, was such a failure in the U. S. Army during World War II, that in Korea the army relied on penicillin for post-infection treatment rather than on condoms for prevention.[60] Beliefs about condoms themselves complicate frequency of their usage. College students report viewing condoms differently based on whether they are told condoms have a success rate of 95 percent or a failure rate of 5 percent.[61] Leviton also argues that the "continuing perception that condoms are controversial and somehow immoral" has an adverse effect on their use, particularly if they are "viewed symbolically as indicating that one of the partners in a sexual relationship is diseased or unclean."[62] She further argues that condom promotion programs need to "not only provide information about the mechanics of condom use, they must incorporate approaches to remove or modify barriers to use."[63]

In effect, in its attempt to stop adolescent sexuality the Regents's statement that they view "the use of condoms as extremely high risk behavior" adds to the problem of their lack of usage among adolescent populations who engage in penetrative sexual activity.[64] A study on the effectiveness of condoms in preventing HIV infection where one partner was HIV positive and the other partner HIV negative found that HIV negative partners were not infected when condoms were used consistently and correctly.[65] Intent on ensuring that adolescents do not engage in sexual activity, the Regents's statement makes safer sexual activity more difficult for those who do. Further statements in the *Instructional Guide* also, presumably unwittingly, discourage adolescents taking responsibility for prevention of disease and unwanted pregnancy. The benefits of an abstinent lifestyle include: "free[dom] from pregnancy and venereal disease, free[dom] from the bother and dangers of the pill, IUD and other contraceptives."[66] By characterizing condoms as risky and contraception as a bother, the *Guide* sends a message to students that it is inconvenient to be sexually responsible. By prohibiting discussion of these options, the *Guide* does nothing to facilitate the protection of sexually active youth. Yet, clearly a fear that young people are at risk for HIV is behind the very need for this education in the first place.

This simplification of sexuality, indeed, has hampered attempts to effectively deal with both unwanted teen pregnancies and disease in the public schools, and elsewhere for that matter. Perhaps part of the reason that, in New York State, the condom causes such controversy is that the condom can have the effect of creating a disturbance in the way the *Guide*'s construction of sexuality works, though I will also argue in a moment that the debates over condoms once again limits "sex" to "penetrative sex," most often conceived of as heterosexual. However, the condom can challenge a number of assumptions about sexuality. Where the *Guide*'s version of sex might see sex as something in need of being tamed and tied to the family, the condom can stand as a symbol both disputing the need for that tie as well as disputing the version of sex that is seen as irrational and spontaneous. The kind of spontaneous sex feared by the curriculum is defined out of the realm of the considered, rational, and even planned; hence, the need for marriage to control it. If sex is viewed as spontaneous then any suggestion that it is mediated by any number of relations—cultural, technological, rational—is obscured. But the introduction of a concrete artifact whose use must be negotiated challenges the notion of sex as nonrational. Condom usage can become a site of problematization of many aspects of sexuality. As such it highlights the ways in which the claim to spontaneity diminishes the possibility of conceiving of sex as an ethical relation, one which includes deliberation and forethought.

Condom use may help to reinforce the deliberative aspect of sexuality and encourage students to learn to engage comfortably in discussions about sexuality. The autonomous subject to whom much of the information about condoms is directed is rarely taught to engage in discussion or negotiation with a partner about condom usage. Curricula assuming this independent sexual agent do not address sex as a relation, except in the context of marriage. The curricula ought to reflect a notion of the subject and of sex that underscores sex as a relation and explains how sex is mediated by a variety of factors, each of which is, in turn, mediated by communication, verbal or other, between interested parties. The *Guide* fails to acknowledge that sexuality is tied to the social fabric in more ways than through its connection with marriage. By only recognizing its tie to marriage, sex education focuses its subject and its audience far too narrowly to be able to address the variety of concerns it needs to address in order to insure that all students can safely and responsibly communicate with their current and future sexual partners. By its use of a particular construction of sexuality the *Guide* actually impairs the ability of stu-

limits their ability to develop intersubjective capacities. This in turn fosters unsafe sex.

The condom is a relatively simple technological advance that, with proper use, could, and has in populations who use them consistently, decrease the spread of HIV.[67] Yet, this relatively simple technological advance is cred. the curriculum with undermining the family and bringing a halt to cherished notions of adolescence. By freeing young people from the "moral cost" of sexual activity, birth control technology undermines traditional morality. Somehow within this conception of morality the cost of sexual transgression must be visible and apparent for all to see. Without this reinforcing punishment one might never know when one was in the company of a transgressor. Without the mark of pregnancy or disease the sexually transgressive appear the same as the moral.

Similar to the mark of venereal disease, condoms exist as physical artifacts of a transgressive act. They mark that an act is intended to take place and that that act is sufficiently risky to require that the actors take precautions. Condoms mark the presence of sexual desire and, even when that desire is not being acted upon, they mark the intention to have and to fulfill that desire. According to Cindy Patton, "To plan for sex or consider how one might wish to engage in it is cultural treason against the idea that sex is unspeakable."[68] I would add that it is not simply sex which is unspeakable, but a particular range of sexual activities that are defined out of the realm of acceptable sex that are unspeakable. According to the *Guide*, sex is quite "speakable"— it will happen during marriage and it is worth waiting for. But it is only this constrained meaning of sex that is given the privilege to speak and even then, admittedly, not in great detail.

Gayle Rubin's conception of a hierarchy of sexual meanings and activities is helpful here. She argues that the most normalized range of sexual activities involve a married couple with no use of contraception, sex toys, and so forth. She delineates the ways in which different sexual identities and activities fit into this hierarchy in ways that encourage sexual passivity in women and encourage women to defer to men's sexual desires.[69] She further argues that gender has been a useful category for looking into why these activities are parceled out as they are on the hierarchy, though calls for an analysis of how sexualities themselves, irrespective of gender, are produced, given meaning, and ranked.[70] But gender is central to understandings of sexuality. If the rectum is the grave of masculinity, for instance, it is largely so because to be penetrated is to be feminine, "to abdicate power."[71] Further, as Judith Butler contends, our very notions of gender are inextricably tied to the maintenance of heterosexuality. Curricula, then, that posit sex as necessarily heterosexual sex are also subtly positing correct gender behaviors. Condoms can complicate the ways in which this sexual hierarchy is maintained. First, because they can take the risk for disease out of some of the practices which are categorized as both moral and health risks. Second, condoms have something of a leveling effect on sexual activities in that they lower risk for contagion regardless of the genders, races, marital status, and so on of their users. Unfortunately, gender norms also hamper the ability for young women to comfortably demand condom usage from their partners. Feelings of suspicion, lack of trust, and a general discomfort with discussing sex with partners all complicate the potential positive aspects of condom usage.

Condoms as a solution to AIDS have their own problems as well, since they require both a recognition of sexual activity and a recognition of relational responsibilities. In a cultural context in which much discussion of sex is either taboo or strongly frowned upon, it is often difficult for people to acknowledge their sexual plans in advance of their sexual activities. It is particularly difficult for girls who tend to claim they do not plan for sex, but are instead swept away by the moment. Boys, on the other hand, do claim to plan for sexual activity in terms of securing a private place, though they tend not to extend this planning to using condoms or engaging in less risky sexual activities. The difficulty of discussing sexual activity as a site in need of relational ethics is complicated by the ways sex not sanctified by marriage is viewed as an activity by definition lacking morality. Where sex is defined as immoral a discussion of ethics is precluded. So if the project of sex education were to be to educate students about the possibilities of a range of sexual activities we would expect to find that range described and supported. What we find instead is a particular form of sexual activity constantly taking over for the meaning of sex. Heterosexual intercourse within marriage comes to stand in for what many curricula describe simply as sex. Marriage then becomes a ceremonial stand-in for ongoing relational ethics. That there are problems with ethical relationships within marriage goes unaddressed, but the moral weight of marriage itself gives an ethical stamp to sexual relations within marriage that is denied sexual relations outside of marriage.

So a discussion of sexuality that solely concentrates on sex in marriage manages to narrow the questions of what constitutes a relational ethic of sexuality. The ethic is defined not by the fact of engaging in sex but by the fact of engaging in sex in marriage. Marriage and its perceived relationship to a stable society become what is at stake in personal sexual relationships. While there may be much that is good in this kind of definition, it does become quite problematic for those it leaves out, as well as for those for whom marriage is not a sufficient protection against a variety of ills and diseases.

One way that certain gay communities have managed to slow the spread of HIV has been to frame the practice of safer sex as something one does for the good of the community. The difference between this community and the community cemented by heterosexual marriage is that the gay community is at least partially predicated on pleasure and sexual relationships (though not all members of the community agree to or approve of this characterization). But safer sex campaigns have been most effective in areas where the gay community is large, organized, and where there is widespread perception that safer sex is important to the community. These highly articulated and diverse communities are not widespread enough for this particular pattern of safety to work well in other communities, nor does it unfailingly work in the gay community, but the successes do point to the importance of linking together pleasure and respect. A glaring problem, partially due to the absence of this linkage in public school curricula, is the lack of condom use among younger members of the community or young visitors, many of whom may be in or just out of high school. A San Francisco study found that 42.9 percent of young gay men between the ages of seventeen and nineteen had engaged in unprotected anal intercourse, raising a concern that young gay men have yet to understand the safer sex message developed by older gay men.[72] A gay community, under different social conditions, might be more publicly vocal about the need for mainstream communities to better prepare their gay adolescents for the responsibilities of membership in gay communities.[73] Sexuality identity or activity may enable one to be a member of a number of different communities and may point to alternative ways to think about community. Because people may move in and out of a variety of communities and consider themselves to be members in a variety of different capacities, communitarian observations on the importance of embeddedness may need to be more flexible. Curricular decisions that are based on the needs of a localized community would do better to consider the range of communities affected by their decisions. This need not limit the ability for curricula to reflect local sensibilities entirely, but it does point to the permeability of community boundaries and the responsibilities of communities to one another.

Other Sex

While condoms are one option for continuing sexual activity in the age of AIDS, their place at the top of the safer sex hierarchy is a problematic reinscription of the kind of penetration domination that Diorio argues against. The debate over the place of condoms in public school AIDS education has managed to keep the definition of sex as a penetrative act.

Whether it is an argument that solely concentrates on abstinence or an argument that only advocates for condom use, sex is seen as penetrative. According to supporters of abstinence curricula, abstinence is important because it will stop the spread of HIV and because it will stop the growing number of teen pregnancies. In either case, sex is clearly a penetrative act if these two outcomes are the result of abstaining from sex. Likewise, condom supporters argue that adolescents are sexually active and are thus at risk for pregnancy and HIV unless they use condoms. Again, penetration is clearly the assumed activity.

If, following Diorio and other safer sex educators, the definition of sex were broadened to include not only penetrative but also other genital and nongenital activities, students could be encouraged to continue their sexual pleasures in ways that are risk activities for HIV, other sexually transmitted diseases, or pregnancy. Continuing to define sex as penetrative activity causes a number of problems. It ignores the sexual activity that adolescents engage in as long as it is not penetrative and continues to define sex as what happens in marriage. Petting, mutual masturbation, and the like can be considered pale attempts at "real" sex. This means that these activities are not readily available as viable alternatives to penetrative intercourse—they are perceived as lesser equivalents.

This kind of "copulation domination" feeds into a number of other problems. Female students overwhelmingly bear the burden for contraception and the cost of not using contraception. By continuing to frame sexuality around a penetrative activity that puts female students at a greater risk for HIV and pregnancy, schools do not contribute as much as they could to addressing the needs of female students. In addition, by continuing to frame sexuality as a necessarily penetrative act, schools do not address female sexual pleasure in the fullest sense that they could. Arguably, schools have little intention of addressing pleasure and sexuality, except to warn students that the pleasure is not worth the risk. But if schools began to reframe sexuality as pleasurable activities that do not necessarily put students at risk for HIV, that is, nonpenetrative activities, students would have greater options in being sexual while avoiding risk.[74] By proliferating the possibilities for what "sex" can mean, schools can also make a move to minimize the discriminatory character of sex education and AIDS education.

Because students are presumed to share identities and life plans, the *Guide*'s message only addresses a limited group of students. But all students, whatever their identities and activities, need to have access to the kind of lessons that will help them minimize their risk for HIV. Students need to be encouraged to think about both their relationship with their own identity and their relationships with others, not in abstract, general and absolutist terms, but within specific, particular, and contingent terms.

Adolescents may be considered irresponsible because the very way in which they are encouraged to develop their ethical behavior subtly discourages responsibility. By discouraging the articulation of particular concerns about students' relationships with each other, the *Guide* makes the task of developing ethical relationships of any configuration much more difficult. Instead of encouraging students to negotiate their ways through the many kinds of relationships in which they are likely to find themselves, the *Guide* would have them believe that marriage alone is safe.

By not engaging with students on the level of contingent identities the *Guide* does not encourage students' abilities to situate themselves within the questions it raises. By keeping to a formulaic approach students are not encouraged to feel comfortable with adding their own specific concerns and questions to those raised by the *Guide*. Specifically, the *Guide*'s assumption that its audience will remain abstinent until marriage discourages students who do not fit that description from being able to attend to their own concerns. This is potentially the case not only for gay and lesbian students but for sexually active heterosexual students as well. Certainly any students who have questions about their own sexual feelings or activities will not find room to voice those concerns, but will rather be encouraged to defer such concerns and activities until marriage. The solution for this would not be to encourage students to sort out their feelings and categorize their activities and identity categories from which to make sense of the world. Rather, students should be encouraged to both attempt to account for their identities and activities and account for the implications those identities and activities have on others.

The inability of the *AIDS Instructional Guide* to make its message accommodate particular situations has the effect of keeping students' engagement at an abstract level. Students are not encouraged to reflect on their own positions vis à vis the *Guide*'s message and thus are not encouraged to insert themselves and their own situations into the scenarios the *Guide* presents. Even though one might intuitively suspect that sex is a relational activity, students are not encouraged to approach the topic of sex with their partners or partners-to-be except in the context of peer pressure when the desiring partner is cast as the villain. While it is not unreasonable to suggest that one should examine one's own position before engaging in dialogue, students are encouraged to have the concretization of their own position be a prior condition to dialogue and one that, in effect, prevents dialogue. Once students have decided to be abstinent, that abstinence is no longer up for debate. Students are taught to be autonomous and uncompromising, not a particularly useful stance in terms of developing communication skills for a variety of situations. Students who consider themselves abstinent, for instance, do not think they need to plan for sex and will likely not be prepared should the occasion arise.

The issues of adolescent sexuality, sexual identity, and HIV all interact to create a series of complex conflicts within schooling. The *AIDS Instructional Guide* does not allow for multiple conceptions of what it means to be sexually engaged. In not allowing students to problematize the *Guide*'s narrow construction of adolescent sexuality, the *Guide* imposes an identity on students. Thus, rather than engaging in reflection as to the meaning of sex, its relation to adolescents and their abilities to relate to one another, the *Guide* simply posits a conception of adolescence that would avoid these questions. This particular conception of adolescence has the effect, as identities do, of creating boundaries and marking those who do not fit as "other." The very reason for the *Guide* in the first place is a concern that adolescents may be at risk for HIV infection. By making the sexually active adolescent an "other," the *Guide* is largely working against its very own purpose.

But if one were to counter the *Guide* with the suggestion that it needs to be more inclusive of identity categories in its lessons this would only in part solve the problem and would also add new difficulties. Identity categories themselves are limited in their ability to handle human complexity; they tend to be insufficiently specific in terms of accounting for activity. In addition, they are problematic, as William Connolly points out, insofar as "doubts about self-identity are posed and resolved by the constitution of an other against which that identity may define itself."[75] Instead of being engaged in the whys or whats of the grounding of identity, we should focus on "the *ways* to cultivate care for identity and difference in a world already permeated by ethical proclivities and predispositions to identity."[76]

What HIV education should entail is not simply role-playing pre-given moral decisions but interacting with others to develop relational stances toward moral problems and communication. Students would need to be encouraged to not only reflect on their own positions going into any dialogue but be willing to have their positions challenged and to in turn challenge the positions of others. Connolly argues that these challenges are already bound up with our conceptions of identity, that we face these challenges both within our own identity and in relation to others. He argues:

Recognition of these conditions of strife and interdependence, especially when such recognition contains an element of mutuality, can flow into an ethic in which adversaries are respected and maintained in a mode of agonistic mutuality, an ethic in which alter-identities foster agonistic respect for the differences that constitute them, an ethic of care for life.[77]

Connolly sees promise in the ways identities are dependent on others to maintain their boundaries, in that those relations are both crucial to the concept of identity and also indicative of the contingent quality of identity. Connolly argues that because "[one] is not exhausted by [one's] identity . . . this abundance . . . can help [one] to recognize and attend to the claims of the other in oneself and to the claims of alter-identities."[78] Thus the very shortcomings of identity and the contingency of identity become part of what binds people together. This model of identity avoids the kind of exclusionary identity that the *Guide* relies on.

With regard to HIV education for adolescents, understanding contingency of identity can be helpful in encouraging them to acknowledge their sexual activity even when it seems contradictory to their status as adolescents. Like nongay people who engage in sexual activity with members of the same sex, adolescents may engage in sexual activity and yet deny it because they have been taught that adolescents should be abstinent. Adding an element of contingency to both students' conceptions of their sexual identity and of their identity as adolescents removes some of the obstacles to students' engaging in discourse ethics involving sexual issues. With regard to HIV education this means that we need to take care against reinscribing the very conditions of moral discourse that prevent students from engaging with the issues in meaningful ways. This involves not only critically evaluating HIV education programs but also critically reevaluating our definitions of adolescence, sexuality, and education.

Curricula can help students examine the assumptions that tend to construe adolescent sexuality as a problem, that create the community and sex as heterosexual. The conflicts caused by adolescent sexuality are only in part the result of sexual activity among adolescents. These conflicts are largely the result of clashing definitions, resistances, and positions not given an opportunity to articulate themselves. Approaches that stress contingent identity have the potential to transform the HIV prevention curriculum's construction of students from passive vectors of disease to interactive social and sexual agents.

Notes

1. Marie Schumacher, *HIV/AIDS Education Survey* (Alexandria, Va.: The National Association of State Boards of Education, 1989), 12.
2. Schumacher, *HIV/AIDS Education Survey*, 11.

3.The National Abortion Rights of America League (NARAL) Foundation, *Sexuality Education in America: A State by State Review* (Washington, D.C.: NARAL, 1995), iv.

4. NARAL, *Sexuality Education in America*, 16.

5. Statistics describing sexual behavior require the same cautious interpretation as do all attempts to represent human interaction quantitatively. Where relevant I have cited statistics from the same time period covered by the chapter.

6. Anne Grunseit and Susan Kippax, "Effects of Sex Education on Young People's Sexual Behaviour" (New York: World Health Organization, 1994).

7. M. Zelnick and F. Shah, "First Intercourse among Young Americans," *Family Planning Perspectives* (March-April 1983) quoted in U.S. Congress. Senate, Committee on Governmental Affairs, *AIDS Education of School-Aged Youth*, 101st Congress, 2nd sess., 1990, 119.

8. Alan Guttmacher Institute, *Sex and America's Teenagers* (New York: Alan Guttmacher Institute, 1994), 20.

9. C. A. Bachrach, M. C. Horn, W. D. Mosher, and W. F. Pratt, "Understanding U. S. Fertility: Findings from the National Survey of Family Growth, Cycle III," *Population Bulletin*, 39, no. 5 (December 1984) quoted in *AIDS Education of School-Aged Youth*, 119. By 1994, 75 percent of teens reported using contraception, most often a condom, the first time they had vaginal-penile intercourse, see Alan Guttmacher Institute, *Sex and America's Teenagers* (New York: Alan Guttmacher Institute, 1994), 33. However, among students who had had multiple sexual partners, only 41 percent reported condom usage at last sexual intercourse. See "Preventing Risk Behaviors among Students," *Centers for Disease Control HIV/AIDS Prevention Newsletter* (October 1992): 2.

10. Hart quoted in Laura C. Leviton, "Theoretical Foundations of AIDS-Prevention Programs," in *Preventing AIDS : The Design of Effective Programs*, Ronald O.Valdiserri (New Brunswick, N.J.: Rutgers University Press, 1989), 163.

11. M. Zelnik and J. Kanter quoted in John DeLamater, "An Interpersonal and Interactional Model of Contraceptive Behavior," in *Adolescents, Sex, and Contraception*, ed. Donn Byre and William Fisher (Hillsdale, N.J.: Lawrence Erlbaum, 1983), 37.

12. George Cvetkovich and Barbara Grote, "Adolescent Development and Teenage Fertility," in *Adolescents, Sex, and Contraception*, 115.

13. Alan Guttmacher Institute, *Sex and America's Teenagers* (New York: Alan Guttmacher Institute, 1994), 22–28.

14. Christopher Bagley and Pierre Tremblay cited in Mike King, "Suicide Watch," *The Advocate*, 12 November 1996, 41.

15. Walter Dowdle quoted in U.S. Congress. House. Subcommittee on Human Resources and Intergovernmental Relations. *Children and HIV Infection*, 101st Cong., 1st sess., 1989, 170–171.

16. Leviton, "Theoretical Foundations," in Valdiserri, *Preventing AIDS*, 224.

17. Leviton, "Theoretical Foundations," 224.

18. Liane Summerfield, "Adolescents and AIDS," *ERIC Digest* ED 319742 (1990).

19. Michelle Fine, "Sexuality, Schooling, and Adolescent Females: The Missing Discourse of Desire," *Harvard Educational Review* (February 1988): 34. See also Joseph A. Diorio, "Contraception, Copulation Domination, and the Theoretical Barrenness of Sex Education Literature," *Educational Theory* (Summer 1985): 239–254.

20. Fine, "The Missing Discourse of Desire," 32.

21. Fine, "The Missing Discourse of Desire," 50.

22. Fisher et al. quoted in Fine, "The Missing Discourse of Desire," 31. See W. Fisher, D. Byrne, and L. White, "Emotional Barriers to Contraception," *Adolescents, Sex, and Contraception*, 207-239. Paul Epstein also points to other outcomes from programs that presume adolescents to be sexually active and encourage them to use condoms—researchers at Johns Hopkins found that students who had participated in a sex education program that included information on condom usage had an increased rate of abstention from sex and a delay in onset of sexual activity. In Paul Epstein "Condoms in Schools: The Right Lesson," *New York Times*, 19 January 1991, 31.

23. Diorio, "Copulation Domination," 239.

24. Diorio, "Copulation Domination," 242.

25. Diorio, "Copulation Domination," 244.

26. Diorio, "Copulation Domination," 247.

27. Diorio, "Copulation Domination," 251.

28. Dianne L. Kerr, Diane D. Allensworth, and Jacob. A. Gayle, "The ASHA National HIV Education Needs Assessment of Health and Education Professionals," *Journal of School Health* (September 1989): 304.

29. Kerr, Allensworth, and Gayle, "ASHA HIV Needs Assessment," 304. This list is not exhaustive—other items include death and dying.

30. Kerr, Allensworth, and Gayle, "ASHA HIV Needs Assessment," 306.

31. Leo Bersani, "Is the Rectum a Grave?" in *AIDS Cultural Analysis/Cultural Activism*, ed. Douglas Crimp (Cambridge: Massachusetts Institute of Technology Press, 1989), 197–222. See also Anne Koedt, "The Myth of the Vaginal Orgasm" in *Radical Feminism*, ed. Anne Koedt, Ellen Levine, and Anita Rapone (New York: Quadrangle Books, 1973), 198-207.

32. Paula Treichler, "AIDS, Homophobia, and Biomedical Discourse: An Epidemic of Signification" in *AIDS: Cultural Analysis/Cultural Activism*, ed. Douglas Crimp (Cambridge: Massachusetts Institute of Technology Press, 1989), 31–70.

33. "Koop Defends Views on AIDS Education," *New York Times*, 3 February 1987, III, 12.

34. Maureen Dowd, "Dr. Koop Defends His Crusade on AIDS," *New York Times*, 6 April 1987, II, 8.

35. U.S. Department of Health and Human Services pamphlet, *Understanding AIDS* (Washington, D.C.: U.S. Government Printing Office, 1988).

36. Nora Kizer Bell, "Women and AIDS: Too Little, Too Late?" *Hypatia* 4, no. 3 (Fall 1989): 5.

37. Rebecca Cole and Sally Cooper, "Lesbian Exclusion from HIV/AIDS Education: Ten Years of Low-Risk Identity and High-Risk Behavior," *Sex Information and Education Council of the United States Report* (December 1990/January 1991): 18.

38. Cole and Cooper, "Lesbian Exclusion," 18.

39. Dianne L. Kerr, Diane D. Allensworth, and Jacob. A. Gayle, "The ASHA National HIV Education Needs Assessment of Health and Education Professionals," *Journal of School Health* (September 1989): 304.

40. Sandra C. Quinn, Stephen B. Thomas, and Becky J. Smith, "Are Health Educators Being Prepared to Provide HIV/AIDS Education?: A Survey of Selected Health Education Professional Preparation Programs," *Journal of School Health* (March 1990): 95.

41. USNY SED, *AIDS Instructional Guide*, 107.

42. USNY SED, *AIDS Instructional Guide*, 106, 145.

43. Diorio, "Copulation Domination," 246.

44. USNY SED, *AIDS Instructional Guide*, 91.

45. USNY SED, *AIDS Instructional Guide*, 92.

46. USNY SED, *AIDS Instructional Guide*, 92.

47. USNY SED, *AIDS Instructional Guide*, 108.

48. USNY SED, *AIDS Instructional Guide*, 108.

49. USNY SED, *AIDS Instructional Guide*, 108.

50. USNY SED, *AIDS Instructional Guide*, 108.

51. USNY SED, *AIDS Instructional Guide*, 125.

52. USNY SED, *AIDS Instructional Guide*, 125.

53. USNY SED, *AIDS Instructional Guide*, 125.

54. USNY SED, *AIDS Instructional Guide*, 125.

55. USNY SED, *AIDS Instructional Guide*, 122.

56. USNY SED, *AIDS Instructional Guide*, 122.

57. USNY SED, *AIDS Instructional Guide*, 15.

58. Gary Nadel quoted in United States Senate, Committee on Governmental Affairs, *AIDS Education of School-Aged Youth,* 101st Congress, 2nd sess., 1990, 8.

59. Nadel, *AIDS Education of School-Aged Youth*, 7.

60. Cutler quoted in Ronald O. Valdiserri, *Preventing AIDS : The Design of Effective Programs* (New Brunswick, N.J.: Rutgers University Press, 1989), 28.

61. Leviton, "Theoretical Foundations," in *Preventing AIDS*, 49.

62. Leviton, "Theoretical Foundations," 160.

63. Leviton, "Theoretical Foundations," 164.

64. USNY SED, *AIDS Instructional Guide*, 162.

65. I. A. Vincenzi, "A Longitudinal Study of Human Immunodefiency Virus Transmission by Heterosexual Partners," *New England Journal of Medicine* 331, no. 6 (1994): 431–446. Another study found a 3 percent infection rate. See A. Saracco et al. "Man-to-Woman Transmission of HIV: Longitudinal Study of 343 Steady Partners of Infected Men," *Journal of Acquired Immune Deficiency Syndromes* 6 (1993): 497–502.

66. Vincenzi, "A Longitudinal Study," 15.

67. Part of the fallout from anti-condom sentiments appears to be a lack of interest in improving the simple, though fallible, condom. The female condom was one of the first innovations in condom design brought about by HIV and a recognition that women have difficulties getting their partners to agree to condoms. The point of this section is not to insist that condoms are the answer but rather that their part in attempting to minimize risk among adolescents has been severely curtailed by the meanings and messages attached to education on sex and AIDS.

68. Patton, *Sex and Germs*, 131.

69. Gayle Rubin, "Thinking Sex: Notes for a Radical Theory of the Politics of Sexuality," in *Pleasure and Danger: Exploring Female Sexuality*, ed. Carole Vance (New York: Routledge, 1984), 267–319.

70. Rubin, "Thinking Sex," 277.

71. Leo Bersani, "Is the Rectum a Grave?" in *AIDS Cultural Analysis/Cultural Activism*, ed. Douglas Crimp (Cambridge: Massachusetts Institute of Technology Press, 1989), 212.

72. John Zeh, "New Wave of HIV Infection Hits Gay Youth," *Open Classroom* (Fall 1991): 3.

73. Zeh, "New Wave of HIV Infection," 3.

74. While Surgeon General Elders was often criticized for being the "Condom Queen," her comments on the need for public schools to address masturbation did her in.

75. William E. Connolly, *Identity/Difference: Democratic Negotiations of Political Paradox* (Ithaca, N.Y.: Cornell University Press, 1991), ix–x.

76. Connolly, *Identity/Difference*, 10.

77. Connolly, *Identity/Difference*, 166.

78. Connolly, *Identity/Difference*, 120.

Part III: Complex Identity and Curricular Debate

5

Local Values and the Open Closet

In the spring of 1992, at the height of the culture wars, controversy broke out in New York City public schools over the inclusion of lessons on gay- and lesbian-headed families in the teachers' guide for first graders in the new "Children of the Rainbow" multicultural curriculum. The public debates that ensued drew together a remarkable variety of cultural anxieties centering on sexuality but expanding to include race and ethnicity, parental rights, and local control of schools. Conservative attempts to put discussion of sexuality back into the closet seemed to have had the opposite effect as spirited public discussion opened the closet even further. Though these openings have been far from uncontested, one aspect of the conservative effort to close the closet had the ironic effect of making gayness more central to heterosexuality's own self-definition. If heterosexuality had indeed been a stable norm prior to issues like gay inclusive multiculturalism, it was only tenuously so. That gay and lesbian people were represented in the controversy as being both outside school communities and potentially lurking within shows the vacillation between homosexuality as a universalizing identity, where anyone could be implicated, and a minoritizing identity, where only a distinct few are definitely homosexual.[1] The tension between the two possible "places" of homosexuality within communities, then, meant that strategically, even those conservative critics of inclusion of gay issues into multiculturalism were faced with having to account for whether sexual minorities were actually already present in the school community or whether they were dangerous outsiders.

Concern over sexual minority-related issues not only occasioned an attempted solidification of "heterosexual" community but it also acted, for the conservative Right, as an opportunity to advocate for "legitimate" racial and ethnic minorities by casting the gay community as white and affluent. The Right's interest in "legitimate minorities" marked a switch in tactics. Only a year prior to the 1992 controversy over Children of the Rainbow, conservative critics had attacked "One Nation, Many Peoples: A Declaration of Cultural Independence" which they claimed had promoted a "cult of ethnicity."[2] In a quick turn around, conservative criticism of Children of the Rainbow was based on a defense of racial and ethnic minorities against the illegitimate claims of sexual minorities. Thus, the debate over Children of the Rainbow partially normalized racial and ethnic difference at the same time that it also "heterosexualized" race and ethnicity.

The debate over Children of the Rainbow was also about AIDS as controversy paralleled many of the same complaints over school policy and authority that had arisen in 1986 over the admittance of an HIV-positive seven-year-old into a city school. In that situation, the dispute demonstrated not only a public suspicion of expert knowledge on transmission of HIV, but also a local suspicion of expert opinion and centralized authority.[3] Because the controversy over Children of the Rainbow often incorporated fear of AIDS/HIV, it demonstrates a move away from concern over the risk of HIV to a concern for the social risk posed by homosexual families to the "heterosexual community." Further, the earlier case provided a potent precedent for rebellion from central authority that would fuel opposition to the Rainbow curriculum.[4]

Controversy and New York City's "Children of the Rainbow" Multicultural Curriculum

At the same time dispute over the curriculum attempted to clearly state which minorities might legitimately find representation in schools, the debate itself also opened a public conversation about sexuality, identity, and diversity. The stakes were clearly quite high as supporters of the gay inclusive multicultural curriculum argued that representation of gay- and lesbian-headed households would help children of same sex parents feel more comfortable in schools and help all students to understand that homophobia was unacceptable. Opponents of the curriculum argued that including sexual minorities in a city-sponsored, if not mandated, curriculum indicated disrespect for racial and ethnic minorities and took valuable class time away from the real struggles against racism and ethnocentrism. In addition, conservative opponents feared that schools would turn their children away from family values and heterosexuality. In short, the Children of the Rainbow curriculum had the potential to challenge the authority of the family in areas that many parents already felt uncomfortable about in terms of the AIDS curriculum guide that had also been challenged on the grounds of violating parental rights.

In my analysis of the controversy that occupied the New York City school community from April 1992 to February 1993, I parallel work on AIDS that details the vast and contradictory discourses that attach themselves to and make up the response to the AIDS epidemic. As work in AIDS discourse analysis contends, we need to take seriously the range of meanings that are articulated through crises.[5] The local production of knowledges and resistances offers educational policy makers and implementers a way to make these local responses a central concern. At the same time, the controversy over Children of the Rainbow shows, like controversies over AIDS education, that local control itself is not enough to insure that minorities within the school community will be represented or that schools are open to shifts in identity and practices. Given the role of education in nurturing and making possible identities for students, it is crucial that curricula consider homosexuality and heterosexuality beyond a limiting binary opposition.

Power, Authority, and the Conflict over Local Values

The controversy over Children of the Rainbow raised the question of the limits of power for each level of New York City schools and whether those liberal procedural limits are able to accomplish the substantive, democratic tasks for which they were devised. New York City has attempted, in recent decades, to decentralize authority and leave greater decision making about curricular and administrative issues up to local districts, primarily in an effort to eliminate corruption and discrimination in an increasingly diverse city. Thus, the central board may put out a curriculum guide but the local boards can alter it to suit their needs. The Decentralization Law of 1970 rearranged school boards into two levels. Locally elected community school boards, roughly equivalent to the concept of school district, are in charge of elementary and junior high schools. These local boards oversee the implementation of curricula in elementary, junior high, and high schools. A central school board, made up of appointees from the president of each borough, two mayoral appointees, and a schools chancellor (appointed by the mayor and confirmed by the central board), has authority over issues affecting the city's high schools and development of curricula. Contact is maintained between the two layers of authority by periodic conferences generally in the form of meetings with representatives from each community school board and the central board. Within individual school districts, community advisory boards determine the locally sensitive changes to relevant curricula in the elementary, junior high, and high schools.

The twin purposes of decentralization reforms were to challenge discrimination by keeping authority at as local a level as possible. In the case of the Rainbow curriculum there was not an inherently tolerant or democratic outcome entailed by this procedural power distribution. Local or community control of schools is one way to attempt to overcome the tensions between state interest in education and parents' desire to have their children brought up in a way that reflects the parents' way of life. Having parents and local community members involved in schooling decisions is meant to cut down on potential clashes in value between state policy and local ways of life. But the provision for community control of curricular issues can be seen as a procedural attempt to sidestep substantive issues that generate controversy, especially when the state is intent on making curricular changes in areas of study that are potentially controversial. Thus while state and city curricula involving sex education, AIDS education, and multicultural education all provide for community control of the specific ways in which the curricula are implemented, this provision of community control has often been interpreted to mean that curricular issues that offend "local" sensibilities can be removed from the schools. Among the most common topics removed from sex education curricula are references to homosexuality. It is therefore not surprising that sections of a multicultural curriculum that attempted to include tolerance for gays and lesbians were most endangered by local review boards. Thus, a mechanism was in place for local sensibilities to drastically alter the purpose of the curriculum, not simply to tailor it to local tastes.

A short history of the Rainbow curriculum's development helps to explain that the curriculum was not very remarkable given the long-standing policy supporting its basic intentions. The Children of the Rainbow curriculum was a first grade teacher's guide to implementing a multicultural curriculum introduced in New York City schools in 1992. While use of the guide itself was not specifically mandated, policy does require that school districts find some locally appropriate way to cover the same issues, including teaching tolerance of lesbians and gays. According to the history of the curriculum listed in the beginning of Children of the Rainbow, it constitutes an extension of the Policy for Intergroup Relations established by the board of education in 1985, which first included sexual orientation as a protected class.[6] This policy formed the basis of the "Statement of Policy on Multicultural Education and Promotion of Positive Intergroup Relations," accepted with a report and recommendations of the Human Relations Task Force in February 1989 to develop multicultural curricular materials.

Gay and lesbian educators had been attempting to become part of the development of multicultural education in New York City since the policy was instituted in 1985.[7] But it was not until 1992, very late in the review process of *Children of the Rainbow* that a lesbian teacher was invited to add material that addressed sexual orientation. Her additions were not given to reviewers and at least some of the objections to the gay and lesbian materials came from people who had worked on the review and were surprised to see controversial material in the final draft that they had not seen in review drafts.[8] This gaffe does not seem to have spurred the vast majority of protests; there was already a precedent for removing even seemingly mundane references to gay relationships in New York City's AIDS curriculum—a lesson discouraging drug use began: "Michael and Bill have been going together for one year" but was changed to "Michael and Bill are very good friends."[9] Given the intensity of the objection to *Children of the Rainbow*'s attention to gays and lesbians, it is important to remember that the text of the *Children of the Rainbow* was a teacher's guide. It was not intended to be read by children, it was only intended to give background information and suggestions on how teachers might design a multicultural curriculum for first graders that included lessons on learning respect for all kinds of families.

However, the finer points of policy language and the audience to whom they were addressed were not as important as a fear that the curriculum was trying to make students not only tolerant of sexual minorities but willing to consider homosexuality as a possible life choice. Protests against the *Children of the Rainbow* began. Mixing criticism of the AIDS curriculum with criticism of the *Children of the Rainbow* curriculum, fifty people marched in City Hall Park chanting, "No way José, don't teach our children to be gay."[10] Members of Concerned Parents for Educational Accountability "spoke of AIDS education and pedophilia in the same breath."[11] Pointing to a passage in the *Children of the Rainbow* curriculum one parent argued, "Now they're going to think that if any man touches me and I'm a little boy, it's O.K., or if any woman touches me and I'm a little girl, it's O.K."[12] The passage in question recommends that children actually meet gay people: "children need actual experiences via creative play, books, visitors, etc. in order for them to view lesbians/gays as real people to be respected and appreciated."[13] Part of the objection to the curriculum was that it suggested that respect was not enough and instead initially pushed for "celebrated" lesbians and gays. In revision, "celebrated" was changed to "appreciated," but that change did not address the conservative protestors' concern that the curriculum required too much of children. In this discussion, "respect" came to mean a neutral stance toward its object and, indeed, as I will show later, "respect" was a sufficiently neutral outlook that its object did not need to be specified. Students could be taught to be respectful of everyone, rather than having to learn in detail about specific groups. Respect was a capacity that did not require knowledge, nor did it require a positive component. "Celebration" clearly goes far beyond respect and, although it was revised to "appreciation," the positive valuation remained, albeit less festively. Raising the bar for intergroup cooperation troubled parents and community members who, although generally opposed to acts of violence and disrespect, did not want the place of sexual minorities to be given a positive valence.

Additional objections were lodged against the four children's books included in the teacher's bibliography in the Children of the Rainbow curriculum. These books were meant as aids to help teachers, and, like the rest of the curriculum, the books were only intended as a guide, not necessarily to be used in the classroom. The books objected to were *Daddy's Roommate, Heather Has Two Mommies*, and *Gloria Goes to Gay Pride*. There is an additional book, *Asha's Mums*, that is not referred to by critics of the curriculum. Of the four books originally included in the teacher's bibliography, only this unmentioned book, *Asha's Mums*, still remains on the teachers' reading list. It is also the only book whose content may not be apparent from the title—perhaps reviewers thought it was about Asha's flowers. Interestingly, *Asha's Mums* is also the only book of the four that deals directly with the kind of difficulty a child might have in having two mothers. It is also the only book of the four with substantial representation of people of color. Asha's teacher won't accept a permission slip for a field trip signed by two women. The teacher is cut off by students' questions each time she starts to say whether she thinks having two mothers is acceptable. So although Asha's friends wind up accepting the two mothers, the teacher never actually endorses her mothers' relationship, nor is the word "lesbian" ever mentioned. Institutional acceptance remains questionable for Asha's mums, but it is clear that Asha's friends are very supportive.

The Discourse of Tolerance in the Culture Wars

Citing widespread criticism of the curriculum, Queens District 24 board president Mary Cummins openly declared herself in rebellion and refused to implement the curriculum. According to policy, she was allowed to forego use of the Children of the Rainbow and choose an alternative, but she also refused to ensure that alternative curriculum materials that taught respect for gay and lesbian families would be provided. In addition, angry at the heavy hand of authority in the implementation of Children of the Rainbow, Cummins refused to attend a conciliatory meeting with Schools Chancellor Fernandez. Under the Decentralization Law of 1970, District 24's board was required to attend this meeting, but they did not. This gave Fernandez his strongest reason for dissolving 24's board, which until then had only rebelled against a non-mandated curriculum guide.[14] Fernandez dissolved the District 24 board, appointed trustees, and was overruled by the central board within a week. When his contract was up for renewal later that year, the central board voted against renewal and Fernandez stepped down. While Fernandez had based his use of power on his advocacy of tolerance, Cummins too used a claim of tolerance to justify her rebellion from central authority.

Indeed, "tolerance" became a shifting and multivalent term throughout the controversy. Conservatives like District 24's Cummins managed skillfully to rearticulate their concerns as "tolerant" and indeed a superior form of tolerance that could accommodate both diversity and conservative values. Cummins's take on tolerance centers on the general principle of tolerance and respect for everyone without the need to specify to whom one should be tolerant, why, and under what conditions this tolerance ought to be cultivated.

As a strategic reversal to cover over an essentially intolerant message, this shift worked well. Even in the midst of heavy-handed wielding of her power she maintained her aura of "feisty"[15] "Grandma"[16] going up against the political machinery of the Dinkins administration and those who desired a "Sodom on the Hudson,"[17] where a neighborhood-filled New York City used to flourish. Certainly there was a fair degree of sentimentalizing and patronizing of Cummins's age and gender, but her successful position as grandmother and object of nostalgia was quite at odds with her powerful statements on the gay conspiracy overtaking New York City school politics. Her public letters to Fernandez positioned her as a lone crusader daring to address the distant chancellor. Thus Fernandez, who was attempting to have public schools take up the mission of teaching diverse groups to get along, was represented as the uncaring bureaucrat who would trade away children's innocence for political points with the "sodomist" voting block. Cummins managed to corner the market on morality and claim that while teaching tolerance of everyone else, Fernandez's curriculum was not tolerant of her way of life.

Cummins argued in her public letter that the Rainbow curriculum guide imposed standards "which are not in consonance with those of our communities."[18] In addition, Cummins accused the central board of "taking liberties without community input."[19] While Cummins's criticisms of the board were intended to represent her as fighting off the encroaching outside authority of a board under the sway of a gay conspiracy, she was exercising her own authority to keep parents in her district from reviewing the guide and from having a public hearing on it. Despite this maneuver, Cummins continued to base her rebellion on the right of parental authority and a claim to minority status herself, contending that forcing information about homosexuality on school children was just like "what Hitler did before the war, before the Holocaust. He took the youngest children, probably in the first grade, brainwashed them for a couple of years and sent them home to snitch on their parents."[20] But Cummins had not consistently advocated for parental input into public schools. Prior to the Rainbow curriculum controversy, Cummins had been the force behind a suit to remove parental input from the hiring procedure for school principals.[21] Nor was Cummins justified in characterizing the Children of the Rainbow curriculum as having been entirely the product of the central board without community input since "every school district in the city was invited to participate in designing the new multicultural curriculum."[22]

Locality, Nostalgia, and the Gay Conspiracy

The conservative response to sexuality issues in the curriculum contained a clear element of fear about the way society had changed and the part that gay men and lesbians, who were becoming more open, had played in that change. A Queens mother's call for school to teach about "old-fashioned families" and "white picket fences" was just one indication of the nostalgia for times when no one would dare make comparisons between Italians and homosexuals. As Cummins argued, the curriculum should "not demean our legitimate minorities, such as blacks, Hispanics, and Asians, by lumping them together with homosexuals."[23] That Cummins could invoke the ambivalent phrase "our legitimate minorities" is interesting on a number of levels. It marked a turning point in the conservative response to multicultural curricula in general in which, in the face of inclusion of homosexuality, alliance with people of color became more appealing. Cummins's statement was also a literal moment of "legitimating" minorities, marking out which minorities were suitable and which were not in a gesture of alliance that still maintained the center of power.

And there was also a clear element of resentment at the attention that AIDS and the gay community were getting. The Family Defense Council, on whose board Mary Cummins sat, called on members to "Help David overcome the Gay Goliath."[24] Their pamphlets further attest to their victories and to their work on "combating pro-homosexual school curriculums and exposing the gay political agenda," warning readers that "although homosexuals are few in number, they are heavily funded and supported, in part, by our government."[25] In their newsletter, the call for donations is placed directly below an article claiming "AIDS Gets Disproportionate Funding."[26] Other articles document the corporations and organizations that support "radical homosexuals"—"Webster's Dictionary, President Clinton, Clinton's health plan, NYNEX, the American Historical Association"—all of which add up to making the gay community look quite powerful.[27] By refiguring tolerance, which was the only requirement for a substitution for the Children of the Rainbow, as imposition, they were able to cast themselves not only as disempowered masses but, as a minority, binding themselves to "legitimate" minorities, heavily discriminated against by powerful interests. This turn toward a discourse of "minority" and also toward a demand for "rights" marked a shift in the language and strategies of the Christian Right.

While they had been among earlier critics of multicultural education (and, much earlier, critics of integration), conservatives, in particular the newly formed Christian Coalition, saw untapped alliances in churches of color, where many people were supportive of a cultural conservative agenda. The Christian Coalition, following on the work of the Moral Majority, moved conservative Christian social concerns out of the churches and into the political arena. More successfully than the Moral Majority, they also used the language of liberalism and rights to form alliances and to form a sense of minority identity for conservatives in a world whose norms appeared to be fading. While liberalism itself in its insistence on church/state separation may have been the major problem for religious conservatives, the *language* of liberalism had become increasingly popular, particularly gaining momentum in the Reagan years. As the Christian Right saw some of its access to political voice stilled in the Clinton era, a strategic shift was enacted that both increased its base and tempered some of its demands. Despite some tempering, the Christian Right had always found success in preventing legal protection for gays and lesbians. As Didi Herman argues, prior to the 1990s this had largely been accomplished through criticism of gay identity and practices, with particular focus on purportedly lurid acts among gay men. But in the 1990s most strategies shifted to counter gay and lesbian demands for rights.[28] Literature of the Christian Right during this period highlights, according to Herman, the relative wealth and power of gays and the relative poverty of African Americans and Hispanics in order to undercut the gay movement's claim to minority status.

According to literature from the Right:

Homosexuals claim they are economically, educationally and culturally disadvantaged. Marketing studies refute those claims. Homosexuals have an average annual household income of $55,430, versus
$32,144 for the general population and $12,166 for disadvantaged African-American households. More than three times as many homosexuals as average Americans are college graduates . . . a percentage
dwarfing that of truly disadvantaged African-Americans and Hispanics.[29]

This passage cites an oft-cited survey of readers of an upscale mar-
keted gay magazine and, as Alex Chasin has argued, it reflects a sample
of upper-middle-class lesbians and gay men who constituted the reader-
ship of the magazine doing the survey, not a random sampling of gay
communities. More importantly, Chasin demonstrates that use of this
survey represents a strategic attempt by the Right to portray gays and
lesbians as overwhelmingly white and upper class, despite the fact that
the data does not reflect all "homosexuals." [30]

Still the claims from conservatives that the gay movement was all
white and only concerned with financial gains missed the degree to
which AIDS had forced a shift in identity politics, as well as made attention to issues of race, class and gender crucial to political organizing and community service. While not always able to overcome exclusions, AIDS activists were made to realize by people of color who
fought exclusion that their constituency was diverse and that activist
strategies, treatment plans, community organizing and education required a nuanced and complex understanding of identity. Activists and
service providers recognized that identity and activity were not co-
extensive. In addition, they argued that access to medical care, validity
of treatment protocols, the very definition of the infections qualifying
as AIDS were all dependent upon an understanding of the interplay of
race, gender, class, ethnicity, sexuality and a variety of other factors.
That "AIDS does not discriminate" was clear. But it was also clear
that AIDS was not a singular experience that would bring together a
diverse range of people in a common experience because the variation
and complications of HIV infections across social positionings meant
different things and were experienced in different ways.

The diversity of people with or affected by AIDS simultaneously
worked against and toward the development of a strong identity-based
politics. The very public nature of demonstrations and of the epidemic
itself helped to facilitate both of these moves, one by solidifying the gay
movement into a single issue and the other by opening coalitions with
other affected groups. Gay men organized the first alternative institutional and grassroots responses including the Gay Men's Health Crisis,
guerrilla clinics dedicated to local drug trials and alternative treatments,

as well as buyers' clubs to cut the costs of drugs and to enable greater access to unapproved treatment. While initially these responses were based in the gay community, intravenous drug users and groups disproportionately at risk for opportunistic infections because of poverty also involved themselves in accessing services and developing programs. The kinds of connections between issues were evident in ACT UP protests that made connections between racism, homophobia, and inaccessibility to medical care and in the Gay Men's Health Crisis estimates that the majority of people who use its services were not gay. Because AIDS activism and services focus on prevention of HIV infection as well as services to those with HIV, one of the main messages is that all are affected by the epidemic.

Indeed, a number of local AIDS services changed their names, omitting "gay" out of concern that populations most in need of services would be unlikely to seek help if they might themselves be considered gay. While this too implies that people of color and poor people are not themselves gay, it also reflects a growing concern that, while the gay community was first to organize local services, they were not the only ones needing services. In a context in which racism defines most social interactions, identification by sexuality is not as important as identification by sexuality. For instance, young black gay men identify as black first and gay second, preferring to maintain strong ties to the black community, despite the homophobia they may have felt. Their close feelings of familial and historical belonging also offset the racism they felt from the gay community, even if they also felt homophobia from the black community.[31] In other words, then, the Christian Right's strategy of whitening the gay movement also played on the problem of racism within gay communities and homophobia within communities of color.

Why Talking about the Closet Keeps the Closet Open: The Failure of Discourses of Containment

The Religious Right posited gays not only as privileged white people but also as a distinct, but increasingly powerful minority—and one that they preferred stay private and in the closet. The assumption that gay men and lesbians were a distinct minority was also behind school curricula addressing homosexuality as if it were only the concern of a small, distinct minority of students. However, I will argue, following Eve Sedgwick, that the closet occupies a more central position to the constitution of all sexualities. Thus, homosexuality is not a marginal force existing along side of heterosexuality but is central to the consti-

tution of heterosexuality itself. Sedgwick contends that "an understanding of virtually any aspect of modern Western culture must be, not
merely incomplete, but damaged in its central substance to the degree
that it does not incorporate a critical analysis of modern
homo/heterosexual definition."[32] Silences, Sedgwick contends, surround
the closet, not just one silence, "but a silence that accrues particularity
by fits and starts, in relation to the discourse that surrounds and differentially constitutes it."[33] This section will serve to outline the silences
and ignorances that continue to proliferate, as well as the silences that
have had to shift when part of the closet is opened.

Sedgwick contends that the closet is the site of origin of unstable
binaries beyond those of hetero/homo. Indeed the closet and the open
secret—knowledge in some sense known but not circulated, an active
ignorance—form the structure of a range of other binaries. The tension
between visibility and invisibility, ignorance and knowledge, and childhood and sexuality is central to examining the power effects attending
the heterosexual/homosexual binary. The suspicion entailed by the invisibility of deviance within communities has the double effect of ac-
knowledging the constant presence of sexual difference while at the
same time encouraging the performance of increasingly visible alle-
giances to heterosexuality. This allegiance to heterosexuality is performed through advocacy of "family values" or through advocacy of
pre-heterosexual abstinent behavior—particularly in the form of "just
say no." Students are not simply encouraged to personally decide to be
abstinent but are encouraged to voice this as a public statement against
deviance, including class lessons in which students actually practice
verbalizing "no" or attempt to find new and creative ways to do so. This
kind of visible if somewhat embattled performance of heterosexuality is
also present in the New Right campaign for a return to "family values."
The connection between the visible and invisible may provide a site of
destabilization of the heterosexual/homosexual binary in a way that
makes that binary and the careful boundary between the two terms increasingly difficult to maintain. Attempts to banish homosexuality,
through publicly invoking it, actually make homosexuality more visible
and contribute to the destabilization of heterosexuality. The point is not
that the inadvertency of subversion of the binary is enough on its own,
however. Institutional and policy changes need to be made to ensure
that proliferation of identity possibilities are nurtured, rather than actively repressed. George Chauncey's work on the history of gay life in
New York points to the ways laws instituted in the late 1940s prohibiting homosexual behavior in public places removed from sight gay
communities that had flourished since the early 1900s.[34] While he and
Sedgwick point to the ways that homosexuality and other sexualities

emerge even when under prohibition, the point is not to make the closet an object of nostalgia or to suggest that all prohibition will be its own undoing and that is all we need to know. But the fact of inadvertent subversion and shift even in what might usually be considered firm categories points to the possibility of progressive change.

Sedgwick's distinction between minoritizing and universalizing models of identity is useful to point out moments in curricular disputes that lend themselves to destabilizing the homo/hetero binary. The minoritizing model of identity marks out homosexuals as a distinct and quantifiable subgroup different from heterosexuality. The boundaries between the two identities are kept stable and clear in this model, which tries to conceive of homosexuality as something outside and away from the heterosexual norm. But Sedgwick contends that the universalizing model of identity may provide a more useful look at the complementarity, reliance, and mutual fragility of each term. According to Sedgwick's universalizing model of the hetero/homosexual binary, both terms

> actually subsist in a more unsettled and dynamic tacit relation according to which, first, term B is not symmetrical with but subordinated to term A; but, second, the ontologically valorized term A actually depends for its meaning on the simultaneous subsumption and exclusion of term B; hence, third, the question of priority between the supposed central and supposed marginal category of each dyad is irresolvably unstable, an instability caused by the fact that term B is constituted as at once internal and external to term A.[35]

Sedgwick's deconstructive reconceptualization of the relationship between homosexual and heterosexual helps to explain not only the benefits of anti-homophobia education to those in the self-identified gay minority but also to show the inevitable links and overlaps between all sexual identities and groups. This is not necessarily to argue that school policies that address the needs of gay and lesbians cannot helpfully use the minoritizing discourse. One example of the positive possibilities of the minoritizing discourse is the Harvey Milk School in New York City, whose purpose is to enable gay and lesbian students to graduate from high school. The school was founded to enable students subject to constant harassment because of their sexual orientation to stay in school. But even the Harvey Milk School shows the inevitable complications of identity-based approaches because a substantial proportion of its students do not identify as gay, but are instead gender nonconforming and thus subject to harassment on those grounds, not on the grounds of sexual orientation per se.

The predominant discourse in public school curricula that addresses homosexuality is the minoritizing discourse. The Children of the Rainbow multicultural curriculum portrayed gay- and lesbian-headed households as distinct minorities and did not attempt to trouble the boundaries of sexual identity. The controversy generated, however, does. And I want to suggest that there is something in the public nature of the curricular disputes, as well as something about their focus on extending even minoritizing information about sexuality to children, that generates particular anxieties about the sexual orientation of children. The controversy over Children of the Rainbow provided the space for parental fears that their children would not be like them and also reflected conservative anxieties that heterosexuality is not as certain as it seems. The moment that heterosexuals have to assert themselves as "heterosexual" or as members of "traditional families" the universalizing discourse creeps in, and heterosexuality is no longer alone in the public eye and imagination.

Gay Visibility, Family Values, and the Embattled Heterosexual "Minority"

Because HIV is so closely associated with homosexuality, objections to AIDS education in general blended together with conservative objections to the gay-inclusive Children of the Rainbow multicultural curriculum. These objections showed the inability of conservatives to see homosexuality as anything but sexual, even though the first grade lessons that caused the controversy only described the variety of family structures possible, including same-gender couples. The overlap perceived between the two curricula becomes apparent in Queens board president Mary Cummins's objection that the Children of the Rainbow lesson teaches "our kids that sodomy is acceptable but virginity is something weird."[36]

In the course of their objections to gay-inclusive curricula, conservatives began to cast themselves as embattled minorities and to suggest that gays are part of a powerful liberal, affluent majority. If the concept of sexual identity turns from clear-cut minority/majority distinctions to the more universalizing account wherein the terms of identity categories become more unstable, conservative concerns are not unfounded. The worldview of heterosexuals is altered in ways that challenge the heterosexual family as natural and inevitable. Conservatives have often argued that inclusion of information on homosexuality represents an assault on the family and nature (this may seem hyperbolic, but my point is they are quite accurate). The increased visibility of homosexuality has encouraged the assertion of visible heterosexuality, often in the call to return to "family values." Certainly other social shifts or perceived shifts have led the New Right to trumpet a return to the family but "family" rather than "traditional" indicates a particular attempt to bring heterosexuality into the public in a way that provides a refuting reply to the call for gay pride. This is after all, heterosexual pride, but it is a pride that seems to feel it has not had to assert itself in quite this way before. As a public movement that bolsters heterosexuality against homosexuality, the new "family values" is firmly cognizant of homosexuality as its enemy.

New Right mobilizations to secure positions on school boards and to work on parental advisory committees charged with tailoring sex and AIDS educational curricula to local tastes shows the centrality of school policy decisions to the conservative agenda. Indeed, in the late 1970s, 1980s, and early 1990s, the greatest victories of the New Right had been in sex-related issues,[37] particularly those regarding homosexuality and young people. The Anita Bryant–led repeal of a nondiscrimination policy that included sexual orientation in Dade County, Florida, was called "Save Our Children, Inc." Like the 1978 unsuccessful attempt in California to outlaw gay and lesbian teachers in public schools, the Briggs Amendment, Save Our Children argued that nondiscrimination policies opened the doors to gays recruiting children. The early 1990s saw a return to these tactics in Oregon, where the Oregon Citizens Alliance "depicted a male teacher in drag standing at the front of a classroom, with the caption, 'If gay rights becomes law, what prevents this type of thing from happening?'"[38] Another flyer opposing gay rights showed a young male child being pressured by another male child to have sex. The caption reads, "How can it be wrong? The police chief says it's OK. Our teachers say it's OK. The newspaper says it's OK. Even the governor says it's OK."[39] Taken together with the success of Clinton's inclusion of gays and lesbians in his presidential campaign, clearly conservatives were concerned that gay and lesbian political power and visibility would open new possibilities for children's and adolescents' identities. Further, the concern that schools would be a central institution in respecting these choices was evident in the centrality of education to scare campaigns.

While the intention of the opponents of New York City's gay-inclusive Children of the Rainbow multicultural curriculum was to ensure that information about gay outsiders did not make it into classrooms, substantial anxiety about the possibility of children becoming gay bleeds over into the seeming concern that outsiders will be allowed in. In other words, part of the anxiety is that those who are considered insiders will turn out to have been nascent outsiders all along. This fuels the dramatic worry over what information about homosexuality will do to children and also points to the boundaries of heterosexuality. These fears about gayness encroaching on previously seemingly nongay areas is a recognition that gayness is now, on the one hand, more visible and thus more likely to be a possibility of a lifestyle that may be lived in public and gayness is also, on the other hand, always potentially invisible. There is no way to recognize the basic gay or lesbian in the street (at least the activists helpfully attire themselves in distinctive ways) so the ability to sort sexualities is more complicated than a simple heterosexual/homosexual binary allows. What the debate generated from parents, then, was a site to perform their own sexuality and the public decisions and debates to remove or revise information on homosexuality served as a public ritual of heterosexual bonding. Unless one firmly asserts "family values" the potential that one's sexuality is in question is heightened.

Much of the response to these controversies does lead into a kind of politics that solidifies the binary of heterosexual/homosexual, but there is also the persistent intrusion of the universalizing discourse of sexuality as each term calls into question the isolation of the other. Instead of solidifying these identities another option is present through the persistent relation of gay to heterosexual and invisible to visible that broadens the range of diversity possible within communities and warns against too easily presuming the limits of community. The cost of this strong limit on community appears to be the persistent anxiety of invisible difference within. The controversies in New York City that entangled gay-inclusive multiculturalism with AIDS and a general fear of nonheterosexuality opened the conversation about community membership and about sexuality in ways that turned homosexuality from a lurking menace to a real substantial threat to previously seemingly fully accepted ways of life.[40] Even while much of this change in perspective is still couched in terms of intolerance, the shift has occurred. While a backlash is possible, it begins from a different place than before. Heterosexuality no longer has unquestioned hegemony and homosexuality is no longer so clearly on the outside.

This broadened conversation did not extend to public school curriculum, however. The Children of the Rainbow curriculum was revised, changes include substituting "same gender parents" for "lesbian/gay parents."[41] Other passages that formerly included specific reference to lesbian/gay parents now read "each type of household."[42] What appears to be missing most from the curriculum, even in its original form, is a concern for the sexual identity of children. The Children of the Rainbow curriculum, despite protestations to the contrary from concerned parents, squarely positions homosexuality as something adults do, a form of family that children might belong to but not an identity children ever have to consider for themselves. Certainly children of gay and lesbian parents may experience intolerance from classmates and schools should help to prevent this. But gay and lesbian youth also face substantial peril at the hands of public schools and unsympathetic families. Gay, lesbian, bisexual, and transgender students report suffering harassment at schools, many in full view of teachers who do not stop the harassment.[43] A recent settlement in Wisconsin where school administrators agreed to pay $900,000 to a young gay man harassed throughout his school career, while administrators did nothing to intervene, may discourage school districts from passively allowing homophobic assaults. Teenagers surveyed about bias reacted more negatively to gays and lesbians than to any other group, some threatening violence.[44] Lesbian and gay youth report crimes at school at three times the rate of heterosexual crime victims.[45] Unlike other minority groups who may find relief from harassment at home, 25 percent of gay and lesbian youth are forced to leave home because of their sexuality.[46] Further, gay and lesbian youth make up to 25 percent of all youth living on the street.[47] Sexual minority youth are very likely to report isolation and are two to three times more likely to have considered or committed suicide than their heterosexual peers. Fifty-three percent of transsexual youth report having attempted suicide.[48] There is also reason to believe that fears about being gay impel some men to be homophobic, presumably lessening those fears would make the potential victims of gay-bashing rest easily and would reassure those men whose anxiety fuels their violence. Further, the kind of violence and isolation caused by homophobic activities affects all students. Heterosexism in schools, families, and communities is an indication that sexuality involves an unsettling array of possibilities that are significantly more complicated for students of all sexual identities and activities. That heterosexism and homophobia are so widespread and constantly in practice is also a reminder that, in attempting to maintain itself as the only sexual possibility, heterosexuality calls its singularity into question.

Thus it is not surprising that debates over the relationship between education and sexuality were construed as part of the culture wars during the controversies over the AIDS curriculum and Children of the Rainbow. The very arguments and turmoil these issues brought out helped stimulate the largest turnout in school board elections in twelve years. An estimated 12.5 to 15 percent of those eligible voted in the elections.[49] This was nearly double the usual rate and 90 percent greater than the previous board elections.[50] The implementation and arguments over the curricula may not have been the finest version of democracy in practice, but the very acts of making public issues that were heavily in contention inspired people on all sides of both debates to become more politically active and to vote in elections that usually do not stir interest. The Christian Coalition's use of grassroots organizing seemed to have shaken up gay activists who had not been as concerned as they might have been with issues not directly related to AIDS and gay inclusion in curricula. Progressive coalitions formed and lobbied for progressive candidates. The focus on sexuality did broaden to include other issues of concern, including minority access to education and reading scores. In the end, both sides claimed victory (it was, perhaps, the one thing they agreed on). The Christian Coalition claimed that 51 percent of its candidates had been elected to school boards.[51] Progressives claimed to have won in "every area that was contested," getting progressive candidates onto conservative boards and winning a majority in two key conservative districts.[52] The results did not settle any of the social issues that had sparked political activity on both sides, but the results did guarantee that debate would continue. While conservatives had been attempting to remove issues from children's consideration, they, if unintentionally, began a more visible public conversation on those very issues they did not consider appropriate for public discussion.

Notes

An earlier version of this chapter was published as "Performance Anxiety: Sexuality and School Controversy." *Philosophy of Education 1996*, edited by Frank Margonis, (Urbana, IL: Philosophy of Education Society, 1997), 281-289.

1. Eve Kosofsky Sedgwick, *Epistemology of the Closet* (Berkeley: University of California Press, 1989).
2. Robert K. Fullinwider, "Multicultural Education: Concepts, Policies, and Controversies," in *Public Education in a Multicultural Society: Policy, Theory, Critique*, ed. Robert K. Fullinwider (Cambridge: Cambridge University Press, 1996), 8.
3. Dorothy Nelkin and Stephen Hilgartner, "Disputed Dimensions of Risk: A Public School Controversy over AIDS," *Milbank Quarterly* 62, Suppl. 1, (1986): 118–142.
4. Nelkin and Hilgartner, "Disputed Dimensions," 136.
5. See Paula Treichler, "AIDS, Homphobia, and Biomedical Discourse: An Epidemic of Signification" in *AIDS: Cultural Analysis, Cultural Activism*, ed. Douglas Crimp (Cambridge: Massachusetts Institute of Technology Press, 1988), 31–70.

6. New York City Board of Education, *Comprehensive Instructional Program First Grade Teachers' Resource Guide Review Draft* (New York: Board of Education Publications, 1994). Note: this is not the original "Children of the Rainbow" curriculum guide, but a revision. However, the page setting out the policy's history has not been revised. Interestingly, what has been revised is the positioning of the curriculum. Chancellor Cortines, listening to calls for emphasis on a core curriculum instead of a multicultural curriculum, took the Rainbow, revised references to gay- and lesbian-headed families and redubbed the curriculum "core" rather than "multicultural."

7. Andrew Humm, "Re-building the 'Rainbow'—The Holy War over Inclusion in New York City," unpublished paper, 1–2. The late Dr. A. Damien Martin, a cofounder of Hetrick–Martin, had been a member of Chancellor Green's Multicultural Advisory Board.

8. Humm, "Re-building the 'Rainbow,'" 5.

9. Humm, "Re-building the 'Rainbow,'" 5.

10. Melinda Henneberger, "Supporters of AIDS Pledge Criticize Other Programs," *New York Times*, 6 September 1992, 51.

11. Henneberger, "Supporters of AIDS Pledge," 51.

12. Henneberger, "Supporters of AIDS Pledge," 51.

13. Henneberger, "Supporters of AIDS Pledge," 51.

14. Steven Lee Myers, "School Board in Queens Shuns Fernandez Meeting," *New York Times*, 1 December 1992.

15. According to a *Sixty Minutes* episode on "Children of the Rainbow," *New York Times* coverage and others.

16. This is her nickname at Christian Coalition gatherings and what associate Howard Hurwitz calls her in his column "Inside Education" in the *Times Newsweekly* (N.Y.).

17. Quoted from a public letter by Cummins in Steven Lee Myers, "Values in Conflict," *New York Times*, 6 October 1992, B6.

18. Quoted in Liz Willen, "School Furor," *Newsday*, 23 April 1992, 3.

19. Willen, "School Furor," 3.

20. Myers, "Values in Conflict," B6.

21. Donna Minkowitz, "Wrong Side of the Rainbow," *The Nation*, 28 June 1993, 901.

22. Willen, "School Furor," 3.

23. Quoted in Steven Myers, "Queens School Board Suspended in Fight on Gay–Life Curriculum," *New York Times*, 2 December 1992, B4.

24. Family Defense Council pamphlet.

25. Family Defense Council pamphlet.

26. Howard L. Hurwitz, *Family Defense Council Newsletter*, 27 March. 1994, 4.

27. Hurwitz, *Family Defense Council Newsletter*, 4.

28. Didi Herman, *The Antigay Agenda: Orthodox Vision and the Christian Right* (Chicago: University of Chicago Press, 1997), 113.

29. Tony Marco quoted in Herman, *The Antigay Agenda*, 116.

30. Alexandra Chasin, *Selling Out: The Gay and Lesbian Movement Goes to Market* (New York: Palgrave, 2000), 33–40.

31. See James T. Sears, "Black–Gay or Gay–Black? Choosing Identities and Identifying Choices," in *The Gay Teen*, ed. Gerald Unks (New York: Routledge, 1995), 135–158, and Kenneth P. Monteiro and Vincent Fuqua, "African–American Gay Youth: One Form of Manhood," in *The Gay Teen*, ed. Gerald Unks (New York: Routledge, 1995), 159–188.

32. Eve Kosofsky Sedgwick, *Epistemology of the Closet* (Berkeley: University of California Press, 1990), 1.

33. Sedgwick, *Epistemology of the Closet*, 3.

34. George Chauncey, *Gay New York: Gender, Urban Culture, and the Making of the Gay Male World, 1890–1940* (New York: Basic Books, 1994).

35. Sedgwick, *Epistemology of the Closet*, 10.

36. Mary Cummins quoted in Melinda Henneberger, "Supporters of AIDS Pledge Criticize Other Programs," *New York Times*, 6 September 1992, 51.

37. Matthew C. Moen, *The Transformation of the Christian Right* (Tuscaloosa: University of Alabama Press, 1992).

38. John Gallager and Chris Bull, *Perfect Enemies: The Religious Right, the Gay Movement, and the Politics of the 1990s* (New York: Crown Publishers, 1996), 46.

39. Gallager and Bull, *Perfect Enemies*, 52.

40. The revision of "Children of the Rainbow" attempted to unentangle AIDS from gay inclusive multiculturalism by removing all references to HIV and AIDS. See Tracy Phariss, "Public Schools: A Battleground in the Cultural War," in *Gay/Lesbian/Bisexual/Transgender Public Policy Issues: A Citizen's and Administrator's Guide to the New Cultural Struggle*, ed. Wallace K. Swan (New York: Harrington Press, 1997), 75–79.

41. New York City Board of Education, *Comprehensive Instructional Program First Grade Teacher's Resource Guide Review Draft* (New York: New York City Board of Education Publications, 1994). On page 377 this substitution is made, but specific reference is also made to "lesbian/gay parents" who "might worry that revealing their sexual orientation could lead to prejudice."

42. *Comprehensive Instructional Program First Grade Draft*, 183.

43. See Richard A. Friend, " Choices, Not Closets: Heterosexism and Homophobia in Schools," in *Beyond Silenced Voices: Class, Race, and Gender in United States Schools*, ed. Lois Weis and Michelle Fine (Albany: State University of New York Press, 1993), 209–235, and Cris Mayo, "Education by Association: The Shortcomings of Discourses of Privacy and Civility in Anti–Homophobia Education," in *Preparing for Benjamin: Lesbian and Gay Issues in School*, ed. Rita Kissen (New York: Rowman & Littlefield, 2002), 81–90.

44. Kevin T. Berrill, "Anti–Gay Violence and Victimization: An Overview" in *Hate Crimes: Confronting Violence against Lesbians and Gay Men*, ed. Gregory M. Herek and Kevin T. Berrill (London: Sage, 1992), 19–45.

45. Gary David Comstock, *Violence against Lesbians and Gay Men* (New York: Columbia University Press, 1991).

46. Hetrick–Martin Institute, *Factfile: Lesbian, Gay, and Bisexual Youth* cited in *Gay and Lesbian Stats*, ed. B. L. Singer and D. Deschamps (New York: New Press,1992), 77.

47. U. S. Department of Health and Human Services. *Report of the Secretary's Task Force on Youth Suicide, Volume 3 Prevention and Interventions in Youth Suicide* (Rockville, Md.: U.S. Department of Health and Human Services, 1989).

48. *Report of the Secretary's Task Force on Youth Suicide, 3.*

49. Donna Minkowitz, "The Wrong Side of the Rainbow," *The Nation*, 28 June 1993, 901.

50. N'Tanya Lee et al., "Whose Kids? Our Kids! Race, Sexuality and the Right in New York City's Curriculum Battles" *Radical America*, 25, no. 1 (March 1993): 17.

51. Christian Coalition flyer.

52. Minkowitz, "The Wrong Side of the Rainbow," 901.

6

Public Sex: The Abstinence Oath and Secondary Virginity

As we saw in earlier chapters, proceduralist liberals and communitarians each limit the range of discussion about identity in the public sphere. Proceduralist liberals want to avoid bringing in identity differences that lead to irreconcilable differences and communitarians argue that public schools need not recognize more than the dominant way of life of a community. The private sphere then becomes the place where difference and dissent may flourish, and thus both liberals and communitarians contend that public schools have no responsibility to explicitly teach about minority or dissenting identities. This chapter will argue, however, that sexual identities, including minority and dissenting sexual identities, do make their way into the public sphere. These identities often make this public showing through the unexpected route of conservative curricular materials. One such conservative route is New York City's "Abstinence Oath" which follows in the tradition of "just say no" campaigns and contains the same potential for shifting spaces of sexuality as other public declarations of sexual identity or intention. As we have seen in the previous chapter, the closet is a difficult thing to close especially if it is constantly evoked publicly in an attempt to keep it closed. Similarly, it is difficult to prohibit speaking of sexuality—adolescent, adult, gay, straight, for example—because the prohibition broadens the spaces of its consideration and discussion. Both oaths examined in this chapter, one for teachers and the other for students, attempt to use a simple pledge to stem the tide of complex sexual meanings and practices. But both oaths continue to broaden the space of sexuality because they bring talk about sex into public spaces.

This chapter will contend that New York City's Abstinence Oath and the *Sex Respect* curriculum's "secondary virginity" highlight public aspects of sexuality and the perpetual need to articulate sexual meanings and identities to make them legible. The Abstinence Oath highlighted the suspected untrustworthiness of public school AIDS educators and the deep ambivalence of policy makers at having to use them in public schools. Behind this unwillingness is also a reluctance to taint or trust school employees with the delicate task of informing students of the risks of HIV and the range of prevention behaviors. The actual taking of an oath, as a public statement, is meant to tie these outsiders more closely to the schools and create obligation between the outsider and the school administrators. At the same time, as many outside AIDS educators noted, the oath destroys the possibility of any link between the educators and the school. Their message is already suspect, the sexuality of their lessons already beyond acceptable limits. The oath, then, highlights the inappropriateness of what was potentially possible to be said about sexuality. In short, the oath highlights the gaps that will be contained in the lessons given to students after the oath is taken. Like encouraging students to say no, like a marriage vow as protection against HIV, the abstinence oath uses words to prevent action in the hopes that public declarations will be enough to guarantee compliance, obligation and, at least in the majority of the central board's eyes, safety. Each of the three strategies contain similar assumptions regarding identity: one is what one says one will do. A student who says no will abstain from sex and will remain protected from HIV. A couple who marries will have waited until marriage for sex and will remain faithful thereafter and will remain protected from HIV. An educator who swears that abstinence will be the stressed message in any lesson on HIV prevention will adhere to the pledge and give students information that the board deems will keep them safe. In none of these scenarios do complications of identity, activity, context, or meaning invade the safety of spoken words and the identities and activities that will, in practice, flow from them.

In addition, the Abstinence Oath places teachers, whether outside educators or public school teachers, at a disadvantage in their attempts to bring students a range of information about prevention of HIV infection. Even if they are well aware that their students are engaging in sexual activity, the oath requires that lessons on prevention stress abstinence as the most effective means of preventing HIV transmission. This message may undercut attempts to encourage students to engage in safer sexual activities by implying that those activities are only a second-best solution. As previously mentioned, studies on condom usage among college students find that the way condom effectiveness is described to students has an effect on the condom usage rate. The more condoms are described as ineffective, the less likely students are to use them. In addition, the message on abstinence has the effect of limiting the range of what might be considered by students to be sexual activity. To abstain from sex to minimize risk for HIV ought to mean to avoid sexual activities in which there is an exchange of bodily fluids, but it ought not to mean abstaining from sexual activities as a whole. Recent surveys indicate a rise in rates of oral sex among New York City teens, perhaps as a result of fears about HIV and intercourse (the rise includes males and females). But many of these teens refer to oral sex as something one can do when "sex" is too dangerous. By defining oral sex out of the realm of sex they appear to be neglecting the possible risk factors for HIV in oral sex. While schools do provide flavored condoms without lubricant for use in oral sex, few students appear to be using them (schools do not provide dental dams).

Abstinence, Censorship, and the Oath

This section will first briefly recount the rocky development of the Abstinence Oath and then comment on the oath as a barrier to education that casts suspicion on educators and puts an unfair burden on students. The Abstinence Oath was instituted by New York City's central board and was intended to ensure that outside educators would adhere to state and city policy mandating that abstinence be stressed in lessons on AIDS prevention. The board initiated the oath during Fernandez's attempt at revising AIDS curriculum to better address the needs of the city's adolescents who were at a nationally disproportionate risk for HIV infection.

The conservative atmosphere of New York City's central board and community boards was reflected in revisions to the New York City AIDS curriculum. While the Rainbow curriculum issue was percolating in the community school boards, the central board began barring curricular materials in AIDS education. In reference to having to review Fernandez's AIDS curriculum and the "Children of the Rainbow" curriculum one central board member said, "I almost threw up at some parts—the idea that my children were going to hear this. It was the introduction of things at a *very* early age—the issue of anal sex, explicit language regarding sexual intercourse."[1] The central board voted 4-to-3 to bar a video, *AIDS, Just Say No*, that they had funded in 1987 and that had been used in New York City schools ever since. In addition they voted to bar a pamphlet issued by the New York City Department of Health, which contained sexually explicit information and whose intended audience was young people not in school, largely made up of homeless youth and young sex-workers.[2] The disgust at which the above-mentioned board member reacted to information on sexuality is a reminder that sex does not have a certain place in education, is not a legitimate area of study, even in an epidemic that disproportionately affects New York City youth.

In addition, the board's decision to limit information provided to youth without parents, on the grounds informed by their parental discomfort at sexual information, neglects to recognize the specific needs of those young people, many of whom are sex workers. Fernandez was deeply concerned that this vote would open the way for the central board to act as censors of AIDS educational materials, though board member Petrides assured Fernandez that further decisions would be left to the chancellor.[3] Though the board's decision was based on its desire to keep in compliance with New York State law that had, since 1987, called for public school AIDS programs to stress abstinence, the timing of its decision was years late. Chancellor Fernandez's supporters presumed that the vote was intended by conservative board members to water down the effect of Fernandez's plan to make condoms available through public high school health resource rooms.

The conservative board members, now with a majority on the board, were no longer willing to see curricular materials that even presented abstinence as one in a range of options for safety. The banned video did not specifically use the word "abstinence," nor did the video argue that abstinence was the most effective means of protection against HIV, but neither did the video advocate for teen sex. In explaining how teens should negotiate their sex lives under threat of HIV, one person in the video suggests, "It just means it's better to wait, that's all, until there's a cure or a vaccine. I'm not planning on having sex until I get married."[4] The banned Health Department pamphlet, *Teens Have the Right*, had been distributed to groups working with runaways and dropouts and had not been designed for public school use.[5] However, excerpts from this pamphlet also are not as anti-abstinence as the board vote suggested: "If you don't want to have sex, you don't have to. If you want to get close, you can try other things that feel good and are safe like hugging, holding, kissing and touching. Use your imagination!"[6] However, the pamphlet did provide specific information on how to have safer sex, if teens decide to.[7] Thus, the banned pamphlet attempted to cover a range of possibilities for students to consider, from refusal of intercourse to alternatives to intercourse to refusal of any sexual activity. Rather than constituting a strict prohibition, the video and the pamphlet encouraged students to examine the complexity of their sexuality and make considered judgments on how to proceed with more safety.

Despite the quarreling between the central board and the schools chancellor, according to revised state policy, the final determination of curricular materials' appropriateness still lay with the local districts' advisory boards. As with the squabble over the Rainbow curriculum, this battle about authority over curricular decisions belonged to neither the central board nor the chancellor. The debates on the central board level, then, were largely symbolic.

Regardless of the finer points of policy, the central board adopted a series of rules that would eventually be incorporated into an oath that outside educators would be required to sign before being allowed to do AIDS education in New York City public schools.[8] The rules stipulated that:—All written and oral instruction relating to AIDS prevention must stress that abstinence is the most appropriate premarital protection against AIDS, and no such instruction shall ever portray abstinence and "protected sex" as equally "okay."

Whenever students are assembled for classroom or other instruction relating to AIDS prevention, the written and oral instruction presented to them on that occasion must devote substantially more time and attention to abstinence than to other methods of prevention.

All written or oral instruction relating to AIDS prevention must emphasize that no other mode of prevention can provide the same 100 percent protection against H.I.V. infection as abstinence and must fully and clearly disclose the various risks and consequences of condom failure.

No outside organization or individual shall be allowed to take part in any aspect of any New York public school's AIDS education program unless such organization or individual has furnished the Chancellor a signed written agreement that such organization or individual will comply with each of the foregoing rules.[9]

The final provision, known as the Abstinence Oath raised the hackles of outside educators, many of whom were concerned that their range of educational options, particularly those directed at sexually active students, would be severely curtailed.[10]

Critical of the central board's unwillingness to face up to the risk HIV posed for adolescents, Manhattan Borough President Ruth W. Messinger joined in the Civil Liberties Union suit against the board and asked Dinkins to join the city to the suit as well.[11] Fernandez contended that, taken as a whole, the city's AIDS curriculum did meet the state policy's requirement on abstinence and that, once again, the central board was attempting to micromanage the city's schools by requiring that each individual lesson stress abstinence.[12] Fernandez supporters hoped that the board would back down from a policy that would mean a dramatic drop off in the number of outside agencies willing to participate in the city's AIDS education program requiring an oath.[13]

A compromise proposal was offered by Petrides and Impellizzeri that would have required that the total time spent on abstinence in lessons about AIDS prevention be greater than the total time spent on other methods of prevention. Rather than requiring that each piece of educational material individually stress abstinence, the compromise only required that the overall message of each lesson stress abstinence.[14] Petrides and Impellizzeri's lawyer, wrote the compromise and likened the stance on abstinence to a horse race, "If two horses are racing down the track from September through June, the abstinence horse always had to be a lot further ahead than the condom horse."[15] The conservative board members also announced that they were willing to revise their earlier resolution to restore harmony on the board.[16] However, amidst the claim of interest in harmony, the central board banned additional AIDS educational materials, in contradiction to Petrides's promise to Fernandez that additional decisions would be left up to the chancellor. A pamphlet from the Gay Men's Health Crisis containing information on how to avoid HIV during homosexual sex and a syllabus published by the Hetrick-Martin Institute for Gay and Lesbian Youth were banned.[17] These materials were not used by teachers but rather by outside educators. Both of these materials supported the decision of students to be sexually active, were specific about safer sexual practice and provided nonrisky alternatives that did not require penetration or exchange of bodily fluids. That board members found these materials addressed to gay students offensive marked but a short step from deciding that inclusion of any gay-related curricular material was offensive—a step already being taken at the local board level.

In a continuing effort at compromise on the AIDS curriculum, Fernandez drafted a revision to the AIDS curriculum that removed references to contraceptive cream and anal intercourse from the fourth and fifth grade AIDS curricula, as well as references to cleaning needles and syringes.[18] In the end, the curriculum was passed with condom references still in fourth grade, more abstinence language throughout the guide, and a change in a sixth-grade lesson on drug abuse, discussed in chapter 5. The lesson had begun: "Michael and Bill have gone out together for a year." It was changed to read: "Michael and Bill are very close friends."[19] The reference to two young men involved with one another was not related to a lesson on sex. In the lesson, Michael is afraid that Bill is being pressured by his friends to smoke crack. That the central board found inappropriate such an example, when they had just released a multicultural curriculum that included teaching tolerance of gays and lesbians, was another early indication that the board was not united on the Children of the Rainbow curriculum.

With much enmity on either side of the debate over the oath, the central board, with some liberal members absent and Fernandez out of town, called a special meeting and passed its own version of the oath. It included a rationale that alluded to the fact that contractors doing business with the city had to sign an oath that they would abide by minimum wage and antidiscrimination laws.[20] This rationale attempts to parallel omissions on information about safer sex with nondiscrimination issues, underscoring the board majority's view that information parents would deem in contradiction to religious teachings was discriminatory whereas omitting specific information on sexual activity and homosexuality was not, in the board's opinion, discriminatory.

Despite the board's attempt to normalize drastic limits on what teachers and AIDS educators could discuss (or in what proportion) by positioning education as a regular business transaction between the city and an outside contractor, protests quickly mounted. A spokesperson for 200 of the city's AIDS education groups, Terry Lewis, said that most of the groups would not sign the pledge. She argued that the central board was entirely out of touch with the realities of adolescent sexuality; estimates held that 80 percent of adolescents in New York City had had sexual intercourse.[21] Health Commissioner Dr. Margaret A. Hamburg said that she would not require Health Department employees who worked in public schools to sign the oath, instead she would find them places where they could conduct their educational programs outside of public schools.[22] Hamburg had Dinkins's support for this decision and it gave him further opportunity to express his displeasure with the board's decision.[23] Petrides and Impellizzeri declared that the "rebellion" convinced them that there had been a problem in trusting that outside educators would follow state policy. Impellizzeri wondered, "Do they really want to cover up the dangers of condom failure?"[24]

This question ignores the main reason for condom failure: human error, either in neglect of proper usage or through an inability to negotiate condom use with a partner or inability to access condoms easily. The question further implies, as does the oath, that abstinence does not fail. A simple pledge by educators sidesteps difficult questions students may have and a simple decision by students to remain abstinent is definitionally secure. Each of these pledges is treated by conservatives as providing a more certain answer to the problem of HIV than the range of solutions and understandings of identity that were articulated through banned curricular materials. The banned videos and pamphlets each stressed a range of possible activities, including abstinence, for students particularly at risk for HIV. By suggesting this range and emphasizing the need for each person to assess their risk, take responsibility for their own safety, and negotiate with their partners, these banned materials invited students into critical examination of the knowledges they would need to protect themselves and their partners from HIV. Thus, the act of speaking about sex was left to students who had been exposed to a range of options. After the institution of the oath, the message of the abstinence regulation became the message of the teachers, which was supposed to be uncritically passed onto the students who would equally uncritically apply it to their lives.

Faced with objections from educators concerned about the limits placed on their teaching ability, conservatives declared that they would not "budge on the issue—even if no one signed the pledge." Thus the conservative members of the central board were willing to defend abstinence even if it meant an end to public health providing AIDS education to New York City's schools. The debate over the oath also confirmed conservative suspicions that educators were stepping around state regulations on AIDS education. In effect, the oath underscored New York State's regulations on AIDS curriculum, but the public nature of the oath and the weight of the obligation entailed by taking the oath pushed the unspoken abrogation of regulation into the public eye. The oath only underscored the already existing suspicions about AIDS educational materials—permitting talk of sex in schools indicated information was already beginning to spin out of the control of parents and the state. Taken together with Fernandez's plan for condom distribution and the Children of the Rainbow curriculum, the sexual mores of city schools appeared to many to be changing in a comprehensive and frightening manner. The hope that an oath would bring this information back under control had embedded within it a theory of education that could see knowledge as bounded by authority. If the schools could be made to stop addressing sex, condoms, and homosexuality, the issues might recede from public view.

In contrast, educators were concerned that students, already partially aware of these topics, would become suspicious that these issues were not being forthrightly addressed. Outside educators objected that they would not be able to answer student questions about sexual activity, without having to continually remind students to be abstinent. Educators feared that this sort of double message would undermine their lessons on safer sex. In addition, by limiting what topics educators could raise in lessons, the burden of finding out information on specific sexual matters fell to the students. Like other "gag orders" on education, the Abstinence Oath required students to know enough about what they were ignorant about to ask questions. But in order to keep in compliance with the balance of education required by the city, educators could not spend their time attempting to teach students the specifics of safer sex. The publicity generated by the controversy over the oath may have had the effect of warning students that what they would hear in lessons would not be the full story, further undermining educators' ability to gain students' trust and confidence.

The oath also had the effect of bringing the concern about student sexuality and sex education into the public, through the spoken or written requirement attending the provision of AIDS education. The oath does make clear that sex is at the base of discomfort over AIDS education. By bringing this discomfort clearly to the fore, the oath attempts, by instituting an initial moment of pledging not to speak about sex, a series of curricular moments where sex will not be spoken of, all of which are marked by the presence of sex as this central concern. Sex does not recede from, but rather more concertedly haunts, the educational project. Indeed, the unspoken (or underspoken) presence of the central concern of AIDS education begins to undermine the educational aspects of that curriculum. An education predicated on the absence of information does not generate confidence in either students or teachers.

Secondary Virginity

The turn to "secondary virginity" in abstinence-only sex education also serves to publicly mark out what is absent in discussion. In the case of pledges of virginity, curricula also open up spaces in schools for a different kind of sexuality, one that requires public assertion of its practice. Like the missing topics opened by the abstinence oath for educators, public avowals of virginity are reminders of the extent to which even a virgin identity is a sexual identity. Further, like the collision of meanings and conflicts that characterize much of the discussion about sexuality in public schools, secondary virginity is also strongly implicated in broader social issues. Where the abstinence oath for educators in New York City shows the conflicts over school authority, this analysis of secondary virginity will illuminate the link between abstinence-based sex education, welfare reform, and normative conceptions of gender, showing that even allegiance to heterosexuality requires substantial work and opens possibilities for multiple definitions and practices.

Secondary virginity is a concept advocated by conservative abstinence-based sex education curricula, including *Sex Respect*,[25] a federally funded sex education program that encourages students, even if sexually active, to return to abstinence and reclaim secondary virginity. Originally funded by the Adolescent Family Life Act of 1981 and the recipient of federal funds for revisions in 1990, *Sex Respect* is among the federally funded abstinence programs attached to religious organizations. In at least one instance, it has been pulled from schools for its sexist content and inaccurate information.[26]

Secondary virginity, the decision to discontinue sexual activity—of all varieties from necking to any form of intercourse—is a concept that carries strong overtones of religious redemption and reconciliation. Attempts in the popular media to trace its origins appear to make secondary virginity a recent, reasonable response to the excesses of the sexual revolution and the relatively new scare of AIDS. In fact, abstinence curricula, including *Sex Respect* and its oft-imitated secondary virginity, were developed as a result of the 1981 Adolescent Family Life Act—well in advance of AIDS and more closely related in time to Reagan and the Religious Right. Nor is this particular version of sex education without historical precedent. Sex education has always been overwhelmingly in favor of abstinence; the "white banner" campaigns at the turn of the century, for instance, had young social purity women approach men, asking them to pledge themselves to sexual restraint.[27] Campaigns for sexual purity also encouraged the National Education Association to recommend that sex education be offered in all public schools. Similarly to what I will argue about *Sex Respect*, early-twentieth-century campaigns enlisted the energies of young women who approached young men on the street to urge them into sexual restraint. This is fairly remarkable as the target of such campaigns was the sort of young man who would approach a young woman for sexual favors (and young women who would "date" for treats and meals). So the tactics of sex hygiene campaigns in part mimicked the very social problem they were seeking to eliminate. In other words, to protect young women from the increasing publicity of sex, advocates of sexual purity sent young women out into the public to convert young men to abstinence.

Welfare Reform and Sexual Abstinence

I want to be different from other girls. I want a guy to look at me in another way . . . I see girls getting into trouble, and I don't want to get hurt. I *want* to be a virgin.

—Betsy[28]

The girls who laughed at me in high school because I was a virgin . . . are now working at a Kmart counter. . . . When people say to me, "You've missed something," I say, Yeah, I missed worrying about being pregnant and getting some STD and . . . dying of AIDS.

—Lakita Garth[29]

According to *Newsweek* in 1994, virginity came back in vogue, no longer taught "with a yawn and a wink," even having the support of President Clinton, whose $400 million campaign against teenage pregnancy turned "virginity into a matter of public health, not just private morality."[30] This move was yet another indication that Clinton was not as progressive as he might have appeared. His support for virginity came one short year after Focus on the Family's "1993 Year in Review" reported that Clinton had "gutted the . . . tiny amount of money for the teaching of abstinence. The funds were diverted into 'safe-sex' programs promoting condom usage."[31] Despite these conservative complaints, the "tiny" amount of money in support of abstinence education was, in 1991, 5.2 million dollars; estimates for 1992, 7.7 million; for 1993, 9 million.[32] In this context of support for abstinence, Surgeon General Elders's brief attempt at steering the federal government's sponsorship of sex education into an emphasis on safer sex and support for masturbation led to her removal from office. Within a few short years, abstinence education became a centerpiece in the war against welfare, as provisions for abstinence education were folded into the gentle-sounding "Personal Responsibility and Work Opportunity Reconciliation Act of 1996," eventually amended to provide over 250 million dollars for abstinence education (5 million more than Clinton had requested).[33]

The complexity of meaning attached to virginity for the young girls quoted above are reminders of the links among sexuality, economic status, and gender. Virginity, for young girls like the above-quoted Betsy, is a way out of the stresses and risks of heterosexual relationships, particularly in an era when parental notification laws make abortion less accessible to young women. But her strategy necessitates avoiding sex because sex leads to the consequences of disrespect from boys, getting in trouble, and getting hurt. Betsy's definition of sexual activity lacks birth control or protection from HIV, and seems to derogate female sexuality. For Lakita Garth, the next woman quoted, the consequences of sexual activity result in a drop in class status. Sexual activity leads to "working at Kmart," again a consequence that covers over the possibility of sexual activity that does not lead to unintended pregnancy. For Focus on the Family, virginity is an embattled concept in an increasingly non-traditional world. Apparently, for Republicans and Democrats alike, virginity/abstinence is one of the keys to successful welfare reform. The welfare reform act included substantial provision of federal funds to support abstinence education "with a focus on those groups which are most likely to bear children out of wedlock."[34] Included in drafts of the act are an array of statistics pointing to the link between single motherhood and poverty, the rising rate of illegitimacy among black Americans, rates of black male criminal activity among young men raised by single mothers, and the rate of criminal activity in neighborhoods with a greater incidence of single-parent households.[35] Rather than focusing concern on the relationship between poverty itself and criminal activity, these statements link single motherhood, and also female sexual activity, with criminality and social decay. In addition, by focusing attention on black family dynamics and configurations without regard to the class context, the statistics strongly imply that African-American sexuality is at the root of the problems of crime and welfare.

Thus the welfare reform's oft-cited black teenage single mother on welfare becomes an occasion to remind all children that "abstinence from sexual activity outside marriage [is] the expected standard for all school age children" and that "a mutually faithful monogamous relationship in the context of marriage is the expected standard of human sexual activity."[36] This policy indicates the willingness of states and the federal government to harness education to the task of normalizing populations, particularly in encouraging students to see the link between sex and money, and encouraging them to "[attain] self-sufficiency before engaging in sexual activity."[37] But nowhere in any of this provision for sexuality education is an attempt to describe sexual activity that does not lead to unintended pregnancy. Sexual activity, not the potentially negative attendant consequences, is the focus of the welfare reform act's provision for abstinence education.

Nancy Fraser argues that AFDC rules installed the state as patriarch of women on welfare. She contends that the differential forms of state support for single men and single women with children conform to dominant social notions of how men and women ought to be treated. Men, she argues, even when in need of support from the state, are conceived as independent, formerly wage-earning, autonomous individuals who ought to be able to spend their money as they see fit and are thus given monetary aid directly. Women, on the other hand, are treated as if they were part of the state's "household." Not to be trusted with cash, they are given food stamps and directed how to spend their aid by the "public patriarchy." Further, their sex lives are watched over by the state, reinscribing cultural understandings of women as sexually irresponsible.[38]

The recent national focus on the problem of single, black mothers on welfare as the central problem of welfare reform reinforced these same ideas about women's irresponsible sexuality, as did the Hyde Amendment's refusal of federal funds for lower-income women's abortions. Parental notification laws limiting young women's access to abortion send the same messages about women's sexual irresponsibility. Indeed, part of the rise in pregnancy among unmarried women is due to the implementation of parental notification laws discouraging young women from obtaining abortions. Thus, policy bent on decreasing teen pregnancy, by decreasing teen access to abortions, has had the effect of adding to the teen pregnancy rate. The rise in the teen pregnancy rate has then been used to justify further policy decisions to emphasize abstinence education and further limit young women's access to information on abortion, since agencies that receive federal funding for sexuality education must not provide information on abortion and must stress ab-stinence. Nowhere does welfare policy recognize that young women need access to more birth control and means to protect themselves from HIV and other STDs. In short, the "public patriarchy" once again demands chastity from those women over whom it watches.

These abstinence-based programs are not new, but, coupled with welfare reform, their problematic effects are more strongly attached to the creation of an ideal female sexual subject whose demonized opposite is the aforementioned black pregnant teen on welfare. In addition, their claims to "education" are dubious as they discourage critical, educational engagement with the subject of sexuality. Instead, these abstinence programs continue the influence of the Religious Right through "gag orders" on sexuality education—by limiting the topic to abstinence and by their continued prohibition of discussions of or referrals to abortion services.[39]

But the uses to which secondary virginity is put are often far from the original conservative, religious intentions. It is worth considering why secondary virginity seems to make sense to conservatives, and how it may work as a reminder to progressive sex educators that their own curricula are a little coy when it comes to articulating values. More important, it is useful to consider how adolescent girls may find secondary virginity an approach to sexuality in ways that conservatives would not fully approve.

But first, a little background: only a few years ago, the Religious Right made a concerted effort to control school boards with the intention of bringing America's schools back into the fold and socializing American youth to understand this as a Christian country. However, the Religious Right was already faced with difficulty making connections with other conservatives who did not share their religious beliefs. The Christian Coalition, in particular, made a conscious decision to alter their agenda to accommodate secular conservatives and to frame their political message within the discourse of liberalism rather than evangelism. The importance of "choice" and "morality" overshadowed earlier talk of "sin" and "adherence to God's law." Thus in local elections, many school board candidates were silent about their religious affiliations and intentions and became known as "stealth" candidates. Once on school boards, they came out as Christian and tried to align public school

curricula with Christian teaching, particularly in the area of sex
education, prayer in schools, and adding creationism to classes on
evolution (or supplanting evolution altogether).

As outrightly and simply conservative as this seems to be, in some
cases, the rhetorical shift toward liberalism affected the substance of
their message and what may have started as a strategy to gain influence
altered attitudes of other members of the Right as well. At least it made
them rethink and repackage their message to make it accessible to others
and to fit it within a framework of tolerance and choice. For instance,
Second Thoughts, a video based on the *Sex Respect* curriculum, offers
Christian and non-Christian versions. Sex Respect itself takes pains to
explain that it has no desire to advocate a particular religious belief and
that all religions value sexuality and love, as do nonreligious people. In
other words, projects that began as firmly religious may now be
grounded in religion, but they are driven by their own conservative,
potentially secular momentum as well. But to maintain the ambivalence
of their religious roots and their liberal upbringing, I want to avoid
reading secondary virginity as purely part of a discourse of religious
redemption and begin to account for its ability to open new possibilities
for public speaking about desire.

Uncertain Definitions of Sex

Beyond the social legitimacy to which secondary virginity may give
students access, I want to account for the popularity of secondary
virginity because of other, potentially conflicted, social forces and
discourses. Secondary virginity appears to be useful to adolescent girls
for reasons not fully accounted for by the original intention of its authors.
Yet, there is reason to be ambivalent about the subversive potential of
secondary virginity. Discourses of the New Right might be seen as
empowering by those teenagers taking them up, but it is important to also
see the normalizing force of these discourses that reinscribe a very
particular conception of femininity and female sexuality. So there is
something progressive about *Sex Respect*'s idea of fluid identities and its
recognition of the ability to reconfigure the body by altering practices.
But the coercive mechanisms that enforce one way of being an
empowered woman are troubling, particularly when that "way" is based
on a lack of knowledge, not a variety of knowledges and practices.

Part of the popularity of secondary virginity is related to the
instability of the term "sexually active." A Brigham Young University
review of studies on teen sexual activity has recently argued that
estimates of teen sexual activity have been exaggerated based on a mis-

definition of "sexually active." The review's authors claim that many of the teens counted as "sexually active" have, in fact, only had sex once, and having had sex one or more times does not mean that they are "sexually active." Indeed, the authors further argue, this limited definition of sexual activity, implying that once teens have had sex they will inevitably have sex again, discourages teens from abstinence by implying that they can no longer rightfully claim "virgin" status. The authors contend that this is a dangerous limitation to put on young people's sexual choices and that curricula would do well to encourage even those students who had had sex to reconsider and achieve "secondary virginity."[40]

Of course, adolescents perpetually reinvent themselves; indeed, the reinvention attending "secondary virginity" follows much the same logic as teens who claim "monogamy for the weekend." A continuing complaint among AIDS educators is that students have seemingly idiosyncratic definitions of "sex," "monogamy," and "virginity," as well as other key terms involved in sex and AIDS education. A few confusions involve the time span of monogamy; according to some teens, it can last a weekend and "monogamously" involve another partner for the next weekend, and so on. In addition, for some teens "virginity" appears to be a concept entirely centered around the vagina, specifically in the context of heterosexual intercourse. In order to then maintain their virginity but still engage in sexual activity, girls have unprotected anal intercourse. Clearly in neither of these two examples are the intentions of curricula reflected in the meanings students take from curricula. But it should be clear from the neglect of curricula to attend to complex definitions of "sex" that these conclusions are not only the result of teen misunderstandings but also the result of curricular evasions of specificity. Abstinence curricula purport to avoid the sticky business of defining sexuality by maintaining a simple message—don't have sex and if you have already started you can stop.

Sex Respect also recognizes that the "just say no to sex" strategy has produced some of its own problems. Just what is sex? How far can the limits of non-sex be pushed until one is indeed having sex? The curriculum thus advocates a form of virginity considerably more specific than simply avoiding "sex"—a suggestion most often interpreted to mean avoid penile-vaginal intercourse. Virginity in the aforementioned program means going no further than a good night kiss. A table included in the *Sex Respect* curriculum suggests that neither male nor female genitals are aroused by the goodnight kiss, though male genitals are aroused by necking and female genitals are aroused by petting and heavy petting. To avoid any temptation to engage in vaginal-penile intercourse, students are instructed to avoid all activities beyond the "goodnight kiss."[41] *Sex Respect*'s model of sex presumes that boys, and girls, once aroused, will be unable to keep from having vaginal-penile intercourse—even though the curriculum recognizes the pleasurable aspects of necking, petting, and heavy petting. Girls' potential for pleasure without risk is elided by messages intent on protecting them not just from the negative effects of "sex" but also from access to passion. These cautions extend to seemingly nonphysical activities like "cool conversations that get too hot."[42] In addition, the curriculum warns against "sitting around dates" that might "end up in tempting situations."[43] Indeed, *Sex Respect* advocates something like dating promiscuity as it encourages young people to date widely rather than consistently with one person. Girls appear to bear the brunt of blame for temptation as pictures of women are most often situated next to warnings about the kind of clothes one ought to wear: "Watch what you wear: "If you don't aim to please, then don't aim to tease" (and here is a little slippage in the logic to preserve the rhyme as sex, which is large defined as a conveyer of disease is construed as a pleasing activity). Further images of women are positioned next to warnings about one's "internal wardrobe" including the need for "good listening skills," "courtesy," and "conversational skills."[44] Boys' pleasure is the guiding model for what must happen if control over desire is lost. Girls do not have sexual agency in this model, except to the extent that their freedom is protected as in the following, "No petting if you want to be free."[45] In addition, the curriculum taps into girls' lack of satisfaction in sexual relationships, in a cartoon scene one character says, "[Secondary virginity] does sound good, because, to tell the truth, I don't enjoy doing it anyway . . . you know you're right, it is like a trap. I do want to be free. I think I'll choose 'secondary virginity.'"[46] Another gender-related tactic suggested to girls in particular is included in a list, "Twenty-five Ways to Say 'No'": "I spent all week deciding what to wear tonight and three hours getting ready. If you think you are going to mess any of this up, you are sadly mistaken."[47]

Sex Respect's lessons also centralize male agency; three of four longer stories of desire deferred feature boys as the main characters. However, the curriculum suggests that boys might be more comfortable with the term "celibacy," even though, in terms of a dictionary definition, "virginity" refers to abstaining from sex before marriage. But as *Sex Respect* notes, "virginity" is more closely associated with females than it is with males—though the hymen is not specifically mentioned in this passage, the indication is that girls have a closer tie with the term because of its physical implications.[48] *Sex Respect* does acknowledge that girls may be sexually aggressive. One cartoon about girls who will call a celibate boy a "wimp" warns, "A threat to a guy's masculinity is a very sensitive blow. The liberation movement has produced some aggressive girls today, and one of the tough challenges for guys who say no will be the questioning of their manliness. Girls can use lines too!"[49] One of those lines is "What's the matter with you? Are you gay or something?"[50]—the only mention of homosexuality outside of the context of AIDS. Whether directing its message to boys or girls, the curriculum notes the role that standards for masculinity and femininity play in teen sexuality. *Sex Respect* attempts to refigure masculinity by telling young men "it's wrong for a guy to manipulate a girl with lines and use her to reassure himself of his masculinity."[51] In a lesson about restraint of passion in a dating situation, the curriculum echoes feminist concerns in the question "why should a person, particularly a girl, wear clothes which advertise her as a person rather than as a sex object?"[52] While the message that all sexual activity ought to be delayed until marriage clearly excludes the majority of teenagers, including gay and lesbian teens for whom marriage is not an option, the suggestions that teens actively criticize gender roles and expectations may provide surprisingly critical openings for renegotiating identity.

Standards of Beauty and Saying "No"

Young women in particular are engaged in critical evaluation of sex roles, expectations, and standards of bodily beauty that are in part facilitated by secondary virginity. As *Vogue*'s recent article on secondary virginity notes, young girls feel pressure to conform their bodies to standards of beauty and to have their bodies displayed in sex in ways that also conform to idealized images of women engaging in sexual activity. Since these standards are unreachable for most women and since this means that sex, for women, is a performance in which their pleasures and emotions are not present and their bodies are present only as stand-ins for the ideal, sex is largely unappealing. Thus secondary virginity allows these young women a way out of an arrangement that magnifies anxieties they already have about their bodies and appears to give them nothing in return: no pleasure, fear of pregnancy, fear of STDs.[53] As the article points out, these young women:

> Had come of age in a country divided against itself, a country that fairly dripped with sex but one in which abortion was threatened and birth control pills were still not advertised, a country with a deep and enduring ambivalence—some would say antipathy—toward female sexuality and bodies, and these young women had taken it all in. They were obsessed with their own bodies, measuring every pound and blemish against models of perfection they saw in magazines and TV.

And with this preoccupation came a definite shame about being sexual at all, a sense that it was not only dangerous, given all the diseases, but also somehow unseemly for women.[54]

Secondary virginity's appeal is tied to insecurities about bodily appearance and a recognition that female sexuality is not fully socially acceptable. Thus these young women are engaged in close readings of social anxieties and actively involved in remaking what they find to be the key marker of their status, their sexual purity. Secondary virginity, therefore, parallels "technologies of the body" that examine the constructedness of even the materiality of the body. In *Sex Respect*, virginity is not only a state of mind or conscious decision but it is also a refiguring of the body as a result of this state of mind. As one publication puts it:

If you've never heard of the term "secondary virginity," you may chuckle. Once someone has lost their virginity it can't be reversed. But according to Sex Respect, Inc. you can reclaim your life as it was before and decide you're free to pursue other things. The idea is behave like a virgin and . . . wait until you're ready to get married. Maybe there's a parallel between the term "secondary virginity" and what Christians call "being born again," which we all know is a biological impossibility. [55]

The physicality of this refusal of intercourse is underscored by the use of bodily imagery—"virginity" concretizes chastity, "born again" concretizes faith. These particular figures of physicality link the concrete body with thinking and deliberation. This technology of the body is strongly implicated in gender norms and status concerns. Certainly the history of adolescence is quite different for girls than it is for boys. Most of the qualities culturally associated with adolescence are male: rebellion, hotheadedness, explicit sexuality, risk. Adolescent girls, on the other hand, were supposed to remain pure, passive, and obedient. Until the 1970s, most status crimes—acts only designated a crime based on the age of the accused, and punishment for which may last until the person reaches majority—were differentially punished based on gender. Girls tended (and still tend) to be labeled incorrigible for staying out late while boys attained the same label for more serious crimes of robbery or assault.[56] Thus the rambunctiousness of adolescence is less possible for girls, and more likely to elicit a greater degree of punishment. It should not be surprising, then, to find girls recouping status through virginity.

Nor should it be surprising to find that many girls are trying to avoid the accusation of "slut" by refiguring themselves as "virgin." At the same time, they occupy a potentially slutish space in public, that is, they do discuss the intimate details of their lives and desires, they do display their sexuality (even if abstinent). But to engage in the distinctions between virgin and slut reopens the difficulties of balancing pleasure and danger in a context in which both are linked to sex. As they trace the dilemmas feminism has faced over prostitution and sexual activity, DuBois and Gordon look at "how feminist conceptualized different sexual dangers as a means of organizing *resistance* to sexual oppression."[57] They note that reformers all too often demonized the sexuality of fallen women even as they purported to help them and in so doing made a positive notion of sexuality impossible for all women. DuBois and Gordon argue, "In fostering . . . hostility to girls' sexual activity, the feminists colluded in the labeling of a new class of female offenders: teenage sex delinquents."[58] At the same time, DuBois and Gordon are also critical of "pro-sex" feminists who too easily presumed that sexual freedom translated into freedom in general. This appears to be the same dilemma facing young women today, whose choices entail other implied conceptions of gender and freedom. For secondary virgins, sexuality all too often means degradation and disrespect. But rather than challenging social norms for girls' behavior, they flee from behavior that might brand them "slut." They cannot imagine or do not have access to sexual practices and identities that might challenge the discourse of purity that gives them value but is ultimately an impossible ideal, particularly if that purity is something one ultimately has to "give up" to one's husband.

Passionate Avowals

In addition to the personal decision to become a secondary virgin, secondary virginity requires a public declaration marking a commitment to maintain or return to chastity. The sociality of this rededication also parallels the born-again practice of "testifying." This is not a private decision with private implications, but rather it is meant to be shared through testimony. Indeed, these secondary virgins, through a variety of programs like Best Friends, a girls-only organization, share their stories of sex, their fall, and their redemption to shore up and display their return to the fold. Best Friends is also attentive to other aspects of young girls' school success, particularly among lower-income communities of color, by providing adult mentorship, role models, and basic nutrition and health information. Even so, its messages subtly criticize the family structure of many of the girls themselves in the message that "children deserve to begin life with married adult parents."[59] Girls are thus potentially distanced from their own family as they begin to learn the connections between the successes of the idealized two-parent family and the apparently dysfunctional single-parent family. Unlike *Sex Respect,* which instructs students to avoid sex until marriage, Best Friends encourages girls to remain abstinent until after high school; their focus is thus more strongly on educational achievement than marriage. As one mentor described the program, "it's not about sex, [but about] being a child," that is, being able to concentrate on school and childhood activities, not sex.[60] To underscore the necessary contradiction between the terms "youth" and "sexuality" this particular program further argues that virginity itself is good for girls' physical and emotional health. As one Best Friend participant put it: "It was hard to say 'no' until I became a Best Friends girl. I have all these friends that check on me and say 'how you doin'?' One time I was going to go with this guy who had this great 'line' but they wouldn't let me. I'm really glad. . . . We watch out for each other at Best Friends."[61]

What each of these approaches to secondary virginity or abstinence have in common is the production of new social spaces and relationships in which to articulate identity. "True Love Waits" rings to show evidence of a pledge of abstinence, rallies supporting virginity and group homes of girls sharing sex stories well into the night in a near orgiastic display of desire deferred, or more to the point, desire redirected, all mark the new form of sexual identity that accompanies these refusals of sex. This is a Foucauldian frenzy of talking sex under the guise of not talking sex, but also a warning of the stresses that sex puts disproportionately on young girls and their potential strategies for contravening these pressures without giving up sexual identity. The seeming prohibitions of secondary virginity incite negotiations of sexuality, against perceived dangers while still within the realm of pleasures. These girls make sexual identity a centerpiece of their self-conception and their public display of their bodies. They are untouchable, but on view, and they must constantly renew the status of their visible allegiance to virginity. Some of this visibility also marks the role of commodification, as one journalist observed, the abstinent teens browsing the "concession stands and souvenir booths" were "full of desire for more stuff."[62] News coverage of and a recent *Ms.* article on high school girls involved in the Best Friends program and college-age women involved in other commitments to abstinence display the good clean fun of girls getting together in a sexualized atmosphere whose intention is to keep them in a high state of excitement about their virginity.[63]

These examples underscore the social elements of desire and sexuality. As Gagnon and Parker argue, "Rather than asking what internal forces create desire, the questions are, how is desire elicited, organized and interpreted as a social activity? How is desire produced and how is desire consumed? . . . Desire . . . becomes a social rather than an individual phenomenon."[64] Decisions about desire and about the desire to wait are made in the context of repeated social choices and, very often in each of these programs, in a homosocial context. Both the social element and the element of choice are crucial to the particular form these sexual identities take. True Love Waits, *Sex Respect*, and the Best Friends program all centralize choice as a paramount concern for adolescent development. Even in their articulation of "traditional values," these curricula position themselves as a freely made choice in a society they claim increasingly pressures young people to have sex. Thus, the prohibition of sexuality is an active choice in identity-formation that marks the maturity and rationality of the individual. Abstinence is not a presumed quality of adolescent life, but rather a state that requires thought, deliberation, action, and continued commitment.

These examples show that identity can be created through productive refusals and it is crucial to ask why "nine out of ten of the girls under sixteen surveyed by a teen services program at Atlanta's Grady Memorial Hospital 'wanted to learn how to say no.'"[65] Certainly saying "no" is compatible with a critical, educational approach to sex education and the crucial difference between an educational approach and a conservative approach is that education should give girls and boys access to resources and strategies that encourage them to make real, considered choices. The implicit norm in conservative curricula, however, is not choice, but "be a good girl (or boy)." Understanding one's sexual identity as fluid, then, in conservative curricula is not meant to question socially prescribed sexual subject positions for girls and women, but rather to reinscribe them. However, even as conservatives attempt to stem the tide of adolescent sex, they inadvertently create new spaces and new varieties of adolescent sexual identity—varieties produced out the refusal of sex.

These identity formations and spaces draw attention to the persistent alterations of sexual meanings and practices that occur despite "gag rules" in classrooms and curricula. As such they serve as reminders that students are actively involved in the articulation of their identities in spaces not often recognized by curricula as "sexual." The identities incited by the oath taking and testifying festivals of secondary virginity point to the centrality of context and relationships to sexual identity and understandings. The spaces for articulating and contesting identity entailed by curricula and curricular debate are places where identity is enacted. Students do not come to places and relationships as fully formed in their sexual identity, but rather, through discursive meanderings, they change and alter their practices and the meanings of those practices. As thrilling in their libidinal excess as these spaces and identities are, they also multiply dangers. Without information and strategies to encourage protection from HIV and STDs, contraception, and sexuality in general, these spaces of sexual identity are quite problematic. These difficulties are inherent in educational programs whose intent is to limit and even prohibit the discussion of sexual information. These prohibitions broaden and mark new spaces in which to consider and discuss identity but also neglect the level of specific information students need to negotiate their identities and relations. While *Sex Respect*'s secondary virginity oath for students attempts to use a simple pledge to stem the tide of complex sexual meanings and practices, it also highlights public aspects of sexuality, even potentially against its own intentions. But it also provides students with little information about safer sex beyond:

> Remember . . . when a person has a sexual relationship, they are having contact with everyone their partner has had sex with! If anyone has been exposed to AIDS . . . it has been nice knowing you. So long![66]

Thus an extremely dangerous effect of curricula advocating secondary virginity is that they spend all their energy on encouraging students to take oaths but little energy on considering what students ought to do should the oath fail them. The actual taking of an oath, as a public statement, is meant to create an obligation, even a contract, between students. An oath uses words to prevent action in the hopes that public declaration will be enough to guarantee compliance, obligation, and, assuming the oath to be kept, bodily safety. But at the same time, oaths mark out what is not said. The oath, then, highlights the inappropriateness of what was potentially possible to be said about sexuality. In short, the oath highlights the gaps that will be contained in the lessons given to students after the oath is taken. This strategy makes an assumption regarding identity: one is what one says one will do. A student who says no will abstain from sex and will remain protected from HIV. A couple who marries will have waited until marriage for sex and will remain faithful thereafter and will remain protected from HIV. In neither of these scenarios do complications of identity, activity, context, or meaning invade the safety of spoken words and the identities and activities that must flow from them.

Remaking Bodies and Sex

As Judith Butler has argued, "To claim that discourse is formative is not to claim that it originates, causes, or exhaustively composes that which it concedes; rather, it is to claim there is no reference to a pure body which is not at the same time a further formation of that body"[67] This helps as a reminder that concerns for purity—sexual or otherwise—suppose an interest in and a recognition of the pervasiveness of impurity and desire. So the discourse of secondary virginity presumes that subjects are tempted to make things with and through bodies and simply suggests another—equally productive—thing to do. This neither ends the preoccupation with bodies nor with desire. But secondary virginity does suggest that bodies may be made different, that is, formerly open to temptation they may be made into seemingly material boundaries against desire. And this may be the crucial difference between calls for virginity or purity that evoke or performatively re-create boundaries and those which excise the supposed stuff of desire: desire is still present behind the boundary. In the case of secondary virginity, while concrete bodily alteration is evoked, the remade boundary is quite clearly and repetitively discursive. The quest for a return to fictive purity is a quest that can also be generalized to the impossibility of control of bodies. This is not to suggest that desire is natural and will always out, but that the kind of rationalized control behind secondary virginity is an impossible aim, especially in the context of education in which critical thinking and feeling subjects will interact with the lessons. The version of the story of sexuality in conservative sex education curricula is itself suspect for wanting to install too much control at the level of bodies and desire to accomplish a task (prevention of STDs, pregnancy, AIDS) that does not require such a level or locus of control. That is, students do not need to completely make over their bodies in order to decide to protect themselves.

In addition, curricula advocating secondary virginity not only suggest that there is a normative body but that only that normative body can ethically engage with others. This puts a double burden on non-conforming, nonrededicated virgins: their bodies are out of control and they are definitionally incapable of ethical behavior. So curricula advocating secondary virginity do a few things to bodies: first, they clearly brings bodies into education as a reminder that there are, in fact, concrete, material bodies in school. In addition, they are reminders about the extent to which bodies are made as much as simply present. Indeed, they may push the limits of the body as preexisting well beyond their intention and instead give a fully normative and discursive account of the body. This move may also have the effect of pulling secondary virginity's ontological and normative ground out from underneath itself. In other words, its slip is showing. The message, in the end, is that ethics requires a particular formation of body that itself requires a continued recourse to discursive support because, oddly, the body itself is not a thing, but a series of acts and relations. Thus the attempt to return students to a pure body leaves them fully mired in discourse that must continually assert that body that cannot exist without their efforts at describing and thus instantiating it.

What is most interesting about young women's (and no doubt young men's) interaction with the curricula is their continued use and refiguring of the lessons. They do remake themselves, refigure their bodies and activities in relation to sexuality. And they may occasionally do so in ways that continue to remake the possibilities. They are at once identifying with the normative constraints but also expanding the ground on which those constraints proceed. For girls whose rededication to virginity is a refusal of commodification of bodies and desires, a discourse of secondary virginity gives them an opening to begin to state their case differently. For students whose desire is not heterosexual, secondary virginity may give them an unintended out. In addition, the pleasure enjoyed by testifying to one's virginity may encourage that the prohibition itself becomes the impetus for one's pleasure. As Butler argues, "the prohibitive law runs the risk of eroticizing the very practices that come under scrutiny of the law."[68] But in the case of students advocating secondary virginity and/or virginity, not only are the sexual practices outlawed potentially eroticized by students but also the very apparatus of the law itself is eroticized. The moment of denying desire becomes a vehicle for stating desire and connecting with others.

But as policies and curricula attempt to have students construct normative bodies, it also implicitly outlines the non-normative body, what is not in the curriculum must be an unthinkable and undesirable body, the desiring and/or sexual active body. As Butler might argue, this curriculum describes which bodies ought to matter and, at the same time, those that do not.[69] For students who do not abstain and for students who do not intend to organize their sexuality around heterosexuality or marriage, conservative curricula do not provide enough information or support. To abstain from sex to minimize risk for pregnancy, HIV, and STDs may usefully mean avoiding sexual activities in which there is an exchange of bodily fluids, but it need not mean abstaining from sexual activities as a whole. Students appear to be using this strategy even in areas in which curricula are abstinence-based. Recent surveys indicate a rise in rates of oral sex among New York City teens, perhaps as a result of fears about HIV and intercourse (the rise includes males and females).[70] But many of these teens refer to oral sex as something one can do when "sex" is too dangerous. By defining oral sex out of the realm of sex they appear to be neglecting the possible risk factors for HIV in oral sex. While schools do provide flavored condoms without lubricant for use in oral sex, few students appear to be using them (schools do not provide dental dams, though one survey indicates that "boys and girls were equally likely to be the receiving partner" in oral sex[71]). Thus, even in their strategies to continue what might be termed sexual activity, if not sex itself, students are using the message of sex education curriculum to frame their activities as "not sex" even as they are engaging in what, post-impeachment, is popularly considered to be "sex." The clear problem is that if what they are doing is not sex then they do not have to worry about the potential for negative consequences associated with sex to be associated with what they are doing. So while these students may be refiguring their bodies and activities to fit an abstinent norm, they are nonetheless exchanging bodily fluids that are potentially risky.

And finally, it may be useful to think of the secondary virginity as "the hyperbolic conformity to the command [that] can reveal the hyperbolic status of the norm itself."[72] In this case, the hyperbolic response of the curriculum may also underscore the hyperbolic cultural reliance on virginity as a marker of ethicality and the hyperbolic use of virginity to denote normative adolescence. That secondary virginity seems a plausible and useful response to many only indicates the degree to which anxieties about young people's sexuality have yet to be adequately addressed, either by policy makers or by young people themselves. Secondary virginity may give them a little breathing room and a way to express their creativity and desires, but without fuller access to a range of options, it also acts as a reminder that a little knowledge is a dangerous thing.

But these identity formations and spaces do draw attention to the persistent alterations of sexual meanings and practices. As such they serve as reminders that students are actively involved in the articulation of their identities in spaces not often recognized by curricula as "sexual." The suspicion incited by the Abstinence Oath and the testifying festivals of secondary virginity point to the centrality of context and relationships to sexual identity and understandings. The spaces for articulating and contesting identity entailed by curricula and curricular debate are places where identity is enacted. Students do not come to places and relationships as fully formed in their sexual identity, but rather through discursive meanderings that change and alter their practices and the meanings of those practices. However, when curricula lag behind these identity and postidentity practices, they are less able to address the kinds of concerns students may have about sexuality.

Notes

Earlier versions of this chapter were published as "Gagged and Bound: Sex Education, Secondary Virginity and the Welfare Reform Act." *Philosophy of Education 1998*, edited by Steve Tozer, (Urbana, IL: Philosophy of Education Society, 1999), 309-317 and "Secondary Virginity and Passionate Disavowals: The Mended Body in Abstinence Education" in *Body Movements*, edited by Svi Shapiro and Sherry Shapiro, (Cresskill, New Jersey: Hampton Press, 2002), 167-186.

1. Segarra quoted in Stephen J. Dubner. "The New Team: The Education of Ninfa Segarra," *New York Magazine*, 17 January 1994, 28. Segarra's comment echoes the overlap between the AIDS curriculum and the Children of the Rainbow curriculum that occurred during public controversies over each. Information in the AIDS curriculum addressed the definition of anal intercourse in later elementary school years, while Children of the Rainbow introduced gay and lesbian families to children in kindergarten. She may have meant that kindergarten was very early to be discussing anal intercourse, though the curriculum does not do so. However, if she considered fourth or fifth grade too early, research indicates that she is incorrect. Because the large numbers of people who develop AIDS in their twenties were likely exposed to HIV in their teens, many educators and public health authorities recommend beginning AIDS education in the elementary years. See Mary E. Walsh and Roger Bibace, "Developmentally–based AIDS/HIV Education," *Journal of School Health* 60, no. 6 (1990): 256–261. Walsh and Bibace, using developmental psychology research on children's understanding of illness, argue that children ages five to seven have vague fears, little understanding of the body's internal workings, and thus need to be reassured of their safety. From ages eight to ten, however, children are more aware of gender roles, sexuality, and have an understanding of causes of illness. Walsh and Bibace suggest introducing "broad categories of prevention," though technical details may be beyond the limits of their understanding. Children at this age, they note, also form prejudices against people with AIDS, tending to blame "homosexuals," "druggies," and "teenagers who do bad stuff" for the disease. From age eleven onward, they advocate fully detailed information on preventative behaviors and transmission. For similar suggestions see also: D. L. Kerr, "Adolescents, AIDS, and HIV: The Future Starts Now," *Journal of School Health* 59, no. 6 (1989): 277–278; Coalition of National Health Education Organizations, "Instruction about AIDS within the School Curriculum: A Position Paper," *Journal of School Health* 58, no. 8 (1988): 323; Centers for Disease Control, "Guidelines for Effective School Health Education to Prevent the Spread of AIDS," *Morbidity and Mortality Weekly Review* 37, supplement 2 (1988): 1–14, among others.

2. James Dao, "School Board Bars Material about AIDS," *New York Times*, 28 May 1992, B1, B7.

3. Dao, "School Board Bars," B1.

4. Quoted in Dao, "School Board Bars," B7. It is troubling that the video encourages students not to *plan* on sex before marriage, when teens who do not plan on having sex tend not to plan for contraception or safer sex.

5. Dao, "School Board Bars," B7.

6. Dao, "School Board Bars," More recently, Chancellor Cortines (who only lasted six months) moved the entire AIDS education offices out of Manhattan and over to Brooklyn in an effort to gain more control over their work. At issue was Gay Men's Health Crisis educational materials that were openly available to participants, including high school students, at an AIDS education conference. In contrast to the moves made by the central school board in 1992, these materials were not supposed to be available to high school students through school-sponsored events. Thus, the Gay Men's Health Crisis was clearly at fault for, at least, having misunderstood who would be attending the conference and Cortines's disapproval could have been predicted. Whether moving the offices to Brooklyn was warranted given the misunderstanding is another issue and one that points to the sort of overreaction, whether because of policy or because of policy enforcers' deep-seated discomfort with the issue of sexuality.

7. Midge Decter, "Homosexuality and the Schools," *Commentary* (March 1993), 25. The pamphlet also includes (thanks here to Decter's copious quoting): "Use a latex condom for any sex where the penis enters another person's body. That means vaginal sex (penis into a woman's vagina, oral sex (penis into the mouth), and anal sex (penis into the butt). Use a dental dam (a thin square of rubber), an unrolled condom cut down one side, or plastic food wrap for oral sex (mouth on vagina) on a woman. Hold it over her vagina to keep her fluids from getting into your mouth." Decter, of course, does not approve and wonders how many New Yorkers would approve of AIDS education done in this way.

8. James Dao, "Critics Decry New AIDS Education Rules as Censorship," *New York Times*, 29 May 1992, B3.

9. Quoted in Dao, "Critics," B3. New York City's lack of effort at preparing teachers to do AIDS education was behind many of these difficulties. Though Fernandez's revision stipulated that teachers receive in-service training on AIDS education, it was expected that this preparation would take a full year. New York City had been doing little to prepare its teachers since 1987 when the state mandated AIDS education and mandated teacher training for AIDS education. If, like many other districts across the country, New York City chose to rely on outside experts then the difficulties the central board was attempting to solve were difficulties partially of their own creation. The majority of the central board had stated discomfort with the issues raised by AIDS education and it is at least this sort of discomfort that inclines districts toward getting outside help. By using outsiders, teachers and administrators can distance themselves from the controversial issues raised and, should parents get stirred up, the school district can either bar the outsiders from coming back or respond to parental complaints by appealing to the expert status of the outsiders.

10. Paul Epstein, "Condoms in Schools: The Right Lesson," *New York Times*, 19 January 1991, 31. Epstein discusses a study by Johns Hopkins in which high school students delayed sexual activity after being taught about condoms.

11. Epstein, "Condoms in Schools," B3.

12. Epstein, "Condoms in Schools," B3.

13. Joseph Berger, "School Board May Alter Sexual Abstinence Policy," *New York Times*, 3 June 1992, B3.

14. Joseph Berger, "New AIDS Plan in Schools: Emphasis on 'No,'" *New York Times*, 4 June 1992, B3.

15. Berger, "New AIDS Plan in Schools," B3.

16. Berger, "New AIDS Plan in Schools," B3.

17. Berger, "New AIDS Plan in Schools," B3.

18. Mary B.W. Tabor, "Fernandez Revises His AIDS Curriculum Proposal," *New York Times*, 24 June 1992, B3. Gresser was absent at the vote, Petrides abstained, Segarra had been pressured by Ferrer to vote for the curriculum, and Impellizzeri had been pressured by Queens borough president Golden (and was under pressure because of a speech she made to a Catholic Club arguing that inner-city families were not moral role models for their children), and thus the curriculum passed.

19. Joseph Berger, "Board Agrees on Teaching about AIDS," *New York Times*, 25 June 1992, B1. This reference was apparently an attempt by the AIDS curriculum developers to adhere to the stipulation that all curricula must reflect diversity, including homosexuality.

20. Berger, "Board Agrees on Teaching about AIDS," B2.

21. Melinda Henneberger, "Educators Fight New York Panel on AIDS Pledge," *New York Times*, 28 August 1992, 1.

22. Henneberger, "Educators Fight AIDS Pledge," 1, B2.

23. Henneberger, "Educators Fight AIDS Pledge," 1.

24. Melinda Henneberger, "Two on Board Defend AIDS Oath," *New York Times*, 29 Aug. 1992, B2.

25. Coleen Mast, *Sex Respect: The Option of True Sexual Freedom* (Bradley, Ill.: Respect, Inc., 1990)

26. Bonnie Trudell and Mariamne Whatley, "Sex Respect: A Problematic Public School Sexuality Curriculum," *Journal of Sex Education and Therapy* 17, no. 2 (1991): 125–140; and Mariamne H. Whatley and Bonnie K. Trudell, "Teen-Aid: Another Problematic Sexuality Curriculum," *Journal of Sex Education and Therapy* 19, no. 4 (1993): 251–271.

27. John D'Emilio and Estelle B. Freedman, *Intimate Matters: A History of Sexuality in America* (New York: Harper & Row, 1988), 153.

28. Michelle Ingrassia, "Virgin Cool," *Newsweek*, 17 October 1994, 60.

29. Lakita Garth quoted in Anne Taylor Fleming, "Like a Virgin, Again," *Vogue*, February 1995, 71.

30. Ingrassia, "Virgin Cool," 60.

31. James C. Dobson, "1993 in Review," Focus on the Family webpage (reference to an amendment to Title XX of the Public Health Service Act).

32. U.S. Congress, House of Representatives, Committee on Energy and Commerce, *Adolescent Family Life Amendments of 1990*. 101st Congress, 2nd sess, 1990.

33. U.S. Congress, Senate, Committee on Appropriations, S. 1061, 105th Congress, Action as of 24 July 1997, LEGI–SLATE Report for the 105th Congress, 21 Oct. 1997.

34. H.R. 3734 "Personal Responsibility and Work Opportunity Reconciliation Act of 1996," Sec. 912, 104th Congress, 2nd sess., 1996. This act became PL 104-327, popularly known as the Welfare Reform Act.

35. H. R. 4, sec. 100. 104th Congress, 1st sess., 1995.

36. H.R. 3734, sec. 510(b)(2). 104th Congress, 2nd sess., 1996.

37. H.R. 3734, sec. 510(b)(2). 104th Congress, 2nd sess., 1996.

38. Nancy Fraser, "Women, Welfare and the Politics of Needs Interpretation," *Unruly Practices: Power, Discourse, and Gender in Contemporary Social Theory* (Minneapolis: University of Minnesota Press, 1989), 144–160.

39. Ronald K. Bullis, "'Gag Rules' and Chastity Clauses: Legal and Ethical Consequences of Title X and the AFLA for Professionals in Human Sexuality," *Journal of Sex Education and Therapy* 17, no. 2 (1991): 91.

40. Joseph A. Olsen, Stan E. Weed, and Gail M. Ritz, "The Effects of Three Abstinence-based Sex Education Programs on Student Attitudes toward Sex Education," *Adolescence* 26 (Fall 1991): 631–641.

41. Mast, *Sex Respect*, 7.

42. Mast, *Sex Respect*, 82.

43. Mast, *Sex Respect*, 83, 82.

44. Mast, *Sex Respect*, 82

45. Mast, *Sex Respect*, 30.

46. Mast, *Sex Respect*, 89.

47. Mast, *Sex Respect*, 92.

48. Mast, *Sex Respect*, 82.

49. Mast, *Sex Respect*, 85.

50. Mast, *Sex Respect*, 86.

51. Mast, *Sex Respect*, 84.

52. Mast, *Sex Respect*, 87.

53. Anne Taylor Fleming, "Like a Virgin, Again," *Vogue*, February 1995) 71–72.

54. Fleming, "Like a Virgin, Again," 72.

55. Bethany Christian Services webpage, "Abstinence," www.bethany.org/bethany/secondtht.html. n. d., [cited 2 April 1997].

56. Sharon Thompson, *Going All the Way: Teenage Girls' Tales of Sex, Romance, and Pregnancy* (New York: Hill & Wang), 145.

57. Ellen Carol DuBois and Linda Gordon, "Seeking Ecstasy on the Battlefield: Danger and Pleasure in Nineteenth-Century Feminist Thought," in *Pleasure and Danger: Exploring Female Sexuality*, ed. Carole S. Vance (London: Pandora Press, 1989), 31.

58. DuBois and Gordon, "Seeking Ecstasy," 38.

59. Best Friends Foundation pamphlet, 4.

60. ABC News, 19 December 1997.

61. Best Friends Foundation Unofficial Page, http://marian creighton.edu/~scarlett/govt/ n.d., [[cited 2 April 1997].

62. Erica Werner, "The Cult of Virginity," *Ms.*, March/April 1997, 42.

63. Ibid., 40–43.

64. John Gagnon and Richard Parker, "Introduction," in *Conceiving Sexuality: Approaches to Sex Research in a Postmodern World*, ed. John Gagnon and Richard Parker (New York: Routledge, 1995), 13.

65. William Bennett quoted on Sex Respect webpage, www.lochrie.com/sexrespect/GeneralIntro.html n. d., [cited 2 April 1997].

66. Mast, *Sex Respect*, 51.

67. Judith Butler, *Bodies That Matter: On the Discursive Limits of "Sex"*, (New York: Routledge, 1993), 10.

68. Butler, *Bodies That Matter*, 109–110.

69. Butler, *Bodies That Matter*, 16.

70. Tamar Lewin, "Fearing Disease, Teens Alter Sexual Practices," *New York Times*, 5 April 1997, 4.

71. Shuster cited in Lewin, "Fearing Disease," 4.

72. Butler, *Bodies That Matter*, 237.

Conclusion

Curious Alliance

The controversies, policies, and student activity I have described demonstrate the complex way in which sexuality not only splits communities but also forms communities, not only provides a place to attempt to close down school-related conversations about sex but also opens spaces for desire. Sexual identity and practice are more complicated than most school curricula represent and young people continue to form and reform sexual identities and activities. A particularly potent new formation is that of alliances among and between sexual identities as they work to improve school climates in Gay Straight Alliances.

Gay Straight Alliances meet in about 2,000 schools nationwide. They are currently the most prevalent queer-friendly extra-curricular sexuality-related activity, excluding the obvious. In a cultural climate where many still believe homosexuality and bisexuality to be unethical, these alliances of gay, straight, bisexual, transgender, queer, questioning, and heterosexual students are important reminders of the central role of ethics in forming and maintaining communities. Gay Straight Alliances also mark an interesting turn in identity-based political movements. They show how people make associations and find common cause across and through identity categories, despite the limitations of curricula or external social divisions. Alliances are therefore important because they underscore the degree to which identity is a social process of recognition and negotiation. For instance, people are not simply heterosexual: they must act in particular ways or they will be criticized as being "gay" or "queer," they must associate with other socially recognized heterosexuals or their own sexual orientation will be called into question; they must also act in "correctly" gendered ways. Schools have had an important role in providing the space for the creation of the new kind of community and association Gay Straight Alliances create. So too has the curiosity of students been crucial to the formation of these communities formed around sexual identities.

This conclusion will focus on the activities that happen within schools to challenge the limitations of curricula. While conservative challenges to inclusion of information on sexuality has often argued student are not ready for sexual freedom and choice and that sexuality leads to unethical relations between young people, I argue here that sexuality has enabled the growth of caring communities curious about one another's sexuality and curious about their own sexual identities. Further, the communities and identities encouraged by Gay Straight Alliances model ways of interacting with diverse others and remaining open to new possibilities for identity and community that may emerge. While student energy has been the most important motivator for these groups, nonetheless the particular space of school has provided the opportunity for groups to form. After showing how the ideas and practices of Gay Straight Alliances demonstrate some of the central themes of queer theory, I turn to an analysis of the policy that provided the space and student accounts of their experiences in GSAs. I examine the Equal Access Act, which has provided space and time for extra curricular public school groups and which has been particularly important for student associations that interrogate sexuality and sexual norms. Then I turn to accounts of students involved in GSAs, examining how they describe shared querying of normative sexuality and curiosity at possible innovations. What they say will show us that they are deeply aware of the associational element of identity, and very aware of how to navigate the often crushing normalizing power they experience in schools. But without the space in which to examine their lives and relations, the curiosity binding these students would have less opportunity to expand into ethical self- and community-formation.

Queer Theory and Curious Associations

While gay straight alliances may not all have key texts from queer theory on their shelves, they nonetheless engage in practices well in keeping with queer theory's central ideas. Queer theory has helped to blur the lines between identity categories and pointed out the transgressive and progressive potential in all forms of sexual identity, including heterosexuality (straight, but not narrow). In much the way queer theory contends sexuality is indeterminate, in play, and constantly negotiated, student groups made this negotiation and play central to their conversation. Students stress the "querying" aspect of queer, some calling their groups "Gay, Straight, and Questioning Alliance" or "Gay, Straight, Questioning, and Queer Alliance." One Internet site, another kind of a space in which alliances form, describes itself as a "guide to being young, and lesbian, gay, bisexual, transsexual or not-quite-straight."[1] GSAs are made up often of people who have not yet made up their minds about sexuality but are in the midst of "questioning," "coming out," and other processes that they themselves recognize as unfinished. Groups provide these students with an opportunity to share their complications with others, some keeping identity perpetually open, others deciding in a supportive atmosphere that with community it is easier to be a sexual minority. Generally these groups work against the presumption of a clear division between outsiders who care and insiders who need to be cared about. Many groups discourage people from identifying themselves or others with a label, though the groups themselves are clear that people with labels exist and should be respected. A recent meeting of sexual minority students, for instance, began with one student explaining that "lgbt" (lesbian, gay, bisexual, and transgender) students and their allies were welcome. Another student responded by saying, "what about 'c, q, and i' people?" He then explained that he did not want curious, questioning and/or queer, or intersex people to feel left out. Discussion briefly centered on the group's need to be careful to avoid exclusion, as they had only just begun to explicitly include transgender people and had been taken to task for that exclusion last year.

Foucault's conception of subjectivity helps explain the kind of alliance identity these groups understand themselves to share as he explains that subjectivity is derived through relations of power and knowledge, not as static products from a power that comes from above. Rather, subjects and identity categories are themselves effects of power and, in turn, have power effects on one another. His work details how the subject confesses, that is, speaks to and within power. Thus our mechanisms for knowing the truth about ourselves are part and parcel of how subjects are constrained and disciplined under regimes of knowledge, as well as how subjectivity is made possible. In other words, to return to the oft-quoted, "where there is power, there is resistance," normative power produces subject possibilities through the production of discourses that make subject positions possible and then outlines the contours of appropriate positions.[2] But because all subject positions are the production of normative power, Foucault's concept of subjectivity opens the possibility that minority identities are not the only ones that need to be scrutinized. Further, his ethics demands that power relations among subject positions be examined. His concept of subjectivity and identity requires a critical engagement with all terms of identity and with the relationships among people who inhabit and create them.

Thus relations are central to the project of sexual associations and innovations. Even calls for sexual autonomy clearly centralize relations in their projects. For instance, Michael Warner has argued that we need to return to sexual autonomy, privileging individual activities against what he calls the shame of sexual hierarchies. Warner argues that queerness and its attendant autonomy is an ethic "not only because it is understood as a better kind of self-relation, but because it is the premise of a special kind of sociability that holds queer culture together. A relation to others, in these contexts, begins in an acknowledgment of all that is most abject and disreputable in oneself. . . . The rule is: Get over yourself."[3] Thus the seemingly autonomous self is necessarily connected to a community that is also struggling through the pressures of sexual shame and working out its own various non-normative approaches to sexuality. Jeffrey Weeks also argues that autonomy is necessary for liberating morality from constraints on sexual identities and activities. But he also reminds us that even when we embrace autonomy as a political goal, we need the company of others because "the individual can realize his or her freedom only with and through others."[4] Further, difference and an ethic careful and nurturing of difference are central to freedom, so his ethic *requires* a diverse community. Weeks argues that sexual relations, even as we think of them as sites of autonomy, are also sites of "a transcendence of self."[5] Rather than concentrating on developing individual authenticity, we should follow Foucault where "erotic experimentation and the forging of new patterns of relationship become the main focus for the elaboration of an aesthetics of existence, and of ethical values."[6]

Because Gay Straight Alliances work in a context in which students involved may still be questioning their sexuality, all students understand the centrality of sexuality to identity and the push and pull of community bonds. At the same time they may share curiosity and a desire for experimentation, and because the groups are largely concerned with working against homophobia, they also understand the press of normative sexuality works differently for different people and identities. In other words, gay straight alliances understand and simultaneously embody the minoritizing and universalizing conceptions of sexual identity. Minoritizing concepts of sexual identity, according to Eve Sedgwick, suggest that there are a small number of homosexual persons, whose practices are similar to one another and distinct from the heterosexual majority.[7] Universalizing concepts of sexual identity, closely in keeping with Foucault's work on normative power and subjectivity of any kind, show instead the necessary linkages between sexual identities and "the incoherence" and instability at the base of all identity.[8] Negotiating the pull of normative sexuality and the push of innovation and difference, Gay Straight Alliances give us a way to consider the relationality between identity categories and a way to look at those relations as potential points of possibility and conflict. Student-organized groups build a form of associational identity that takes responsibility for the terms of identity, without allowing them to stop the important conversations about how those terms separate people from one another. These alliances help to name differences, maintain relationships, but do not divorce themselves from historical or contemporary problems that attend identity. Instead, they both fall within the problems of identity and attempt to go beyond them, without devolving into ahistorical liberal individualism and without staying in a potentially nonpolitical transgressiveness. Because these alliances require difference, they maintain their ties through an ethical curiosity, not only of what others who are different might be like but what it might mean to be different from what one is at present. So the students involved in these alliances are drawn into ethical relations with others and with other possibilities for themselves.

These groups rely on curiosity to fuel their ethics in a number of different ways. Most obviously, young people are curious about sexuality and find a safe place to critically discuss sexual issues in Gay Straight Alliances, places that they don't find in curricula. In addition, Gay Straight Alliances, like queer identity, are a curious assortment of groups that do not necessarily have more than the press of normalizing power in common. For instance, Gay Straight Alliances are increasingly incorporating analysis and critique of dominant forms of gender as transgender students and their allies work to ensure they are not excluded from communities. Even though sexual orientation may be the central concern for some students, others may find gender expression more pressing. Students who want only to have gay people respected because they are just like heterosexuals are sometimes initially surprised that other students do not want to live their lives as within the dominant bounds of gender. In short, for some, alliances are a place to critique normative sexuality; for others, they are a place to critique normative gender; and, for others, they offer a site for any combination of critique and stability.

By centering curiosity in their ethical project, alliance groups understand the positive value of difference and the possibilities that difference and innovation open up for new forms of identity and relations. While their curiosity may seem wide-eyed and innocent, these students are fully involved in attempting to sort out sexuality or keep sexuality perpetually complex. These curious students are not disconnected tourists in sexual diversity, but rather they are interested community members attempting to sort out the complications to their connections with diverse others and to take care not to exclude others in ways they themselves have been excluded. They also recognize how their understanding of their own identity alters the way they feel they can work against homophobia. As one young woman explained, "Before I came out I was different. I would always be there for everything. I was pro diversity everywhere. You want me to march for lesbians? I'll march for lesbians, I didn't mind being called gay. It didn't affect me When it turned out it did apply to me, I'm not gonna be there."[9] She realized that the ability to be an advocate depended on a level of safety that she no longer felt and that the school community that appeared welcoming was not. Further, she realized that while it seemed like being gay was "accepted but no one talked about it." She noticed "a GSA announcement and then nothing. I knew all the groups that met but never heard anything else about it. Maybe it was more like an invitation to start a club, but it never started." Another young woman realized that her early discomfort about homophobia got her thinking about her own identity. She explained, that in high school "I know one person who was out, I didn't know I was gay." She had a teacher who "always made these offensive jokes and there were always a lot of people laughing. I felt like I was the only person not laughing" and wondered why.[10] Both of these young women recount the beginning of understanding and the need for community, but they remember most vividly the feeling of isolation in school and the lack of space for that community to form.

Space for Sexual Alliance

Sexuality, difference, and innovation pose particular difficulties for the formation of communities, challenging older, more conservative models of community that stress conformity and tradition. Jeffrey Weeks argues that our understanding of ethics needs to be expanded in order to facilitate the recognition of these communities of sexual difference. He advocates the development of the "rights of everyday life,"[11] including the right to difference which "endorses the value of sexual choices and experimentations which enhance individual growth and sexual exploration, while not offending the equal claims and autonomy of involved and consenting others."[12] He also includes "the right to space," which transcends the private/public divide [through] the development of the possibilities for private life through the growth of public opportunities."[13] Without a right to space, the right to difference and the development of sexual ethics have nowhere to start. For sexual minority students, whose movement through public spaces is often impeded by harassment and homophobia, a space to form alliances is crucial.

The afterschool location of these alliances is as important as the partial, implicit critiques they make of identity politics. Because this generation of students is not living in a time of mass movement politics, social change activities happen in localized and often institutional spaces. These institutionally bound spaces, like afterschool groups or community center alliances, may appear to older generations of activists as an indication of the constraints put on politics and the shrinking of the public sphere. However, the political and social analysis of identity undertaken in these spaces is decidedly less constraining than earlier forms of identity politics. In other words, the spaces of political movements have changed, and so too have the forms of political identity.

The Equal Access Act, passed in 1984, has provided the legal support for gay straight alliances (and a variety of other afterschool programs), opening space for young people to organize interest groups in which they can easily find access and like-minded others. A number of districts have attempted to ban gay straight alliances, following the EAA's guidelines, arguing that alliances are disruptive because they are contrary to local norms. Those challenges have so far been unsuccessful, but they do echo the debate over the act itself. As David Buckel details in his analysis of debate over the EEA legislative debate, sexuality was at once presumed to be inappropriate for schools and thus not covered and also presumed to be already protected, and so unnecessary. But legislators were concerned that a law supporting student organizations might be taken as support for illegal homosexual activities. Debate centered on the distinction between advocacy of rights for gay people and support of illegal activity. One legislator claimed that gay clubs would not be protected by the bill because gay activity "is unlawful."[14] A colleague's question brought him to specify that support for gay rights would only be unlawful if states prohibit homosexual activity. Pushed further, he finally decided that political activity was different from outlawed sexual activity, but the anxieties represented by his inability to see the difference between talking about political rights and engaging in sexual activity has continued to trouble the local understandings of the Equal Access Act.[15]

These discussions over the EAA parallel the ambivalence with which school policy addresses sexual orientation. In part, this ambivalence opens spaces for student negotiation because the official discourse around sexuality is so fraught that it is itself a statement of the problem of sexuality. But the confusion around sexuality has also meant that student groups have trouble finding a faculty sponsor, getting approval from administrators and avoiding the scrutiny of conservative watchdog groups. Given recent coverage of attempts to have a gay straight alliance at El Modena High School, it appears that even discussing the formation of such alliances can bring an entire school under suspicion for homosexuality, as neighboring schools now refer to El Modena as "Homo-dena."[16]

Even as some students manage to carve out spaces in school to consider vital and educational issues around sexuality, the school environment continues to be challenging. Adolescents are responsible for more homophobic violence, even against adults, than any other age group. Schools are still filled with homophobic taunts and violence. Because so many sexual minority students understand school as a hostile place, they are reluctant to make their presence known. The lack of visible and out students means that administrators will often claim that schools have no gay students. One student explained her attempt to start a Gay Straight Alliance after a school mate had come out at an assembly on a field trip. "We went back and wanted to start a gay school group and the principal said what are you talking about? We don't have gay kids here."[17] Another student who had successfully organized a Gay Straight Alliance and had developed a positive relationship with his school administration remarked: "Were we hassled? Oh yeah, even some teachers were ripping down signs."[18] Another young woman recalls that her Gay Straight Alliance was smoke bombed. The school board met to discuss the incident "but they just talked about it all as property damage, they'd never say don't hate someone because they're gay, just don't destroy someone's property. This teacher stood up and said this is happening because they hate gays and we have to talk about it like that."[19] Since curricular measures rarely address homophobia specifically, often the only way homophobia is "officially" addressed is in afterschool programs.

Afterschool groups have themselves met with conservative challenges, though ultimately the Equal Access Act has provided protection. In Salt Lake City, the school board banned the Gay Straight Alliance because sexuality was not a part of official curricula. So the exclusion of sexuality from the curricula became the justification for excluding an afterschool group attempting to fill that void. When the board was made aware that its actions were discriminatory under the EAA, they presumed this was the case if the ban was only directed at the Gay Straight Alliance and so they cancelled all other afterschool groups they defined as noncurricular as a remedy. However, they left in place the Future Business Leaders of America and the Future Homemakers of America, neither of which fit guidelines for curricular groups. The lines between identities appropriate for school and identities not so were decisively draw. It became clear to the student community that a variety of groups were implicitly not offering viewpoints and were serving constituencies the board felt ought officially to be part of the school. According to the brief against the district:

> Included within the list of "not approved" clubs were such clubs as the
> Human Rights Club, Key Club, Native American Club, and Polynesian

Club (all of which formerly met at East High School), the Advancement of Hispanic Students, Ethnic Alliance, Highland Organized for Planet Earth, Juveniles in Highland Against Drugs, and Students Against Drunk Driving (all of which formerly met at Highland High School) and the Black Students Union, Latino Pride Club, Native American Club, Students of the Orient, Young Democrats, and Young Republicans (all of which formerly met at West High School).[20]

As many students understood the actions of the school board to be directed against the GSA, they rallied in support of not only their own largely identity-based groups but the GSA as well. Certainly not all of them were supportive of the Gay Straight Alliance, but engaging in public action against what they all experienced as an unfair policy helped to level—and highlight—the differences between young people, in effect acting as a large, broad-based alliance in their protests. While the initial actions of the school board had been undertaken because of their disapproval of homosexuality as a school topic, all groups were eventually implicated.

Association/Identity: Commonalities, Parallels, and Differences

Association seems to benefit all sexualities. Heterosexual and questioning students point out that allying with gay, bisexual, lesbian, and transgender students can change their ideas about themselves and others. As one self-identified heterosexual student has put it, she is more like the gay students in her high school so she more easily associates with them.[21] Other students experience Gay Straight Alliances as queering their heterosexual privilege, making them realize that the relative ease with which they negotiate their relationships may be part of the heterosexism and homophobia that constrains the lives of their friends who are not heterosexual. Heterosexual members of GSAs also find themselves in a bind: they are reluctant to counter rumors that they are gay (because they do not want to seem disapproving of homosexuality), but they also want to be able to be role models for other straight students. As one explains it, going to a conference of lgbt youth and allies was the first time he had the experience, however briefly, of being a minority. "At first I was a little apprehensive, but the LBGTQ students showed me around, taught me how to dance, offered to let me stay at the hostel with them. We became really close friends. All feelings of alienation were quickly replaced by curiosity for those whose lives were so different from my own and yet so similar to my own."[22]

Students of a variety of sexualities have recounted the ease they found discussing sexuality with friends they knew to be gay, bisexual, or lesbian. Others have also changed their ideas and practices of gender through close relationship with transgender friends. More than a few have remarked that knowing a gay person who had gone through a coming out process compelled them to more carefully interrogate their own sexuality. These interactions are not without their difficulties, including the loss of the rare space to be only with gay people, but sexuality-related groups increasingly state the importance of including students still "questioning" or "curious." When I asked an afterschool alliance group how they would improve schools, they specifically expressed a desire for support from schools to support curiosity. One suggested, "If not a pride group, at least hotline conducted by some teachers and brave students who have come out for the students who are scared or maybe just curious."[23] Despite the occasional stated desire to have space just to be with people who know they are gay, lesbian, bisexual, or transgender, students are well aware that not all their allies will be sexual minorities and also that many people will not have fully made up their minds. Thus sexual minority students are perhaps more open-minded than other groups because they recognize the strong possibility that allies will not be completely like them or that sexuality is more complicated than even a "coming out" process can account for.

Some self-identified straight students say that because heterosexuality relies on unquestioned dominance, just knowing there are sexual minorities means that their own heterosexuality means something different. Being friends with gay students means that these straight students feel they need to actively work against the homophobia harms their friends and supports their own identity. Others find themselves perhaps a little overwhelmed by how working in an alliance troubles their own public identity. One explains, "People assume I'm LGBT identified. When I tell them I'm not, first they doubt me, and then they wonder why I would get involved. At school I no longer have an identity separate from the GSA, it's not Nate . . . anymore, it's Nate of the GSA."[24] Two women students also described joining a Gay Straight Alliance in order to help them face rumors going around their school that they were lovers.[25] They had such difficulty dealing with homophobia, even though they weren't lesbians, that they realized they had more in common with gay students in their school than anyone else.

Recent work on Gay Straight Alliances by Jeff Perrotti and Kim Westheimer also raises the issue of "straight" girls in groups. They say that a common complaint from organizers is that GSAs are "just a group of straight girls," but a better way to think of the issue is to consider why it is that girls would find supporting sexual minorities so compelling.

They contend that girls often have to deal with as much hostility from young men as sexual minority students do and so there is a gendered ground for their alliance. Perrotti and Westheimer recount one girl's anger at the suicide of a young gay man, harassed into despair by other boys at his school. "The guys who treated him badly treat us the same way. . . . We know what it's like."[26] So what may appear to be disconnected alliance is actually a form of shared experience based on different, yet related, identity categories. Another young woman points out that because of her gender, her sexual identity is dependent upon her partner, so while GSAs are at least sometimes better places to be, they are still bound up in gender assumptions and lack a full vocabulary and appreciation for bisexual identity.[27] Dissimilarities within alliances continue to be a crucial problem and site of possibilities. Differences in experience and social position mean that, for instance, the commonplace statement that young men are subject to more homophobic harassment than young women needs to be reconsidered in light of young women's greater likelihood to be harassed because they are women, not necessarily with specifically antilesbian content (antilesbian harassment is also, of course, often directed at women of all sexual orientations).[28]

Curiosity about sexuality and sexual alliance also draws groups together and provide the bonds for exploring other aspects of identity. An out of school group, OutRight! points out that "those who come to meeting rarely face question only of sexuality . . . [t]his diversity has given us a formidable challenge. OutRight! makes a concerted effort to provide several facilitators at every meeting, and we try to assemble a pool of facilitators with diverse backgrounds in order to bridge whatever gaps these youth bring with them."[29] GLSEN also stresses the need for local chapters to address issues facing all students in school and to organize against sexism, racism, and classism, as well as against homophobia. But the stress on diversity as a whole has also been used to discourage gay straight alliances. More than one student group has been turned down by school administrators who claimed that the students were being too narrow and should focus on all aspects of diversity, not just issues of sexual orientation. The group at El Modena, for instance, was told by their principal that they could meet but had to find another name.[30] Another group in Indiana was told by school officials that they wanted the Gay Straight Alliance to meet under another name, like "Diversity Club."[31]

While the space of schools has provided the important context for the clubs, the ethical curiosity of students and their advocates has altered school communities. By centering curiosity and a careful consideration of identity categories, students, in effect, embrace the universalizing concept of identity while also addressing the cultural context that creates minoritizing prejudices and positive possibilities for the development of new identity formations. Because these groups are formed with the twin projects of challenging discrimination against sexual minorities and providing students with space to interrogate their own identities and desires, the groups encourage students to see themselves as ethical actors and communities, responsible to themselves and responsible for one another.

Notes

An earlier version of this was published as "Queering School Communities: Ethical Curiosity and Gay Straight Alliances." *Journal of Gay and Lesbian Issues in Education*, vol. 1., no. 3 (Spring 2004), 23-36.

1. Outreach (Australia), www.also.org.au/outreach/welcome.htm, n. d., [cited 30 August 1999].
2. Michel Foucault, *History of Sexuality, Volume One: An Introduction* (New York: Vintage Books, 1990), 95. See also Michel Foucault, *Power/Knowledge: Selected Interviews and Other Writings 1972–1977* (New York: Pantheon Books, 1977).
3. Michael Warner, *The Trouble with Normal: Sex, Politics, and the Ethics of Queer Life* (Cambridge, Mass.: Harvard University Press, 1999), 35.
4. Jeffery Weeks, *Invented Moralities: Sexual Values in an Age of Uncertainty* (New York: Columbia University Press, 1995), 65.
5. Weeks, *Invented Moralities*, 68.
6. Weeks, *Invented Moralities*, 70.
7. Eve Kosofsky Sedgwick, *Epistemology of the Closet* (Berkeley: University of California Press, 1989), 56.
8. Ibid., 55.
9. Anonymous interview with author, 21 September 2002. Street-involved youth have other concerns with identifying as queer, see Suzanne de Castell, *No Place Like Home: The Pridehouse Research Project Final Report*. Human Resources Development Canada. www.sfu.ca/pridehouse, October 2002, [cited 17 Nov. 2002].
10. Anonymous interview with author, 21 September 2002.
11. Weeks, *Invented Moralities*, 140.
12. Ibid., 142.
13. Ibid., 147.
14. 130 Cong. Rec. 19211-52 (1984), Id. at 19224 quoted in David Buckel, "Gay/Straight Student Alliances and Other Gay-Related Student Groups," www.glsen.org/pages/sections/library/schooltools/021.article, n.d., [cited 30 August 1999].
15. Buckel, "Gay/Straight Student Alliances."
16. Harriet Barovick, "Fear of a Gay School," *Time*, 21 Feb. 2000, 52.
17. Anonymous interview with author, 21 September 2002.
18. Anonymous interview with author, 21 September 2002.

19. Anonymous interview with author, 21 September 2002.

20. From the brief prepared by Lambda Legal Defense for *East High Gay/Straight Alliance v. Board of Education of Salt Lake City School District* (U.S. District Court for the District of Utah, Central Division, March 19, 1998) www.lambdalegal.org/cgi-bin/pages/documents/record?record=234, n.d., [cited 30 August 1999].

21. Elizabeth Evers quoted in David Ruenzel, "Pride and Prejudice," *Teacher Magazine*, April 1999, 27.

22. Caleb Baker, "Putting the 'S' in GSA," www.glsen.org/templates/student/section=47&record=899, n.d., [cited 28 August 2002].

23. Anonymous personal communication with author, 21 September 1999.

24. Nate Triplett quoted in Michael Parrish, "The 'S' in GSA: Not Just Lip Service," www.glsen.org/templates/students/section=47&record=1388, n.d., [cited 28 August 2002].

25. Anonymous personal communication with author, 4 November 1997.

26. Quoted in Jeff Perrotti and Kim Westheimer, *When the Drama Club Is Not Enough: Lessons from the Safe Schools Program for Gay and Lesbian Students* (Boston: Beacon Books, 2001), 66.

27. Lindsey Morrison, "Bisexuality: Now You See Me," www.glsen.org/templates/student/record.html?section=47&record=232, n.d., [cited 27 August 2002].

28. Michael Bochenek and A. Widney Brown, "Gender and Homophobia," in *Hatred in the Hallways: Violence and Discrimination against Lesbian, Gay, Bisexual, and Transgender Students in U. S. Schools* (New York: Human Rights Watch, 2001), 34.

29. Hugh Singerline, "OutRight! Reflections on an Out-of-School Gay Youth Group" in *The Gay Teen: Educational Practice and Theory for Lesbian, Gay, and Bisexual Adolescents*, ed. Gerald Unks (New York: Routledge, 1995), 229-230.

30. "Common Questions and Answers about Gay-Straight Alliances," www.glsen.org/templates/student/record.html?section=45&record=965, n.d., [cited 19 November 2001].

31. Terry Horne, "Gay-Straight Alliance Sues High School," *Indianapolis Star*, 30 October 2001.

Bibliography

Ackerman, Bruce. "Why Dialogue?" *Journal of Philosophy* 86 (January 1989): 5–22.

Alan Guttmacher Institute. *Sex and America's Teenagers*. New York: Alan Guttmacher Institute, 1994.

Alexander, Vicki. "Black Women and HIV/AIDS." *Sex Information and Education Council of the United States (SIECUS) Report* (December 1990/January 1991): 8.

Bachrach, C. A., Horn, M. C., Mosher, W. D., and Pratt, W. F. "Understanding U.S. Fertility: Findings from the National Survey of Family Growth, Cycle III." *Population Bulletin* 39, no. 5 (December 1984).

Baker, Caleb. "Putting the 'S' in GSA." www.glsen.org/templates/student/section=47& record=899, n.d. [cited 28 August 2002].

Banks, James A., and Cherry A. McGee Banks. *Multicultural Education: Issues and Perspectives*. 4th ed. New York: John Wiley and Sons, 2001.

Barovick, Harriet. "Fear of a Gay School." *Time*, 21 February 2000, 52.

Bauer, Allison F. *State of the States 2002: Gay, Lesbian, and Straight Educators Network (GLSEN) Policy Analysis of Lesbian, Gay, Bisexual, and Transgender (LGBT) Safer Schools Issues*. New York: GLSEN, 2002.

Bell, Daniel. *Communitarianism and Its Critics*. Oxford: Oxford University Press, 1994.

Bell, Nora Kizer. "Women and AIDS: Too Little, Too Late?" *Hypatia* 4, no. 3 (Fall 1989): 3–22.

Bellah, Robert N. *Habits of the Heart: Individualism and Commitment in American Life*. Berkeley: University of California Press, 1996.

Benhabib, Seyla. *Situating the Self: Gender, Community, and Postmodernism in Contemporary Ethics*. New York: Routledge, 1992.

Berger, Joseph. "Board Agrees on Teaching about AIDS." *New York Times*, 25 June 1992, B1.

———. "New AIDS Plan in Schools: Emphasis on 'No.'" *New York Times*, 4 June 1992, B3.

———. "School Board May Alter Sexual Abstinence Policy." *New York Times*, 3 June 1992, B3.

Bersani, Leo. "Is the Rectum a Grave?" In *AIDS Cultural Analysis/Cultural Activism*, edited by Douglas Crimp, 197–222. Cambridge: Massachusetts Institute of Technology Press, 1989.

Best Friends Foundation Unofficial Page. mariancreighton.edu/~scarlett/govt/. n.d., [cited 2 April 1997].

Bethany Christian Services Page. www.bethany.org/bethany/secondtht.html. n. d., [cited 2 April 1997].

Bochenek, Michael and A. Widney Brown. *Hatred in the Hallways: Violence and Discrimination against Lesbian, Gay, Bisexual, and Transgender Students in U.S. Schools*. New York: Human Rights Watch, 2001.

Buckel, David. "Gay/Straight Student Alliances and Other Gay-Related Student Groups." www.glsen.org/pages/sections/library/schooltools/021.article, n.d. [cited 30 August 1999].

Bullis, Ronald K. "'Gag Rules' and Chastity Clauses: Legal and Ethical Consequences of Title X and the AFLA for Professionals in Human Sexuality." *Journal of Sex Education and Therapy* 17, no. 2 (1991): 91–102.

Butler, Judith. *Gender Trouble: Feminism and the Subversion of Gender*. New York: Routledge, 1990.

———. *Bodies That Matter: On the Discursive Limits of "Sex."* New York: Routledge, 1993.

Byrne, Donn, and William A. Fisher, eds. *Adolescents, Sex, and Contraception*. Hillsdale, N.J.: Lawrence Erlbaum, 1983.

Carlson, Dennis L. "Ideological Conflict and Change in the Sexuality Curriculum." In *Sexuality and the Curriculum: The Politics and Practices of Sexuality Education*, edited by James T. Sears, 34–58. New York: Teachers College Press, 1992.

Carmody, Deirdre. "Regents Require AIDS Instruction for Elementary and High Schools." *New York Times*, 19 September 1987, 1, 34.

Centers for Disease Control. "HIV/AIDS Surrveillance Report," *Centers for Disease Control Page*. www.ede.gov/nchstp/hiv_aids/stats.htm. December 1996, [cited 3 May 1997].

———. "Guidelines for Effective School Health Education to Prevent the Spread of AIDS." *Morbidity and Mortality Weekly Review* 37, supplement 2 (1988): 1–14.

Chauncey, George. *Gay New York: Gender, Urban Culture, and the Making of the Gay Male World, 1890–1940*. New York: Basic Books, 1994.

Childress, James F. "Mandatory HIV Screening and Testing." In *AIDS and Ethics*, edited by Frederic G. Reamer, 50–76. New York: Columbia University Press, 1991.

Coalition of National Health Education Organizations. "Instruction about AIDS within the School Curriculum: A Position Paper." *Journal of School Health* 58, no. 8 (1988): 323.

Cohen, Cathy J. *Boundaries of Blackness: AIDS and the Breakdown of Black Politics*. Chicago: University of Chicago Press, 1999.

Cole, Rebecca, and Sally Cooper. "Lesbian Exclusion from HIV/AIDS Education: Ten Years of Low-Risk Identity and High-Risk Behavior." *Sex Information and Education Council of the United States Report* (December 1990/January 1991): 18–23.

"Common Questions and Answers about Gay-Straight Alliances." www.glsen.org/templates/student/record.html?section=45&record=965, n.d. [cited 19 November 2001].

Connolly, William. *Identity/Difference: Democratic Negotiations of Political Paradox.* Ithaca, N.Y.: Cornell University Press, 1991.

———. *The Ethos of Pluralization.* Minneapolis: University of Minnesota Press, 1995.

"Consumer Reports: How Reliable Are Condoms?" reprint of *Consumer Reports* (May 1995). In Consumers Union of U.S., Inc. Page. www.tezcat.com/~alan/html/condoms /html, n. d., [cited 3 May 1997].

Crimp, Douglas. "How to Have Promiscuity in an Epidemic." In *AIDS: Cultural Analysis/Cultural Activism,* edited by Douglas Crimp, 237-270. Cambridge: Massachusetts Institute of Technology Press, 1988

Cvetkovich, George, and Barbara Grote. "Adolescent Development and Teenage Fertility." In *Adolescents, Sex, and Contraception,* edited by Donn Byrne and William A. Fisher, 109–123. Hillsdale, N.J.: Lawrence Erlbaum, 1983.

Dao, James. "Critics Decry New AIDS Education Rules as Censorship." *New York Times,* 29 May 1992, B3.

———. "School Board Bars Material about AIDS." *New York Times,* 28 May 1992, B1, B7.

de Castell, Suzanne, *No Place Like Home: The Pridehouse Research Project Final Report.* Human Resources Development Canada. www.sfu.ca/pridehouse, Oct. 2002, [cited 17 Nov. 2002].

Decter, Midge "Homosexuality and the Schools." *Commentary,* March 1993, 25.

DeLamater, John. "An Interpersonal and Interactional Model of Contraceptive Behavior." In *Adolescents, Sex, and Contraception,* edited by Donn Byrne and William Fisher, 34–48. Hillsdale, N.J.: Lawrence Erlbaum, 1983.

D'Emilio, John, and Estelle B. Freedman. *Intimate Matters: A History of Sexuality in America.* New York: Harper & Row, 1988.

Desmond, Stephanie. "School Board Defers Vote on Policy to Protect Gay Students: Some Believe Measure Could Allow Teaching about Homosexuality." *Baltimore Sun,* 27 June 2002.

Diorio, Joseph A. "Contraception, Copulation Domination, and the Theoretical Barrenness of Sex Education Literature." *Educational Theory* (Summer 1985): 239–254.

Dowd, Maureen. "Dr. Koop Defends His Crusade on AIDS." *New York Times,* 6 Apr. 1987, II, 8.

Duberman, Martin, Martha Vicinus, and George Chauncey, Jr. *Hidden from History: Reclaiming the Gay and Lesbian Past.* New York: Meridian, 1989.

Dubner, Stephen J. "The New Team: The Education of Ninfa Segarra." *New York Magazine,* 17 January 1994, 28.

DuBois, Ellen Carol and Linda Gordon. "Seeking Ecstasy on the Battlefield: Danger and Pleasure in Nineteenth-Century Feminist Thought." In *Pleasure and Danger: Exploring Female Sexuality,* edited by Carole S. Vance, 31–49. London: Pandora Press, 1989.

Elwin, Rosamund and Michele Paulse. *Asha's Mums.* Toronto: Women's Press, 1990.

Epstein, Paul. "Condoms in Schools: The Right Lesson." *New York Times,* 19 January 1991, 31.

Family Defense Council pamphlet.

Feinberg, Walter. *Common Schools, Uncommon Identities: National Unity and Cultural Differences*. New Haven, Conn.: Yale University Press, 1998.

Fine, Michelle. "Sexuality, Schooling, and Adolescent Females: The Missing Discourse of Desire." *Harvard Educational Review* (February 1988): 29–53.

Fisher, W., D. Byrne, and L. White, "Emotional Barriers to Contraception." In *Adolescents, Sex, and Contraception*, edited by Donn Byrne and William A. Fisher, 207–239. Hillsdale, N.J.: Lawrence Erlbaum, 1983.

Fleming, Anne Taylor. "Like a Virgin, Again." *Vogue*, February 1995, 71–72.

Foucault, Michel. *History of Sexuality, Volume One: An Introduction*. New York: Vintage Books, 1990.

———. *The Use of Pleasure: Volume Two of the History of Sexuality*. New York: Vintage Books, 1990.

———. "Nietzsche, Genealogy, History." In *Language, Counter-Memory, Practice: Selected Essays and Interviews by Michel Foucault*, edited by Donald F. Bouchard, 139–164. Ithaca, N.Y.: Cornell University Press, 1977.

———. "On the Genealogy of Ethics." In *Michel Foucault: Beyond Structuralism and Hermeneutics*, edited by Hubert L. Dreyfus and Paul Rabinow, 229–252. Chicago: University of Chicago Press, 1983.

———. *Power/Knowledge: Selected Interviews and Other Writings 1972–1977*. New York: Pantheon Books, 1977.

Fraser, Nancy. *Unruly Practices: Power, Discourse, and Gender in Contemporary Social Theory*. Minneapolis: University of Minnesota Press, 1989.

Gagnon, John, and Richard Parker. "Introduction: Conceiving Sexuality." In *Conceiving Sexuality: Approaches to Sex Research in a Postmodern World*, edited by Richard Parker and John Gagnon, 3–18. New York: Routledge, 1995.

Gehring, John. "Mass. Stance on Anti-Gay Bias in Schools Stirring Debate." *Education Week*, 17 May 2000, 23.

Gilman, Sander L. "AIDS and Syphilis: The Iconography of Disease." In *AIDS: Cultural Analysis/Cultural Activism*, edited by Douglas Crimp, 87–108. Cambridge: Massachusetts Institute of Technology Press, 1988.

Gross, Jane. "New York State's Curriculum on AIDS Criticized." *New York Times*, 2 November 1987, 19.

Grunseit, Anne, and Susan Kippax. "Effects of Sex Education on Young People's Sexual Behaviour." New York: World Health Organization, 1994.

Gutmann, Amy. *Democratic Education*. Princeton, N.J.: Princeton University Press, 1987.

Health Omnibus Programs Extension Act of 1988 § 2-2500-102 STAT. 3093 (1988).

Henneberger, Melinda. "Educators Fight New York Panel on AIDS Pledge." *New York Times*, 28 August 1992, 1.

———. "Supporters of AIDS Pledge Criticize Other Programs." *New York Times*, 6 September 1992, 51.

———. "Two on Board Defend AIDS Oath." *New York Times*, 29 August 1992, B2.

Horne, Terry. "Gay-Straight Alliance Sues High School." *Indianapolis Star*, 30 October 2001.

Hottois, James, and Neal A. Milner. *The Sex Education Controversy: A Study of Politics, Education, and Morality*. Lexington, Mass.: Lexington Books, 1975.

Howe, Kenneth R. "AIDS Education in the Public Schools: Old Wine in New Bottles?" *Journal of Moral Education* 19, no. 2 (May 1990): 114–123.

Humm, Andrew. "Re-building the 'Rainbow'—The Holy War over Inclusion in New York City." Unpublished paper.

Hunt, Janet G., and Larry L. Hunt. "Here to Play: Families to Lifestyles." *Journal of Family Issues* 8, no. 4 (December 1987): 440–443.

Hurwitz, Howard L., ed. *Family Defense Council Newsletter.* No. 27, March 1994.

Ingrassia, Michelle. "Virgin Cool." *Newsweek,* 17 October 1994, 58–65.

Keegan, Patrick. "Sex Education Raises New Concern for Schools." *New York Times,* 21 October 1987, 1.

Kerr, Dianne. L. "Adolescents, AIDS, and HIV: The Future Starts Now." *Journal of School Health* 59, no. 6 (1989): 277–278.

Kerr, Dianne L., Diane D. Allensworth, and Jacob. A. Gayle. "The ASHA National HIV Education Needs Assessment of Health and Education Professionals." *Journal of School Health* (September 1989): 301–307.

King, Katie. "Local and Global: AIDS Activism and Feminist Theory." *Camera Obscura* (January 1989): 79–100.

King, Mike. "Suicide Watch." *The Advocate,* 12 November 1996, 41–43.

Kirby, D. *Sexuality Education: An Evaluation of Programs.* Santa Cruz, Calif.: Network Publications, 1984.

Koedt, Anne. "The Myth of the Vaginal Orgasm." In *Radical Feminism,* edited by Anne Koedt, Ellen Levine, and Anita Rapone, 198-207. New York: Quadrangle Books, 1973.

"Koop Defends Views on AIDS Education." *New York Times,* 3 February 1987, III, 12.

Kornfield, Michael. "Schools Welcome AIDS Teaching." *New York Times,* 11 October 1987, 12.

Kosciw, Joseph G., and M. K. Cullen. *The GLSEN 2001 National School Climate Survey: The School-Related Experiences of Our Nation's Lesbian, Gay, Bisexual, and Transgender Youth.* New York: Gay, Lesbian, and Straight Educators Network, 2001.

Kymlicka, Will. *Liberalism, Community, and Culture.* Oxford: Clarendon Press, 1989.

———. *Multicultural Citizenship: A Liberal Theory of Minority Rights.* Oxford: Clarendon Press, 1995.

Laumann, Edward O., and John H. Gagnon. "A Sociological Perspective on Sexual Action." In *Conceiving Sexuality: Approaches to Sex Research in a Postmodern World,* edited by John Gagnon and Richard Parker, 183–213. New York: Routledge, 1995.

Lee, N'Tanya, et al. "Whose Kids? Our Kids! Race, Sexuality and the Right in New York City's Curriculum Battles." *Radical America* 25, no. 1 (March 1993).

Levinson, Natasha. "Teaching in the Midst of Belatedness: The Paradox of Natality in Hannah Arendt's Educational Thought." *Educational Theory* 47, no. 4 (Fall 1997): 435–451.

Leviton, Laura C. "Theoretical Foundations of AIDS-Prevention Programs." In *Preventing AIDS: The Design of Effective Programs,* Ronald O. Valdiserri, 42–90. New Brunswick, N.J.: Rutgers University Press, 1989.

Lewin, Tamar. "Fearing Disease, Teens Alter Sexual Practices." *New York Times,* 5 April 1997, A 14.

Martin, Judith. *Star-Spangled Manners: In Which Miss Manners® Defends American Etiquette (For a Change)*. New York: W.W. Norton, 2002.

Mast, Coleen. *Sex Respect: The Option of True Sexual Freedom*. Bradley, Ill.: Respect, Inc., 1990.

McKay, Andrew. *Sexual Ideology and Schooling: Towards Democratic Sexuality Education*. Albany: State University of New York Press, 1999.

Minkowitz, Donna. "The Wrong Side of the Rainbow." *The Nation*, 28 June 1993, 901.

Moen, Matthew C. *The Transformation of the Christian Right*. Tuscaloosa: University of Alabama Press, 1992.

Morris, Ronald William. *Values in Sexuality Education: A Philosophical Study*. Lanham, Md.: University Press of America, 1994.

Morrison, Lindsey. "Bisexuality: Now You See Me," www.glsen.org/templates/student/record.html?section=47&record=232, n.d. [cited 27 August 2002].

Murphy, Julien S. "The AIDS Epidemic: A Phenomenological Analysis of the Infectious Body." In *AIDS and Ethics*, edited by Frederic G. Reamer, 50–60. New York: Columbia University Press, 1991.

Myers, Steven Lee. "Values in Conflict." *New York Times*, 6 October 1992, B6.

———. "School Board in Queens Shuns Fernandez Meeting." *New York Times*, 1 December 1992, B4.

———. "Queens School Board Suspended in Fight on Gay-Life Curriculum." *New York Times*, 2 December 1992, B4.

Nelkin, Dorothy, and Stephen Hilgartner. "Disputed Dimensions of Risk: A Public School Controversy over AIDS." *The Milbank Quarterly* 64, supplement 1 (1986): 118–142.

Nelkin, Dorothy, David P. Willis, and Scott V. Parris. *A Disease of Society: Cultural and Institutional Responses to AIDS*. Cambridge: Cambridge University Press, 1991.

New York City Board of Education. *Comprehensive Instructional Program First Grade Teachers' Resource Guide Review Draft*. New York: Board of Education Publications, 1994.

New York State Department of Education. Bureau of Curriculum Development. *AIDS Instructional Guide: Grades K–12*. Albany: The University of the State of New York, 1987.

Newman, Leslea. *Gloria Goes to Gay Pride*. Boston, Mass.: Alyson, 1991.

———. *Heather Has Two Mommies*. Boston, Mass.: Alyson, 1991.

Nieto, Sonia. *Affirming Diversity: The Sociopolitical Context of Multicultural Education*. 3rd edition. New York: Longman, 2000.

Oakeshott, Michael. "Political Education." In *Rationalism in Politics and Other Essays*, 43–69. Indianapolis: Liberty Press, 1991.

———. *Religion, Politics, and the Moral Life*, edited by Timothy Fuller. New Haven, Conn.: Yale University Press, 1993.

———. "The Tower of Babel," In *Rationalism in Politics and Other Essays*, 465–487. Indianapolis: Liberty Press, 1991.

Okin, Susan Moller. *Justice, Gender, and the Family*. New York: Basic Books, 1989.

Olsen, Joseph A., Stan E. Weed, and Gail M. Ritz. "The Effects of Three Abstinence-based Sex Education Programs on Student Attitudes toward Sex Education." *Adolescence* 26 (Fall 1991): 631-641.

Outreach (Australian website). www.also.org.au/outreach/welcome.htm, n. d., [cited 30 Aug. 1999].

Parrish, Michael. "The 'S' in GSA: Not Just Lip Service," www.glsen.org/templates /students/section=47&record=1388, n.d. [cited 28 August 2002].

Patton, Cindy. *Fatal Advice: How Safe-Sex Education Went Wrong.* Durham, N.C.: Duke University Press, 1996.

————. *Inventing AIDS.* New York: Routledge, 1990.

————. *Sex and Germs: The Politics of AIDS.* Boston: South End Press, 1985.

Perrotti, Jeff, and Kim Westheimer. *When the Drama Club Is Not Enough: Lessons from the Safe Schools Program for Gay and Lesbian Students.* Boston: Beacon Books, 2001.

Pinar, William, ed., *Queer Theory in Education.* Mahwah, N.J.: Lawrence Erlbaum, 1998.

Presidential Commission on the Human Immunodeficiency Virus Epidemic. *Report of the Presidential Commission on the Human Immunodeficiency Virus Epidemic.* Washington, D.C.: U.S. Government Printing Office, June 1988.

"Preventing Risk Behaviors among Students." *Centers for Disease Control HIV/AIDS Prevention Newsletter,* October 1992, 1–2.

Quinn, Sandra C., Stephen B. Thomas, and Becky J. Smith. "Are Health Educators Being Prepared to Provide HIV/AIDS Education?: A Survey of Selected Health Education Professional Preparation Programs." *Journal of School Health* (March 1990): 92–95.

Rawls, John. *A Theory of Justice.* Cambridge, Mass.: Harvard University Press, 1971.

Reamer, Frederic G., ed. *AIDS and Ethics.* New York: Columbia University Press, 1991.

Remafedi, Gary. "Introduction: The State of Knowledge on Gay, Lesbian, and Bisexual Youth Suicide." In *Death by Denial: Studies of Suicide in Gay and Lesbian Teenagers,* edited by Gary Remafedi, 7–14. Boston: Alyson, 1994.

Ross, Judith Wilson. "Ethics and the Language of AIDS." In *The Meaning of AIDS: Implications for Medical Science, Clinical Practice, and Public Health Policy,* edited by Eric T. Juengst and Barbara A. Koenig, 30–41. New York: Praeger, 1989.

Rosser, B. R. Simon. *Male Homosexual Behavior and the Effects of AIDS Education: A Study of Behavior and Safer Sex in New Zealand and South Australia.* New York: Prager, 1991.

Rubin, Gayle. "Thinking Sex: Notes for a Radical Theory of the Politics of Sexuality." In *Pleasure and Danger: Exploring Female Sexuality,* edited by Carole Vance, 267–319. New York: Routledge, 1984.

Ruenzel, David. "Pride and Prejudice." *Teacher Magazine,* April 1999, 22–27.

Sandel, Michael. *Liberalism and the Limits of Justice.* Cambridge: Cambridge University Press, 1982.

Saracco, A., et al. "Man-to-Woman Transmission of HIV: Longitudinal Study of 343 Steady Partners of Infected Men." *Journal of Acquired Immune Deficiency Syndromes* 6 (1993): 497–502.

Schumacher, Marie. *HIV/AIDS Education Survey.* Alexandria, Va.: The National Association of State Boards of Education, 1989.

Sears, James T., ed. *Sexuality and the Curriculum: The Politics and Practices of Sexuality Education.* New York: Teachers College Press, 1992.

Sedgwick, Eve Kosofsky. *Epistemology of the Closet.* Berkeley: University of California Press, 1990.

————. "How to Bring Your Kids up Gay." *Social Text* 29 (1991): 18–27.

"Senate Votes." *New York Times,* 15 October 1987, II, 12.

Silin, Jonathan G. *Sex, Death, and the Education of Children: Our Passion for Ignorance in the Age of AIDS*. New York: Teachers College Press, 1995.

Singerline, Hugh. "OutRight! Reflections on an Out-of-School Gay Youth Group." In *The Gay Teen: Educational Practice and Theory for Lesbian, Gay, and Bisexual Adolescents*, edited by Gerald Unks, 223-232. New York: Routledge, 1995.

Summerfield, Liane. "Adolescents and AIDS," *ERIC Digest* 1990. ED 319742.

Tabor, Mary B. W. "Fernandez Revises His AIDS Curriculum Proposal." *New York Times*, 24 June 1992, B3.

———. "S.I. Drops Gay Issues from Student Guide." *New York Times*, 9 June 1992, B3.

Taylor, Charles. *Multiculturalism and "The Politics of Recognition,"* edited by Amy Gutmann. Princeton, N.J.: Princeton University Press, 1992.

———. "Interpretation and the Sciences of Man." In *Knowledge and Values in Social and Educational Research*, edited by Eric Bredo and Walter Feinberg, 153–186. Philadelphia: Temple University Press, 1982.

The National Abortion Rights of America League Foundation. *Sexuality Education in America: A State by State Review*. Washington, D.C.: NARAL, 1995.

Thompson, Sharon. *Going All the Way: Teenage Girls' Tales of Sex, Romance, and Pregnancy*. New York: Hill & Wang, 1995.

Treichler, Paula A. *How to Have Theory in an Epidemic: Cultural Chronicles of AIDS*. Durham, N.C.: Duke University Press, 1999.

———. "AIDS, Homophobia, and Biomedical Discourse: An Epidemic of Signification." In *AIDS Cultural Analysis, Cultural Activism*, edited by Douglas Crimp, 17–31. Cambridge: Massachusetts Institute of Technology Press, 1989.

———. "AIDS and HIV Infection in the Third World: A First World Chronicle." In *Remaking History*, edited by Barbara Kruger and Phil Mariani, 31–86. Seattle: Bay Press, 1989.

Trudell, Bonnie, and Mariamne Whatley. "Sex Respect: A Problematic Public School Sexuality Curriculum." *Journal of Sex Education and Therapy* 17, no. 2 (1991): 125–140.

U.S. Congress. Senate, Committee on Governmental Affairs, *AIDS Education of School-Aged Youth*. 101st Congress, 2nd sess., 1990.

———. House. Committee on Energy and Commerce, *Adolescent Family Life Amendments of 1990*. 101st Congress, 2nd sess, 1990.

———. House. Subcommittee on Human Resources and Intergovernmental Relations. *Children and HIV Infection*. 101st Cong., 1st sess., 1989.

———. House. Subcommittee on Governmental Operations. *The Federal Response to the AIDS Epidemic: Information and Public Education*. 100th Cong., 2nd sess., 1987.

U.S. Department of Health and Human Services. *Understanding AIDS*. Washington, D.C.: U.S. Government Printing Office, 1988.

———. *Centers for Disease Control HIV/AIDS Prevention Newsletter*. October 1992.

U.S. Supreme Court. *Romer, Governor of Colorado et al. v. Evans et al.* (1996) No. 94–1039.

"Updated: School Districts That Have Disassociated from the Discriminatory BSA." www.glsen.org/templates/resources/record.html?section=115&record=409, 10 December 2001, [cited 4 September 2002].

Valdiserri, Ronald O. *Preventing AIDS: The Design of Effective Programs*. New Brunswick, N.J.: Rutgers University Press, 1989.

Vincenzi, I. A. "A Longitudinal Study of Human Immunodefiency Virus Transmission by Heterosexual Partners." *New England Journal of Medicine* 331, no. 6 (1994): 431–446.

Wallace, Barbara. "A Call for Change in Multicultural Training at Graduate Schools of Education: Educating to End Oppression and for Social Justice." *Teachers College Record* 102, no. 6 (2000): 1093–1111.

Walsh, Mary E., and Roger Bibace. "Developmentally-Based AIDS/HIV Education." *Journal of School Health* 60, no. 6 (1990): 256–261.

Walzer, Michael. "Comment." In *Multiculturalism and "The Politics of Recognition,"* edited by Amy Gutmann, 99–103. Princeton, N.J.: Princeton University Press, 1992.

———. *Interpretation and Social Criticism.* Cambridge, Mass.: Harvard University Press, 1987.

———. *Spheres of Justice: A Defense of Pluralism and Equality.* New York: Basic Books, 1983.

Ware v. Valley Stream High School District, 545 N.Y.S. 2d 316 (1989).

Warner, Michael. *The Trouble with Normal: Sex, Politics, and the Ethics of Queer Life.* Cambridge, Mass.: Harvard University Press, 1999.

Watney, Simon. "School's Out." In *Inside/out: Lesbian Theories, Gay Theories,* edited by D. Fuss, 387–404. New York: Routledge, 1992.

———. "The Spectacle of AIDS." In *AIDS: Cultural Analysis/Cultural Activism,* edited by Douglas Crimp, 71–86. Cambridge: Massachusetts Institute of Technology Press, 1988.

———. *Policing Desire: Pornography, AIDS and the Media.* Minneapolis: University of Minneapolis Press, 1987.

Weeks, Jeffrey. *Inventing Moralities: Sexual Values in an Age of Uncertainty.* New York: Columbia University Press, 1995.

Werner, Erica. "The Cult of Virginity." *Ms.,* March/April 1997, 40–43.

"What Is Sex Respect?" *Sex Respect Page.* www.lochrie.com/sexrespect/GeneralInfo .html, n. d., [cited 2 April 1997].

Whatley, Mariamne H., and Bonnie K. Trudell. "Teen-Aid: Another Problematic Sexuality Curriculum," *Journal of Sex Education and Therapy* 19, no. 4 (1993): 251–271.

Wihoite, Michael. *Daddy's Roommate.* Boston, Mass.: Alyson, 1991.

Willen, Liz. "School Furor." *Newsday,* 23 April 1992, 3.

Young, Iris Marion. *Justice and the Politics of Difference.* Princeton: Princeton University Press, 1990.

Zeh, John. "New Wave of HIV Infection Hits Gay Youth." *Open Classroom* (Fall 1991): 3.

Zelnick, Melvin, and Farida K. Shah. "First Intercourse among Young Americans." *Family Planning Perspectives* (March/April 1983): 64–70.

Zelnik, M., and J. Kanter. "Sexual and Contraceptive Experience of Young Unmarried Women in the United States, 1976 and 1971." *Family Planning Perspectives* 9 (March/April 1977): 55–71.

Index

About the Author

Cris Mayo is assistant professor in the Department of Educational Policy Studies and the Gender and Women's Studies Program at the University of Illinois at Urbana-Champaign. Her primary areas of research are gender and sexuality studies, queer theory, and educational philosophy. She has published in *Educational Theory*, *Philosophy of Education*, and the *Journal of Gay and Lesbian Issues in Education*.